John P Gibson

The right of John P Gibson to be identified as the author of this work has been asserted by him in accordance with the Copyright, Designs and Patents Act 1988.

All characters and events in this publication, other than those clearly in the public domain, are fictitious and any resemblance to real persons, living or dead, is purely coincidental. It is fiction.

All Rights Reserved
No part of this publication may be reproduced, stored in a retrieval system, or transmitted, in any form or by any means, without the prior permission in writing of the publisher, nor be otherwise circulated in any form of binding or cover other than that in which it is published and without a similar condition including this condition being imposed on the subsequent purchaser.

Copyright John P Gibson 2015

This is a first draft and will likely have mistakes throughout. It has not been edited by a professional publishing company.

John P Gibson *High Tide*

Other books by John P Gibson

Dead Next Tuesday
DARWIN
Beaverpots
Blind Spot
Mr. Pincoat
Kamauna 2908
Take Ten
Benchwarmer
LISA'S
TOUT
The Algarve Story
4 String
JC The Legend
The Golden Years
So Simple Who Knew?
2021
Iguana Café
Hot Sun Bar
Bistro Restaurante

These can be purchased at Amazon.com

High Tide

Short Stories

By

John P Gibson

Gone to Trial-Page 5
Kanga-Page 19
Clowns-Page 41
Parasite-Page 55
The Spider Web-Page 67
Lost In Heaven-Page 89
Hell's Game-Page 101
Down Under Slither-Page 115
McDougals-Page 141
Wine Not-Page 167
Beach Impressions-Page 187
A Moving Experience-Page 209
Slide Rule-Page 233
Spring Cleaning-Page 253
Political Positioning-Page 271
Trip Around-Page 295
Loose Change-Page 313
Shop Talk-Page 331
Michelin Star-Page 351
Name Change-Page 375
New Game-Page 397
A Winning Moment-Page 413
The Darkside-Page 429
Blood Brother-Page 449
The Hypnotic Way-Page 469
A Clowning Glory-Page 489
Pool Party-Page 511
Cab Fare-Page 533
The Rail Story-Page 553
High Tide-Page 573

Gone to Trial

"Sorry Mr. Splechette but it looks as though we will have to go to trial."
Just the words Truncal did not want to hear from his very expensive lawyer Mr. Justin Credible with the firm Ditcher Quick & Hyde. It had already been a long and arduos battle with his ex-wife Cerebella. This was all new territory for him as it was for most men when in divorce proceedings; especially the first. What concerned Truncal was his vast fortune and just how much of it Cerebella would get.

John P Gibson   *High Tide*

Not that one hundred and fourteen billion dollars was an incredible amount, Truncal knew several that were wealthy into the trillions of dollars. It was a new world out there and one that demanded that everyone do their utmost to create god forsaken sums of money. Truncal had been on this path now for twenty some odd years after he graduated school. He had thought if he was going to have to earn money, why not be directly involved with the product. He had decided to work in money trading and with the stock market. He was successful early on in his chosen field and became addicted to not only the process but also the actual physical money itself.

Frequenting his large very secure warehouses where most of his money was stored he would salivate while holding the wads of bills in his hands. This had always given him a nervousness that started his sweat glands producing the acrid smelling liquid running down his brow. If he ever thought he was the nervous type when surrounding himself with loads of cash, he certainly was now that their was a woman in his life that could technically take half of his wealth if not more. His sweat never smelled right.

"You're sure of that Justin? Surely there must be a way to appease this bitch?"

Truncal probed his lawyers face for the slightest expression of hope. The last thing he wanted was a large publicized account of the messy divorce he was about to enter into.

"Yes I am afraid so, I have conversed with Steven Wallace and we come to the same conclusion."

Justin always threw me off when he referred to Steven Wallace as I thought it was just one of his partners when in fact it was two separate ones, Steve and Wallace. Confusing to me to say the least.

"The both of them have informed me that your ex wife Cerebella has hired the lawyer firm Dooey Cheatham and Howe. If I thought for a moment we were the best law firm in the city or for that matter the country, Dooey Cheatham and Howe would certainly rank second."

This did not of course instill any confidence in me, it sounded as though it would be a battle of 'Bucks and Fucks' as a certain number of my colleagues would express on many ocassions when we were putting deals together with other unscrupulus corporations.

It all depended on how much money and who would bend over the fastest to get fucked. I was certainly not prepared to be one of the latter ones; I had been screwed over enough times in my life, especially after getting into the money game.
"What do you propose then?"
I thought to play it nieve at the least and hear what it was my lawyer would allow me to hear. I knew him to be someone who used far too many words to get a point across, I guess because he was getting the fifteen hundred dollars per hour, and of course every second counted. Nearly 42 cents per second to be exact.

"Sue, Grabbit & Runne another lawyer firm in town has also contacted us regarding another law suit totally unrelated to the one we are presently conducting."

This I found strange as why would my lawyer bring up a completely different case than the one we were presently engaged in? I would have to do some prying on my part for sure. Maybe it was just a tact to prolong our meeting and of course increase the bill charged for the time put into todays meeting.

"And what does that have to do with our case?"
A simple question and hopefully getting an equally simple and short answer.
"It appears Cerebella has several of these law suits happening. A real pro gold digger I'd have to say."
I heard his slite loud and clear, it took me a bit off guard. I was used to other business leeches taking many for a ride, but not my ex-wife. I always thought her to be a one man woman, even if our marriage had not been close to perfect it certainly was not one short of money.

"Can you elaborate more on this? I mean how much money does she need to live a life of luxury?"
Of course the same question could have been asked of me and many others in a position of wealth. It's just that for me I was plain greedy and had been since a young boy. My parents, grandparents, great grandparents, and even further back all came from big money. I was only doing what I was trained to

do. How could I really fault my ex-wife for changing her ways to mine? If her lawyers could outsmart mine she could, and would more than likely get half of my fortune. A fortune I had spent a lifetime collecting. A fortune that was one of the largest in the world.

"It is not a question of how much she would need to live, but, how much she can actually get. I would believe her intention is to be if not the richest person on this planet, at least close to it."
Justin spoke clearly and slowly as Truncal gazed at his very expensive watch once again. There was another knock on the door as an associate of Justin's stood at the opening with a handful of papers.

"Sorry to bother you Justin, this just came in, thought you might be interested in what it has to say."
"Come in."
He replies as he takes the documents in hand and reads through them flipping pages as he reads. His expression was not comforting in the least.
"I can't believe it."

John P Gibson   *High Tide*

He says as he looks at his assistant standing wondering whether or not he should leave us alone. "Your ex-wife again. Another lawyer firm involved, 'Steal, Cash & Hyde' a real low life of a company."

All I could do was stare at him in disbelief, what the hell was this woman doing? I had married her in part for her intelligence but now I was seriously beginning to think that she was a hell of a lot smarter than I had ever given her credit for. Cerebella had come from a rather poor family background, only a few million to support the four of them. Her parents and a lazy good for nothing older brother named Prostesus Splechette.

I thought over the years I had been more than good to her. I even bought her a box of chocolates for her birthday one year. They weren't the most expensive, but very near the top. I finally had to eat the entire bunch after several months as she had not touched them. The meeting was getting to the point of ridiculous as more than two hours had passed and not a thing had been resolved; at least in my mind.

"When we go to trial what exactly are the grounds for an amicaple break-up Truncal?"
I heard the question from Justin and thought it obvious to everyone that knew us. She was a total bitch and had been shortly after the wedding, and why the hell was my lawyer even talking this way? We had agreed to take this trial to the top to make sure Cerebella did not get anything from me. My lawyers and, I was sure hers as well would benefit the most from this lawsuit.
"I don't think that would be possible Justin, you of all people know what she is like."

Just at that moment another of Justin's associates comes through the door with more paper work in his hand.
"Sorry to bother you Justin, this just came in."
He handed the papers to Justin and left as fast as he had entered, I would thank him later for saving me a few pennies for his quickness.
"Well Truncal, it appears Cerebella is at it again. Apparently she has hired another law firm to sue what appears another of her enterouge. Benz, Tharules & Proffet. One of the more seedy of our breed."

For a slight moment I thought I saw a smile encroch on Justin's face, it must have been my imagination as he continued on.
"She has her claws into a corporation she claims caused serious and ireversable damage to her health."

That would explain her constant coughing towards the end of our relationship, I thought to myself. She had developed this cough along with other ailments, I thought it was all brought on by our continual bickering.
"And what corporation is this?"
I thought to ask as I myself was involved with many and I certainly hoped it was not one that I owned.
"Teleplay, she claims she had damaged her imune system after taking some of the vitamin products they sell."

My wife had been into looking after herself when it came to nutrition and physical training; she was very healthy for most of our time together until just near the end.

"She had complained about her health even though she was taking what was touted as the best vitamins on the market. I had no idea it was that serious."

I was lying of course, I had personally been adding a slow but deadly poison to her daily feast of pills. This news made me happy in that I would not be suspected in any wrong doing; especially by her law firms and mine.
"It's certainly going to be a complicated if not history making trial Truncal, I hope you are prepared for one hell of a ride."

"Don't you worry Justin, I can handle it all, I just hope it won't cost too much in the long run."
I thought I would throw that little hint in just in case Justin was thinking of charging his higher rate to me. He had in the past infered that I was one of his more loyal customers and always eligible for his ten percent discount rate.
"Great then, we go to trial next Tuesday and before then we will go over exactly how it is we want you to respond to questions in the courtroom."

I knew this would involve several more meetings of which his firm would charge me for, it was just part of the game these lawyers played and I would have to go along with it.

"It will give us at least a little more time to prepare for what your wife will surely serve up to us as one of our more , shall we say, delicate cases."

Delicate was a word I was sure it would *not be* once the preceedings were under way. If anything I knew how my now ex-wife operated and it was not with any finesse or dignity at all. Just at that moment another of Justin's associates comes into the room with of course more paper work in his hands.

"Some more information concerning the case Justin."

The young man hands over the papers to Justin whose expression changed again. I was sure I now had a grasp as to what the information might be he was looking at, the meeting had become quite predictable.

"Some more bad news I'm afraid Truncal, Cerebella has commissioned another law firm, Lose, Case & Getzilch. They are a fairly new firm and have a track

record of losing every case they have managed so far."
I couldn't believe it, this was just getting too bizzarre for me, I needed a break and the longer the better.

"I'm afraid Justin I'm going to need a bit of a break from all of this bullshit. I'm going away for a few days to collect my thoughts about this upcoming courtcase."
Justin just looks at me and rifles through the drawer in his desk for a moment. He pulls out a business card and hands it to me.

"Well, if you feel you must Truncal, we can manage with the details while you're away. Here is a company I recommend for travel plans, that is if you are interested? I'm sure you have your own people you deal with."
I read what is on the card; 'Darremta, Ravel, Wythus….. a holiday you will never forget.'
I return the card to Justin without saying a word and make my way to the door. I would use my own people as he suggested. 'Chill with best' a company I had used for years and knew to be at least a little bit honest with their business programs. It would be

more of a cool off period for me as I pushed through my mind all that Cerebella was putting me through. She certainly had become the bitch everone said that she was. I was now at a loss for what to do and I had resided to the fact that my lawyer firm would have to handle everything from here on in. I had often said over my career that money was no object; apparently now it was.

The fact that I was so attached to my wealth made it even harder to deal with. I would talk to the one person on this planet that I trusted about what might transpire from all of this legal posturing; Coles. A young and very intelligent man who had the gift of knowing. Knowing many things about many things. His expertise on most subjects was more than incredible. We met a few years back and instantly bonded as good friends, something a rich man seldom has.

I would be remise in saying that I didn't help him somewhat in his endeavors. I did, and in most circumstances it came back to me in spades. I knew I would be able to trust him as a key person when the trial started. If he could get me out of this one I would be indepted to him for life. I would rather give him my money than Cerebella. Not all of it of course, I would need some for myself.

I tried to relax in my study before a rather simple dinner was prepared for me. I would eat alone as usual except for the ten or so staff standing at the ready around the parimeter of the large dining room. After dinner I would call Coles and run everything by him to get some feedback. I knew he would be in my court once he was up to speed with all of Cerebella's efforts. When the court case was underway it would then be up to Coles Law as to how the end would materialize.

The End

Kanga

The forest loomed over their travels as the three of them continued to climb to the top of the mountain. It was a big mountain, one with several glaciers and below the treeline a forest so thick it gave a perfect place for many species of animals to live, thrive, and hide; several of them deadly; especially to humans. David had made sure his companions and himself had done due diligence when packing for this adventure. It just might be the last one they endeavored.

It wasn't unusual for the three of them to be off in some strange place on this planet, in fact it was their job. To find and report any new species to the main ship, this was their job. A job that any human living had to do if they were to survive. It was not that long ago that their planet had been destroyed; at least it was the atmosphere surrounding the planet that had become deadly to the human species and millions of others that had cohabitated on the beautiful planet for millions of years.

There had been a select few chosen to man the space station 'HOPE' (Highly Optimistic Preliminary Escape) and then to venture out into the stars to find possible planets capable of supporting human life. This just happened to be one of the many out there. David's crew consisted of four others and himself and the selection had not taken long as there were only David and the four others left after the devastation of their planet.

David was a tall and very fit man in his early thirties exhibiting a strong talent for leadership, hence his position as Captain of the small crew and ship called HOPE. He had been a quick selection out of maybe twenty just before the ship left their home planet and before all of the destruction had started. If given enough time there would have been more of them on HOPE, but as the records show, their time for escape was limited to mear minutes.

Bonnie, a twenty something physically fit female who was more than qualified to operate any part of the space station and its many systems including the escape pods that would eventually land them all on a new planet: Like the planet they were now surveying. She was not part of the landing party on this excursion. It was David the Captain, Dan, Keith, and Paul. She was the only female.

Dan was younger in his mid twenties and a real heart throb according to him when in conversation about his conquests back on their home planet. He had a bit of an ego dilema. His selection for the crew was done through his uncle who was one of the more influential people regarding this high priority project.

Keith another young male was actually not chosen directly for the mission, he was one of the many mechanics needed for the mission and just happened to be on the ship when it had to leave. In good shape with long blonde hair he was not that much different to Dan.

Paul the last of the crew was considerably different to the rest as his age would suggest. He was in his eighties with graying hair, eye glasses, and a frail short body that had seen many different experiences over his long life. The reason for his part in the journey was not unlike Keith's. He had been on the ship sleeping in one of the pods as he often did when on board doing his regular inspections.

Paul had been the mastermind not only in the production of the ship but of the plan to escape the planet and find others that might sustain life; especially their lives. It was not his intention to be part of the crew as he had said his age was against him. He had planned all along to die a peaceful death in his home just as the catastrophe would hit their planet.

The intention of course was to have a much larger crew and one that could sustain itself for generations through procreation. The ship had of course everything needed for such a plan and Paul had even designed the garden center where all of the food was to be grown for consumption by the crew on a daily basis. The original number of crew would have been one hundred. A number he thought would be sufficient to continue the species once a suitable planet was found.

Now that they were actually on another planet, and one that looked and felt very similar to the one they had left some five years earlier, it was not certain that enough of them had made the journey to facilitate the requirements for continued growth of the species. Paul knew in the back of his mind it would only be a matter of time before their species would finally die out.
"Paul… Paul… can you read me… can you hear me?"

The muffled and scratchy voice came over the radio in front of Paul and Keith who were always the ones to stay on HOPE while the others did there investigation work on the planet they were now calling home. Several evenings per week were spent thrashing out ideas for a proper name for the planet. A sequence of letters and numbers sounded to impersonal to the crew, everyone wanted a name that would stand out and make this place sound as good as it appeared.

"Yes, we can hear you, where are you?"
Paul turned to Keith who was leaning in close so as he could hear everything that was said. They both then looked to the radio control panel in front of them. The voice of David came through once again with some urgency in his tone.
"We found something... something I think is important... we are trying to take some vids for you to see... hopefully get some samples to bring back with us."

David continued as now a fuzzy and pixilated picture appeared on the vid screen in front of the two. Paul and Keith could just make out a very green undergrowth with large tree trunks working their large roots underneath it. It was dificult at best to make out what David was refering to, it looked like a small mouse, a creature the crew had been used to back on their planet.

This one however had large circular eyes protruding from a small head, small arms and legs with a thick tail. There was no fur or hair anywhere on the body, at least none they could see on the vid screen. Paul was of course recording the vid for future investigation work. Keith was taking hand notes in his large binder where he had many notations about experiments and such.

"Just be careful what you touch and make sure you're masks and gloves are on. We don't want you returning contaminated with some strange virus."
Paul says into the screen as David and Bonnie can be seen working the small creature into a box so it could be brought back for experiments and other observations. The two of them watched the vid screen as the three started their trek back to HOPE, and with any luck not succumbing to any problems along the way.

Once back on the ship and after the sterilization process the three of them took some time to rest a little before the experiments would commence with the little creature they had found out on the planet's surface. They also had brought back a few plant specimens as well. It would be a busy week or so to determin and categorize the results.

"He looks so weird."
Bonnie states the obvious as all of them are looking through the glass panel at the small creature they had brought on board.
"He almost looks like he is smiling at us."
Keith interjects as he starts writing on a pad of paper in front of him.
"And how do we know this creature is a male?"
David says as he also looks into the enclosed glass cubicle where the strange creature is sitting just looking out at the crew who are doing the same; looking back at the creature.

"Not really sure, but just the way he looks and behaves suggests he is a male, that is according to how our species work."
Dan says his bit as he looks on while eating a sandwich.
"Well whatever he is we should really have a name for him don't you think?"
Paul speaks out as he is the only one seated.
"How about Kanga?"
Bonnie says.
"Kanga, what the hell is that?"

David asks as he and the rest of the crew look to her with surprised looks on their faces.

"Well he looks similar to that of the Kangaroo, you know, the one that lived in Australia."
Bonnie elaborates as the others digest the information. The Kangaroo was just another of the many species that had died out on the planet many years previous.
"Sounds good to me."
David says.
"Settled then, we'll call this little guy Kanga. Any objections?"

Paul says as he looks around at the others. They all nod their heads in agreement and then return to staring at the little creature through the glass. He was not any larger than a football and really was something the crew could get attached to.
"I'll continue testing Kanga for the next few days when I'll have a better idea about what he is all about."
David says as he flips through a book he had on the table beside him. It was obvious what would be

occupying the time of the crew, their new found little pet named Kanga.

Life went on as usual, or at least as usual as it could for a small crew of a ship exploring the cosmos. There of course were more excursions out onto the planet surface but Kanga had been the only animal species they had encountered. Not even any insects or aquatic animals. Plant life was abundant and with plenty of fresh water available it looked like a perfect planet to start the colonization of humans.

This of course would be facilitated by Bonnie as she was the only human female available. The topic had been discussed on many ocassions, it would be done by sperm donation by all of the men, this way the strongest and best would impregnate Bonnie to allow for the best and healthiest newborn. Now with the addition of Kanga to distract them the ongoing topic of having sex with Bonnie would take a back seat, at least for the time being. More treks out onto the planet surface and it had now been determined that the air was breathable and the environment would support humans. It would just be a case of categorizing plants that were eatable and those that were not.

It was a few weeks later that everything started to change when Bonnie went to Paul with some health problems she was experiencing. She always came to Paul as he was the more experienced and with his age it was unlikely he would take advantage of her. After some initial testing Paul had come to the conclusion that Bonnie was pregnant.

"Pregnant? Are you serious Paul? How the hell did that happen?"
Her questions to Paul sounded strange as if anyone should know it would have been Bonnie for sure.
"Yes, I am afraid so Bonnie. Could I ask you which of the crew members it was?"
Paul's question seemed legitimate as it had been agreed by the crew as to the proceedure for Bonnie getting pregnant. In Paul's mind it was obvious Bonnie and one of the crew members had been having sex on the sly.

"It wasn't any of the crew Paul, and to be completely honest if I were to have sex with any of them, it would be you."
Paul sat back and a glazed look took over as he stared at Bonnie.

"No serious Paul, we all had an agreement and I have not had sex with any of the crew. Got that?"
"Yes… yes… I've got that."
He replies still thinking what it was she had said about him being the one she would like to have sex with. It would have been difficult as he now had erectile dysfunction, something that came on a few years back.
"This is really weird Paul, how the hell could I possibly have gotten pregnant if I haven't had sex with anyone?"
Her question was a legitimate one as Paul just sat there looking at her.

"Maybe a toilet seat?"
Paul said off the top of his mind as he had no other explanations. Bonnie just gave him that look.
"Well, let me do a few more tests and all I can say is you will have a baby in about nine months."

Again Bonnie just gave him the look and then let out a deep sigh as she slumped back in the chair. There was a long uncomfortable silence that Paul did not know how to deal with.

"Well I know your somewhat confused at this time so lets just give it some time and see how the tests go with the months ahead."

Paul says to Bonnie who was still not paying much attention to what was being said to her. This was not the plan, especially this soon in the journey. If a suitable planet was found and all of the tests came back positive for humans to live, it would be then that she would have been impregnated. This planet still would require due diligence in the testing formats and that could take close to a year or more.

"Come on, lets go to the canteen and get something to eat. Afterall you are now feeding the two of you."

Paul says as he gets up from his chair and stands beside Bonnie as she slowly turns and gives him a painful stare. She stood and then moved along with Paul and out to the ships food dispensary where it was always likely to find another of the crew; especially at this time of the day. They did indeed find someone there; it was David with his eyes glued to a textbook in front of him on the table and a hand around a mug of coffee.

"Can we join you?"
Paul asks as he pulls out a chair for Bonnie who at this point mustered a smile for David. She sat and David finally looked up from his book.
"Why of course you can, and how is everybodies day going?"
He asks as he closes the text book and looks first to Paul, and then to Bonnie.
"Doing just fine aren't we Bonnie?"
Paul replies as he sits down across from David and beside Bonnie.

"Yes… yes just fine David, and you?"
Paul smiled as she was finally coming around and hopefully dealing with situation.
"Just checking on some inforamtion about some tests we have been doing on Kanga."
"Anything we should know about?"
Paul asks as he looks to David.
"Nothing conclusive yet, but a real odd creature for sure."

He tips back his cup and finishes his coffee. He looks to Bonnie, then Paul.
"Can I get you guys a coffee? Real good this morning for some reason."

He rises from the table with his empty mug.
"Sounds good to me, Bonnie?"
Paul replies as he turns to Bonnie.
"Yeah, why not, feeling a bit hungry as well, could you bring me a muffin David?"
She smiles at him as he nods his head and makes his way to the counter for more coffee and a muffin for Bonnie.

"I need to ask you Bonnie, do you want to keep this a secret, you know, about you being pregnant?"
Paul looked to bonnie who paused to think for a moment before she answered him.
"I think it a good idea Paul, it will be obvious enough in a few months, by then I'll have had enough time to figure out what the hell has happened."
"And hopefully sooner than that after I have a few more tests done. You are telling me the truth about not having sex with any of the crew, right?"

Bonnie looks at Paul straight in the eye before she replies.
"I told you Paul, I have not."
Her tone said it all and Paul would leave it alone. She would have to deal with it and he did not want to get her upset. David came up to the table with a tray, three mugs of coffee, and a couple of muffins which he started to place in the center of the table in front of Bonnie and Paul. It was not more than a few moments later and Dan and Keith entered the room and made their way over to the table.

"Hey guys how's it goin?"
Dan asks as he takes a seat. Keith had made his way over to get something from the counter.
"Anybody want anything while I'm here?"
He looks over to the four of them now seated at the same table.
"Yeah, a coffee sounds good, you guys OK?"
He looked around at Paul, David, and Bonnie. They all nodded their heads with the odd OK working it's way out.

"Well, how's our new pet Kanga doing?"
David asks Dan as he sits down next to him.
"He seems fine, still have some testing to do on him, but all-in-all he seems the perfect pet. Too bad we could not find any other life forms."

David replies as he places his hand on the closed book in front of him and takes a drink of his coffee.
"Yeah, I know what you mean, looks good though for us to set up a camp on the surface though. Keith and I have just about finished our testing of the atmosphere and plant species around."

Keith now made his way over with a couple mugs of coffee and places one down in front of Dan as he sits on the other side of David. The five of them sat and talked for a couple of hours and not once did Bonnie or Paul bring up the fact that Bonnie was pregnant. To her wishes, Paul kept silent about it at least until it was obvious to everyone. By that time she had hoped she would have a logical explanation for her unplanned pregnancy.

Life went on within the ship and they were getting close to starting the initial phase of construction of the new base station on the planet they would now call Sierra. Named mainly for it's many mountains and forests.

It was nearly a month after Bonnie and Paul had discovered her pregnancy and with additional tests Paul was no closer to solving the mystery. Bonnie however was complaing of certain pains and her stomach had increased in size dramatically in the very short time. It was a private meeting and examination by Paul that brought the, if not surprising news, very shocking.

"What do you mean I'm going into labour? It's only been one month Paul, this is absurd… are you sure about this?"
Paul just looks at Bonnie and nods his head, he was at a loss for words. It was obvious she was in a state of shock and time was the only thing that would bring her back to reality. At least a reality that she might be able to comprehend.
"We'll have to get you into the operating room right away, I'm afraid I'm going to need help on this one

so at least two of the others will have to know what's going on."

Bonnie looks at Paul with a vacant look as she winces with the now more than regular pains any pregnant woman would experience.
"What ever Paul, let's just get on with it, the pain is getting more intense, I'm not even sure if I can make it to the medical room."
Paul takes Bonnie's arm as she staggers just a bit as they start for the medical room. On the way Paul stops at an intercom device on the wall and calls the others to meet at the medical room.

The pain she was feeling was intensifying as they walked, when they got to the medical room the others were there waiting for an explanation. Bonnie was now in so much pain she hardly noticed the three of them standing in the middle of the room. Paul took Bonnie right over to one of three beds at the back of the large and complicated looking facility.
"What the hell is going on Paul?"
David asks as he and the others move quickly to help Bonnie to one of the tables where they layed

her out and then raised the back of it so she was elevated a bit at the waist.
"Bonnie's gone into labour."

Paul says as he rushes about getting trays of medical equipment, towels, and adjusting the light so as to see better what he was about to do.
"What do you mean labour?"
David asks the obvious question that was on everyones mind.
"She's about to have a baby."
He answers as he starts to take Bonnie's pants off.
"How the hell can she be pregnant?"
Dan asks as Bonnie lets out a shrill scream.

"I thought one of you might know the answer to that one."
Paul says as he now gets Bonnie in position for delivery. She was now screaming at a high pitch and starting to worry the others standing around her. Paul had put on his surgical attire and gloves and moved in to the area between Bonnie's legs. It did not take long and all of a sudden a small head appeared first where Paul took his hand and guided the baby out. At first it looked like any other baby

being born, but the size of it was very small. This would be normal Paul thought as the length of time from conception to delivery was very short.

As Paul cleaned up the newborn and held it with both hands to let the others see it the others nearly gagged as the newborn started to make noises, it looked just like Kanga; except of course smaller.
"What the fuck!"
David says as he steps back a bit from Paul who is still looking the creature over. He then puts it into an enclosed glass pod as he then goes back to Bonnies who is still screaming out.

Paul buries his head back in between Bonnie's legs and goes to work. It was half a dozen Kangas later that she finally stopped her screaming. All the men could do was look into the glass enclosure and stare at the seven very small Kangas. All that could be surmised was that Bonnie must have touched the creature without her gloves on and somehow the creature was able to transmit sperm or whatever it was to Bonnie to facilitate her getting pregnant. It would now be a very interesting post pregnancy as the men had no idea what these creatures even ate to keep themselves alive. It did not take long before the answer was found as Dan and Keith's dead bodies had been found with missing limbs and certain internal organs. Bonnie was doing fine.

The End

Clowns

Eddy made his way around the corner of the building and then started his long walk down the dark alley. It was way past midnight and in this part of town only a few lights worked if any at all at this time. He had made this journey hundreds of times before and knew the protocol better than anyone. The door was just around the corner and if one did not know where it was, it was likely they would walk right on by it without a query, a good thing, as entry through this door was restricted to only a few, and this few were of like mind. Not a sane one. The secret knock on the heavy metal door changed weekly and it was up to the individual to remember

John P Gibson *High Tide*

this or forever lose the right to enter. Eddy approached the door and started the knocking sequence; this week it was a simple one. Three fast knocks, two long ones, a five second pause then four more slow knocks. There was always someone just inside the door at the assigned time per individual.

There was a pause, then the creaking noise of a large bolt action lock sliding just before the heavy door opened slowly. On the other side was a figure that looked dressed very similar to Eddy. The real only difference was the height and breadth of the man. As far as the dress of the two men they were nearly identical; the make-up, the clothing, shoes, and hat. They were clowns.

Not the cheery fun looking clowns one might see at the fair grounds or the circus, but evil looking in everyway possible. Teddy gave the large clown in front of him a special handshake with his large white gloved hand and after the door was closed they would be allowed to speak with each other. Secrecy was of the utmost importance. It was the number one rule amongst this group of highly eccentric individuals. One of the other rules was to have the elaborate makeup and costumes they wore, on nearly a twenty-four hour basis. They both stood near the closed door for a moment as a smile came across their made up faces. Of course the smile was difficult to see as the make-up suggested otherwise.

"Good to see you Teddy, and how are you this fine night?"
The large clown addressed Teddy who just stood before him.
"I'm in great shape Tertius, and you?"
The large clown pulled his white gloved hand back before responding to the question.
"Could not be better Teddy, the gang are all waiting in the parlor, you're the last as usual."

He states as he gestures for Teddy to make his way into the parlor, one of the many rooms in a very elaborate and high end home in one of the more rundown parts of the city. It was unusual at best, but the reasons for it made plenty of sense to those that had congregated around a very large and beautifully crafted round wooden table. Teddy made his way into the lavish room with ornate carved frames bordering an assortment of oil paintings of clowns.

These clowns looked very similar to the ones sitting at the table and all of them now staring at Teddy and Tertius walking their way. There were only two chairs available as the two clowns sat down.

There was silence as the two took their places at the table. Seven was the number of the clowns evenly spaced around the table with small pads of paper and a pen beside each of them, and a bottle of beer with a very creepy clown label on it. The silence pervaded for what seemed an eternity. A very large clock hanging on a wall at the back with a clown face started to chime the hour of midnight. It too was creepy in it's loud melodic gongs.

It was a clown seated across from Eddy and Tertius that started to talk first but not before tipping a very large hourglass up to start the course sand falling to the empty orb below.
"I just want to say it is once again a pleasure to see the full compliment of our society again this week. We have written an agenda for this meeting and I trust I will have your utmost attentiveness."

The clown neglected to stand as he spoke. It appeared for the most part a somewhat casual affair. He continued.
"It has been brought to my attention that a few of you have expressed a concern about our latest acquisition. I realize since we had started this new weekly ceremony it has become more difficult to acquire the necessary components."

The hourglass was now about halfway finished as the clown that was speaking paused for a brief moment to take a drink from the bottle of clown beer. As he finished the bottle he tipped it side-to-side to make sure he had got every last drop before replacing it on the table just as the hourglass finished with the last of the sand spilling into the lower part.

"Thank you Gary, we are all in this together and of course understand what it is you are trying to convey to us. If you could pass the hourglass to Donny so we can hear his thoughts on the matter."
Philip says as he tips his beer back for another swig. He was sitting on the other side of Gary. The hourglass was moved along the table to Donny who

would tip it up to start the process once again and state his observations to the group of clowns who were now finishing their beers as well.

It was a very short and stubby looking clown that appeared from a hallway with a large tray full of clown beers who approached the table and started to place a beer in front of each of the clowns around the table. It was uncanny how all of them had finished their beers at the same time. Once the beers are in place in front of each clown and the empties taken away by the short clown Donny starts in with his agenda.

"I understand your concern Gary but we as a group have only so many options as our resources are starting to dwindle. I believe I had brought up this concern some years back. When more and more groups such as our own start up it is no wonder it has become more difficult to find our ceremonial criteria. But on the positive side, most things in general have improved."

Donny takes a break as he sips his beer. As he replaces his beer to the table he notices the hourglass is still more than half full and he takes the opportunity to continue his monologue.

"It is because of our fervant belief in our benevolent and intelligent leader 'Bobo'."
He turns with bottle in hand to a very large dressed up manaquin in the corner of the room dressed similar to those sitting around the table. A very ghoulish looking clown with the trademark frown instead of a smile. There was an inaudible murmer as they all bowed their heads for a moment. Donny now looks around and takes his last few minutes to conclude his talk.

"My friends we have to know that we have come to the end of our vigil and tonights ceremony might just be the last of its kind. You must all know that over the years you have been doing the right thing, I just want to say before I finish that we should still keep a vigil watch over things just in case this sort of thing starts to happen again."
The hourglass had just finished as he passed it along to the clown next to him. As the clown turned the hourglass over to start he also took a swig of his beer before he started to speak to the others.

"Thank you Donny, I do understand some of the tension in the room, as a big part of our lives will change dramatically after tonights ceremony."
He again takes another drink of his clown beer before continuing.

"The great thing about our society is that we claim no leader than that of 'Bobo' who we all know is just a pigment of our imagination."
"Don't you mean figment, Philip?"
Donny asks as everyone started to giggle just a little.
"Yes of course I did Donny, I was just trying to inject a little humour into the situation that was all."
Philip takes another drink of his beer before continuing.

The smile he had put on just barely made its way through the heavy makeup and enhanced frown across his face.
"Back to the situation at hand, we have an obligation to continue our work indefinitely so that what has happened in the past will never happen again on this planet; anywhere. We have now instilled in our youth the importance of our cult and that it is to be continued through eternity. It also gives us the

chance to test our clown beer so gratiously brewed by our very own Eddy."

Philip turns to Eddy and raises his beer for a toast as the others follow suit. The gurgles and slurps that ensued said it all; the beer was indeed good. Eddy had a few years back come up with the idea of brewing beer with sardines. This of course had not gone over very well with the other clowns until they tried his first batch; it was a hit from the start, and one of everyones favourites.

Once the beer bottles were returned to the table top the last of the sand had filtered its way to the bottom of the hourglass. Philip slid it over to the clown next to him and then sat down. There was silence once again as the clown turned the hourglass over to start the process. He stood and revealed to all his crazy costume and an average height to the rest. Of course there was no smile to be seen.
"I agree with all that has been said and only want to thank everyone and of course Bobo; (he raises his beer to the iconic god before them) for allowing me the privilage to have a positive affect on this planet."

The room was silent as he continued.

"It is not often one can say to almost anyone that his life spent under the direction of such a cause has been truly beneficial and welcoming."

He turned to acknowledge the clowns to his right and the clowns to the left of him before continuing.

"I, as many of you have passed the baton down to my children and I pray they will do the same when the time comes for them."

He takes another drink of beer.

"In many ways it is a difficult night tonight as we know it will be the last of its kind. At least we pray for it to be. Many of our clubs have closed and hopefully never to be re-opened. This last ceremony of course will be televised for the many millions of others that have been helping with this problem over the years and a great thankyou goes out to them for their efforts."

The hourglass had now emptied from top to bottom and the clown slid the hourglass along to the last remaining clown as he sat down; but not before taking another swig of his beer.

"Thank you Tim for your input on this our last night of ceremonies. I will try and keep my oratory short so that we can get on with the rest of the night, it will be a long one once again, but we can be soliced in the fact that after this last ceremony the planet will be a better place for it."
The clown looks around the room for nods of acceptance and then continues.

"It has been expressed that we continue with our weekly get togethers so that we do not lose our focal point and the reason we came together at the start. I agree with this as I know the rest of you do as well. It is agreed then that regardless of the fact that the ceremonies will not continue, at least our meetings and beer sampling will. If anyone has further imput we can discuss anything after the ceremony. I now beckon everyone to finish their beers and follow me into the chamber room for our final ceremony."

The clown starts to move in the direction of a large open hallway with a very large carved wooden door at the end of it. Teddy scurries up beside the clown as they walk.

"Good one Marco, this certainly will be a momentous moment."
The two walk quietly as the others fall in behind them. Once they reach the doors the very small clown was already there to open them, as he did so the massive round room inside had a round raised platform in the middle with a large wooden pole erected in the center.

"Everyone please take your places for the ceremony. Peter could you get the lights please?"
Marco says to the short clown who was now rushing about getting chairs set for the clowns to sit in. He went off to a side wall where there was a large electrical panel where he started to flip switchs. The lights started to come up and one could now see the main center piece and what was attached to the wooden pole. It was a man tied to it with his clothes removed and his head slumped over onto his chest. There was a turntable mechanism obviously built into the platform and the man turned slowly around and around. There were a pile of clothes laying at the foot of the pole, obviously his.

John P Gibson *High Tide*

There lay what looked to be a very expensive three piece suit with tie and fancy black leather shoes. It was unlike the others that had been the focal point of the ceremony. It did not take long and Peter had placed a wooden box on a small side table next to each chair. The clowns took their chairs and opened the lid to the box and then just waited as Marco stood to address them all.

"My esteemed colleagues I now beckon you to start the ceremony as we deal with the last of these vermon that have terrorized our planet for far too long. It will be important of course to make sure you are all on target as we do not want any mishaps like we had last week. Please take your weapons and ready yourself. Peter please start the music."

Peter went over to a side cupboard and opened the door where a large reel-to-reel recording device sat. He pushed a button and the familiar music started to drum out of the many speakers around the room. It was a favourite circus melody playing as the clowns now started to throw the large lawn darts at the near naked man tied to the pole. He started to scream after the first of many darts found their mark. It did not tak long and the man succumbed to the darts impaled in his body and a pool of blood surrounding his clothes on the floor below him. He was the last, the last that the clowns knew of. The last of a breed they hoped would never rise to power again. The last politician.

The End

Parasite

The story of a large biped creature capable of destroying it's large host in more ways than one had made front page news for more than a month and the planet Earth had all of its humans on the edge of their seats waiting for more news on a daily basis. The only reason this was such a newsworthy story was that this information was coming back to the planet Earth from many thousands of drones situated in the atmosphere of a planet not too dissimilar to that of Earth. It was a mere one light year away and had always allowed the probability of supporting humans and of course other life forms.

John P Gibson   *High Tide*

Out of the forty-five billion or so humans existing on Earth, the majority of them had access to vid-screens so as they could watch the almost continous coverage of the events happening on the planet they now had named Savior. It was a beam of light in an otherwise very dark abyss they had lived in for centuries. The powers that be had for a very long time promised that things would change for the better; they of course hadn't, but now with a new planet they could colonize, hope was once again at the forefront.

"Savior one to base three… Savior one to base three… do you read?"
The message was coming through loud and clear at the massive station on Earth called NASA. A relic of an organization that had kept the name for sentimental reasons. 'National Aronautics and Space Administration' had been the first to discover this new planet Savior and of course were very proud to be the first as there were many countries vying for leadership in the 'race for space' as many referred to it as.

"This is base three reading you loud and clear Savior one, what do you have to report?"
The technician says into his headset while watching the vid-screen in front of him. He was just one of thousands in a very large warehouse type room where all of the vids and voice recordings were monitored on a twenty-four hour basis. There was a small amount of crackling heard before the voice from Savior one came across once again.

"We have the additional five hundred drones activated and flying over section five, do you register the video footage yet?"
There was a hum of activity in the room as many technicians moved about and adjusted vid screens, especially the largest at the back of the room being fifty feet wide by twenty feet high. The images started to sharpen as focus was improving. It was a view that many humans had never seen before and most in the room were in awe of what they were watching. It was a landscape so different from that of Earth's but in some ways so familiar as well.

"Varifying vid reproduction and audio... coming in fine Savior one."

The tech replied as now several others were standing behind him and watching the vid screen. The images that presented themselves were very disconcerning as most of what could be seen were vast areas of desert like topography. The original vids of the planet showed extensive areas such as this and the only reason continued exploration prevailed was that there was some life form detected.

Now with the additional vid drones it would be possible to find these life forms and determine their biological make up. The new drones were considerably more high-tech than any other used thus far. The base camp on the planet was not that large and the thirty or so astronauts had been there now for several years. The atmosphere was close enough to Earth's that they could breath and function normally as if they were on Earth when outside the confines of the camp. The strange part of course was that no other life form other than this strange beast could be found. It had the scientists puzzled for sure.

"There… there is one… right there."
One of the scientists at base three standing behind the manned vid screen says as he points his finger at an object scurrying across a level part of the landscape. It quickly ran in behind a large rock outcrop where it stayed. The drones of course could be controlled by computer either from base three or Savior.
"Get that drone over to where it went, we need more video so we can get a better idea on how this creature is put together."

A lone scientist says as he watchs what has transpired over the last few minutes on the vid screen in front of him and the others. The technician plays with some levers and buttons as the view changes and the vid shot now shows a creature huddling behind the rock it was using for refuge. It looked a little strange but with similar characteristics to that of a human; just not as tall and with absolutely no hair on the parts of the body that were exposed outside what looked like a one piece material type clothing. There was no footwear on the short and stubby feet, and nothing else to suggest this creatures status or place of origin on the planet.

"Have we spotted any more of these little guys?"
The question came from the Scientist overlooking the operation.
"Not yet, I have a feeling there can't be too much life on this planet judging from the looks of the landscape."
The technician replies as he continues to study the vid screen without looking back at the scientist.

"Well, keep me posted, I have some other things to deal with concerning the make up of the soil samples we have. It's looking doubtful anything could survive in this environment."
The scientist says as he turns and then leaves the control room to make his exit to the laboratory where he had come from. The rest of the crew continued to watch the vid monitor and the information the drones were sending back to them. It did not take long and one of the techs pointed at the screen.

"There... there... I see something, it looks like another one of those creatures, like the one behind the rock."

Everyones eyes moved to the man's finger as it pointed out a small movement on the screen. It was running along the same path the other one had taken and was now coming in behind the rock with the first one. It looked nearly identical to the first but with a covering somewhat different. The difference being in colour, not the material.
"Now it looks like they are conversing with each other... you know... talking, or at least some kind of verbal communication."

One of the techs says as she looks on with the others. There is silence as they listen for any audio the vid might provide them. There was a faint murmer but nothing intelligible could be deciphered. The looks in the creatures eyes however told the story all too well. They were frightened and were doing their best to find a false haven. It would take closer examination to find out more about these strange creatures they had found on the surface of Savior.

*****

It was six months later and Earth was going through more turmoil and the efforts of those on Savior were now starting to pay off. The physical make up of the small creatures was not too dissimilar to that of the humans conducting the studies. A few of the lead scientists were now able to communicate with the species; even if it was in a small way.

The information was being compiled, and the further along the scientists went with their studies, the more concerned they became. Some basic language similarities allowed the scientisits to at least communicate with this new species on a childlike level. The information they were gathering was not good. This species called themselves Trendor; the closest the humans could get through translation. They were at this time experiencing one of the most horrific environmental challenges they had ever known. The two Trendors had been held in isolation until the scientists were sure it would be safe to deal with them in the same environment.

John P Gibson   *High Tide*

After finding out what kind of nourishment these aliens requiered, it was easy enough to satisfy their hunger. Most of the food the humans were eating worked well for the two Trendors. They started to expand and not look so boney. With the limited conversation it was discovered that the two Trendors now named Chilso and Marfam, the closest the humans could get to the language of the Trendors, had some very important news to divulge.

It appears the devastating ecological phenomenon had been caused by the Trendors. The information started to point clues in their direction as the main fault of the collapse of the system. The hope to colonize this planet with humans was now diminishing rapidly as the tests were proving that there was still more troubles for the planet that was believed to be a good candidate for the placement of humans. As Earth was going through it's problems the massive ships that were built to bring the large population to this planet had been loading for the past few months with an additional six months to go before they were full to capacity.

It was the only option to make the lengthy trip to Savior. No other planets within a distance that would allow the humans survivability existed and now the scientists not only on Earth, but also Savior were at a crossroad as to what could possibly be done to save the human population. With the limited translation of what Chilso and Marfam were trying to convey to the scientists, it was not looking good.

It was more words of warning than anything else. The Trendors had existed on Savior for more than three million years; most of which were lived in harmony with the multitude of other species on the planet. The reason for their demise was believed to be a process by which an alien species arrived and started to change the way the Trendors lived their lives. It was not long and the introduction of classes within the species and the new one created a very different way of life. The trendors were made to work for the new aliens and through sexual domination a different breed of Trendors were then being born into a scary and unrealistic reality.

It did not take long and the devastation the new breeds were causing made it clear and simple that total destruction would ensue if changes were not made. The aliens could see this and at some point saw the light and left the planet to find another that they could infest and dominate for their own purpose.

The Trendors were not able to get back to a lifestyle that was beneficial to them or any of the other species on the planet. Over the course of thousands of years the actions of the Trendors put the planet in a state of deterioration that could not be reversed. Underground was the only option for those that had had the foresight. Even then it would be many that could not survive the new way of living a life on a damaged planet.

The crew on Savior were now realizing the significance of their findings. The similarities of what was happening back on Earth coincided with much of what the Trendors had been saying about their planet. There was an uncomfortable hush in the room as all just looked at the Trendors who had now become silent as well. It was obvious there would have to be some serious conversations.

The End

The Spider Web

Darren came running out of the room screaming in a high pitch of that not unlike a womans. His hands were flayling above him as he continued to the front door of his apartment. He threw the door open and kept running down the hallway to the elevator where he repeatedly pushed the buttons to get the doors to slide open. He was in panic mode and with all of his screaming he had roused the curiosities of most of the tenents along the hallway that shared the more than luxurious condo building in the upscale city of Victoria. A moderately sized city in a province of Canada. It wasn't the first time Darren had done this exact thing, so his neighbours seemed not all that concerned as they peered out from their doorways.

There were no usual questions asked such as; 'Is everything OK Darren?', 'Do you need some help?', 'Should we call the police?.... Again.' Darren was on his own as the elevator doors opened to an empty space that he rushed into. As the CCTV cameras would attest to later, Daren would continue his antics in the elevator.

Once the doors opened in the lobby of the building his screaming was heard by the front desk attendents. The two of them looked up ready to assist then noticed it was Darren. The two – a male and a female in their thirties – went back to what it was they were doing before being rudely disturbed by the screams and over the top body movements of Darren, who was now sprinting his way to the double front doors of the upscale apartment complex. Outside Darren looked both ways then made a decision to run to his left down the street. His screaming finally started to fade in the distance and things started to return to a quietness the building was famed for. One of the reasons people wanted to live at Serene Heights. A multi-condo complex for the above average wage earner.

Darren Driddle had been there for nearly five years, not too long after it had opened to the public. He was one of the first to choose one of the only two penthouse units available. Darren was a arachnophobe. He had been afraid of spiders all of his thirty-five years. He had developed the loudest scream to be heard anywhere. A slim man with blonde wavy hair and clean shaven, he was someone often labeled as a girlyman.

Darren wasn't gay but often came across as one. He had lived alone since he had moved in and the others had grown to like the man until recently when he went off because of a small spider somewhere in his condo. The initial response was of course to help the man, but with his inscesent non-stop screaming whenever he did see one, it was nearly impossible to deal with. Because of his very large inheritance from his Mother who had passed away some years ago he was not in need of a job, nor did he want one. Most of his time was spent in his condo apart from the times when he had seen a spider somewhere in his premises. He was also one of those people who did not have any close friends.

It was just all too strange to those that were there to see it now happen on a more frequent basis. Darren had now run nearly a mile down the road alongside a park and nearing the center of the city. There were many people along the street, many of whom turned to watch him run along screaming. They too looked for a person that might be chasing him; there was nothing of course. No one.

It finally got to him. Exhaustion. His heavy breathing and the fact that he had run nearly a mile had taken its toll on his body. He found a bench to sit down on, but only after searching it methodically for any spiders. It was not long and he heard the shuffling of feet and the squeak of an unoiled wheel approaching. As Darren looked up he noticed an old shriviled up man making his way at a very slow pace with his wheeled walker to the bench where he sat. The old man not more than four feet tall with white wrinkly sagging skin on his face and his hands turned the walker and what seemed like minutes, sat down beside Darren; almost too close as he could smell the all too familiar old people smell.

"You OK there sonny?"
The craggly old voice came at Darren along with a foul smell of halitosis. Darren was about to respond as he looked at the old man and noticed he had hearing aids in both of his ears; he would have to speak loudly he thought. Not a problem as he was still shaken by the event at his condo and his high pitched voice would more than likely be heard by the old decrepid human sitting beside him.

"I'm... a little shaken... I must look a mess."
Darren confides in the old man next to him.
"What is it that is bothering you son?"
He asks almost losing the lower set of his dentures as he spoke.
"Spiders, I ... hate them... and I found another in my condo."
Darren started to shake as he spoke the words to the old man whose glaring eyes behind the far too thick spectacles did their best to keep focus, he did however manage to get his lower teeth back in place.

"I know what you mean, my wife was the same way when it came to those little critters."

Darren turned his head away, he was pretty sure he did not want to listen to what the old man was saying even though he did not use the word spider, little critters said it all.

"She just had to hear the word spider and she went all crazy like. It got to a point where she had to have her own room and on her bedside table she had cans of insect repellent and stuff."

Darren could still not turn to look at the old man, he was starting to shiver and shake all over. He could just picture the scene. The most difficult part was that he would have to return to his condo at some point. Preferably never he thought in the back of his mind, but reality suggested otherwise. Afterall, he was only dressed in his jockey shorts and pink socks.

"In the end the doctor said she died of some kind of poison, he said probably from the spray in the cans on her bedside table."

The old man continued not realizing that Darren was in some sort of trauma. He just kept mumbling on like some old people do.
"And then when I had to have the cleaning lady we had come in and clean up the mess, she downright refused after she saw what the spiders had done in the room."

Darren could only imagine as his imagination took over. As much as he hated the idea, he would have to get home. Home where he hopefully would find the spider gone. Away from his condo forever. The walk back seemed of course to take considerably longer as his pace was a deliberate slow one. He could hear the faint chatter of the old man still as though he was still seated beside him on the park bench.

Once at the main entrance to his building Darren stopped with his hand on the handle of the main door. He was almost thinking of turning and starting all over in a different city, different province, maybe even a different country; one where he could be certain there were no spiders.

He slowly opened the door to see people in the lobby who looked at him in his strange attire. Darren was used to it as this of course had not been the first time he had left his condo barely dressed. As he approached the elevator he looked around to make sure there were no spiders lurking about. There were none that he could see.

The doors slid open with a hiss and swoosh he was familiar with. He looked into an empty elevator as he poked his head in first to look around for any tell tail signs of the eight legged creepy monsters that seemed to stalk Darren far too often.

He gritted his teeth and entered, then pushed the button to his floor. He kept looking around expecting something small and creepy to lower itself down from its web in front of his face. It did not happen. He let out a big sigh of relief as the doors opened, it was like he had been holding his breath the whole time. The hallway looked clear and he then started to make his way to his condo near the end of the hallway. He kept looking over his shoulder and up and down as he walked.

As he approached his door, Darren slowed and stood still a few feet from it. He started to tremble and break out in beads of sweat that rolled down his face. His eyes looked like giant marbles and his shaking started once again. He turned and started at a quick walk; nearly a run, back to the elevator. His idea was to make his way to one of his co-workers place to see if he could stay there until he calmed down.

*****

"Hello… who's there?"
The voice of Darren's co-worker Ed came across the intercom speaker at the entrance to the multi-unit apartment complex about two miles from where Darren lived. It had been a long and somewhat hectic journey.
"Hi Ed, it's me Darren… can I come up to see you? It's rather important."
He says with some anxiety in his voice.
"Yeah… yeah, come on up."
Darren hears the buzz and then the click of the lock on the main doors release. He pushes the large glass door open and enters the foyer to the complex.

It would be another ride up the elevator to the top floor with Darren keeping a close lookout for any spiders that might be lurking about in the corners or on the ceiling. The CCTV camera would of course be capturing all of this and would more than likely give the audience at some point something to talk about when they saw the man dressed in his boxers and pink socks.

After the elevator stopped and Darren checking either way down the hallway he ventured out and along to one of the doors near the end. He quickly rang the doorbell and kept doing so until there was the unlocking of the door as it opened.
"Oh God... Ed, it's so good to see you."
Darren says in a gasping way as he leans in and hugs Ed who is just somewhat taken aback by the whole thing.
"It's... good to... see you too... Darren. What's going on? You seem so stressed... and look at the way you're dressed. You do know it's very cold outside?"

"Please, Ed, can we go inside so I can try and settle down just a little. You don't have any spiders do you?"
Ed now had some idea as to why Darren was here at his condo. He had heard the stories before about Darren's phobia about spiders and had always just shrugged it off as some minor nuisance to allow others to extend some sympathy towards the man.

"I don't think so Darren and of course you can come in, lets get you some more clothes to put on, you must be freezing."
Ed says as he brings Darren into the front room of the condo after closing the door. Darren of course his head turning constantly looking for any crawly creatures that might be lurking about.
"You have a problem with spiders do you Darren?"
Ed thinks to ask as darren seems to be drifting further away from reality. At least the reality in the room they were both in at the moment.

"Yes… yes I… do… I hate the… fucking things."
He answers as he starts to get his breath back.
"I always have… and… there is a… huge fucking one… in my apartment… right now."

He continues on as Ed listens sympathetically not knowing what he could really do to calm Darren down.

"I'll be right back Darren, I'm just going to get some clothes for you to put on... your trembling like a leaf."
Ed turns to go to his bedroom just shaking his head and gratefull he can escape Darren's dilema; at least for the few moments it would take him to retrieve enough clothes to put on Darren to help keep him warm.

Darren still standing looks around the room again to make sure he cannot see any spiders moving about. He was now feeling the cold work it's way through his near naked body. The clothes Ed had bundled up in his arms looked so nice to him he ran over and hugged Ed while he still held onto the pile of clothes in his arms.

"You're welcome Darren, these should get you back to feeling human again."
Ed places the clothes in Darrens outstretched arms.

"Oh thank you Ed, I can't tell you enough how thankful I am for your trouble. I promise I'll make it up to you."
Darren says as he puts the clothes on as quick as he can. It took a few moments and Ed just stood there and watched.

"You really need to get yourself under control here Darren, I mean afterall it is only a spider we're talking about here, and it's likely it's not even poisonous."
When Ed said 'poisonous' Darren started to shake once again, and this time it was not from the cold.
"Yes... I... know Ed, It's just that I have always been terrified of those little monsters."
He hoped this would somehow shed some light on his situation; at least enough to make Ed understand his dilemma with these freaky creatures.

"Well I can't relate Darren, I can pick them up, let them run all over my hands and arms, even put them close to my face and talk with them."
All Darren could do was look at Ed in a state of fear with his mouth agape, and the adrenilan starting too

rush through his veins. If he hadn't been scared before… he certainly was now.

"Sorry Darren… I'm really sorry… I wasn't thinking. Look my place is clean and there are no spiders or for that matter any insects. My cleaning girl does a very thorough job when she comes once a week."
Ed thought this should put Darren at ease, then thought possibly a drink of something might help the situation.

"Darren, would you like something to drink?"
Darren continued looking about the room, then focused on Ed.
"Yes… that would be great."
"What would you like? A beer, something stronger? Maybe a tea or coffee?"
Darren thought for a moment as he again started to look around the room.

"Yeah… a beer… a beer sounds good."
He continues to look about the room while Ed makes his way to the fridge. On his way he decided to ask a few more questions of Darren.

"Do you think maybe my cleaning lady might be able to help? You know, with cleaning your place out completely. She is very good, and I could go with her to make sure there were no spiders when she had finished."

Darren thinks for a moment as he pulls back on the beer. It was obvious he was seriously contemplating the offer Ed had just put forth. It certainly would be better if someone else were to venture into his home before he had to. Especially if it was someone that was qualified at cleaning homes.
"That sounds like a great idea Ed, you sure she wouldn't mind?"
"No, I would pay her of course for her work and I'm pretty sure she could do it today. I'll give her a call to find out."

Ed takes his phone and pushs some keys and then startes talking to someone on the other end. His conversation was short and not only did he have a smile on his face, but Darren did as well.
"She will be here within about fifteen minutes then we can all go over to your place so she can do her work."

Ed says as he puts his phone down on the table.

"I was wondering Ed if it would be alright if I stayed here at your place until she has finished cleaning my place, and I certainly don't mind paying her extra for her work. You do understand I hope."
"Yes of course I do Darren, when she gets here I'll take her over to your place to get her started. Could I get your keys from you?"
Darren reaches for his pocket to retrieve his keys as he fumbles a little and drops them to the floor below. Ed and Darren both bend over to pick them up and knock heads together. They then look up to each other and let out a little laugh.
"You want another beer Darren?"

Ed asks as he rubs his head as he puts the keys into his pocket.
"Yes I think I could use one, I'm still shaking a bit, and I can't get the picture of the spider out of my head."
Ed just looks at Darren with a look of understanding. He too had, in the past been to places that were uncomfortable. He went into the

kitchen to get the beer just as there was the sound of the doorbell ringing.

"Do you want to get that Darren, it'll be Hellen, my cleaning girl."
He says as he continues into the kitchen. Darren makes his way to the front door and with a cautious hesitation opens the door just enough to look out to see who it was. What he saw was a relatively young blonde girl with a somewhat pretty look to her. She was holding a large cloth bag.
"Please… come in, you must be Hellen?"
She looks at Darren from head to toe noticing the clothes he was wearing did not fit very well.
"Yes I am, is Ed here?"

She asks as she peers in past Darren and into the hallway where Ed was now appraoching Darren with a bottle of beer in his hand.
"Oh hi Hellen, so glad you could make it on such short notice. This is Darren, Darren this is Hellen."
He says as he passes the beer to Darren and motions for Hellen to enter.

"Hi Ed, no problem, I had this afternoon off anyway. So lets get a move on then."
She says in a matter-of-fact tone.
"OK then we're off, you going to be alright Darren?"
Darren just looks at the two of them as he takes a drink of the beer before he answers.
"Yeah… yeah… I should be fine, there's more beer in the fridge, right?"
"Yes there are even some imports you might like to try like the sardine beer from Portugal. It shouldn't take us too long, should be back around five then we can go for some dinner. Sound good to you?"
Darren again gives them both a look as he takes another drink from the beer bottle in his grasp. He smiles.

"That sounds good, you can always give me a call when you're done. Nice to meet you Hellen and thank you so much for helping me. I'm sure Ed will fill you in on what the issue is."
Darren looks to Ed with a smile.
"Good enough, lets go then."
Ed says as he escorts Hellen out the door and down the hall. Darren closes the front door and then locks it.

He was alone once again. This time however he felt somewhat safer as he held onto the beer in his hand. He also had a closer look at Ed's home and could see that Hellen did a fantastic job of keeping it spotless. This reassured Darren that when he returned to his place, it would be as clean if not cleaner.

Now all he needed to do was relax as best he could and wait for Ed and Hellen to return from his place. He would settle into the comfy sofa and watch some TV on the large set above the fireplace while drinking his beer; which he noticed was getting empty. He would have to go get another one from the fridge.

After about an hour and several more beer Darren curled up on the sofa and started to doze off. He was feeling considerably better, and thought a short nap should do the trick. Ed had said to him that Hellen and him should have the job done by about five PM, he would make sure he was up and about before that.

****

John P Gibson *High Tide*

It was a strange humming sound that stirred Darren awake as he rubbed his eyes. He looked over to the clock on the wall and it said it was about five minutes to five. He had timed it perfect. It was however the humming sound coming from the TV that he did not understand. It took him a few minutes to get himself together and then walk over to the TV and turn it off He then looked out the window and noticed that it was very dark outside. Something wasn't quite right. It should still be light out at this time of the afternoon. It was a moment later that he realized it was not five in the afternoon, but, five in the morning.

Where the hell were Ed and Hellen? Surely it could not have taken them this long to clean his home of the dreaded spiders? He searched for his cell phone and finally found it in amongst the many empty beer bottles cluttering the coffe table in front of him. After quickly dialing Eds cell phone he sat back and waited. There was no answer, and once directed to Ed's voicemail Darren left a long and concerned message. He then thought to call his land-line, as he still had one where most had given up on the old phone systems. It was the same; no answer as he waited for the voicemail to kick in. Darren left pretty much the same message as the cell phone.

Now he was really in a state, what should he do? There was only one answer and that was to go to his place to see what was going on. He managed to find some warmer clothes of Ed's to wear as the outside temperature was cold. He had no key for Ed's home so he just shut the front door and made his way outside to where he would run as fast as he could to his place. It would take him about fifteen minutes.

Once he arrived at his building, he went into the front doors and to the elevator. He was shivering and a cold sweat started to work its way to the surface of his face. It was mostly due to the fact that he did not know what to expect when he opened his apartment door.

Once off the elevator he walked slower to his door now realizing he had given his key to Ed so Hellen and him could get in. Luckily he had a spare he hid under a stone frog in the planter next to his door. As he fumbled with the key in the door lock, it finally clicked open. He pushed the door ever so slightly while all the time calling for Ed.

The door was now fully open and the room inside was pitch black, he could not see a thing. Darren reached in and around the door to where the light switch was and flipped it on. What he saw sent a cold shiver up his spine and a shrill scream worked it's way out of his trembling mouth. It was only a moment later and thousands of large spiders jumped onto him and started to weave their web all around his body. He fell to the floor and the spiders did the rest of their work quickly and efficiently. What Darren had seen when he walked in were Ed and Hellen suspended in their own spiderweb cocoon with only their heads visible where it was obvious they had died a terrible death.

The End

Lost In Heaven

It wasn't a shock to Tony, he knew in the back of his mind somewhere he would certainly be leaving the place he had been accustomed to for all those years. It was just that this place held no recollection to him what so ever. As a young boy he had of course been tutored in the ways of the Catholic religion. One he had thought to be very similar to others around the planet. As he had grown up in Italy the influence of the religion was very prominent, especially in his family. Tony Barcelli was a forty-seven year old successful entrepreneur in a field that many Italians were accustomed to: The

John P Gibson *High Tide*

Mafia. Of course as a child he had no idea what the organization meant, or what it was all about, this he would find out soon enough as he grew older.

Somehow Tony knew he had moved on in his life, and his recollection of what his life was about before this transformation suggested he had left the human existance he had had for nearly fifty years. But where was he? Why did he feel so good? Why was there no one else here with him? These questions and more kept him in a thought provoking place.

As he walked about the seemingly endless expanse of virtually nothing, Tony started to focus on his thoughts and what it was he had been doing just a short itme before arriving at this place. His brain started to put things in order and he now understood he had died; he had left the world he had been so used to for so many years. The moments leading up to his death started to materialize; almost in a visual 3D fashion right in front of him. It had been a bullet to the head, and his death was swift and painless. This was just part of the way the Mafia worked when one had for the most part done his best within the brotherhood. The strangest part was, when he looked around, he could not see any part of his body; at least the body he had been involved with for nearly fifty years. It was just all too strange to him. There were not even any sounds that he could hear, it was completely quiet except for his thoughts.

Tony decided to just sit and wait; sitting of course in his mind as he still could not see any sort of body that might belong to him. Without his thoughts, it was the most quiet and calm he had ever experienced. The passage of time was even non exsitant. Where the hell was he?

As he sat and contemplated his next move, Tony all of a sudden felt something; something strange but nice. It was a feeling he could not describe to himself as he had never felt it before. It was not threatening in any way, and he was hoping he would continue to feel this way for as long as he possibly could.

It was a feeling of complete calmness with no urgency involved at all, he was just drifting in and out of a blissful state that he did not want to ever end, and if not for what was abot to happen next; it very well might have continued on for eternity. At least the eternity he was familiar with when he had been alive on the planet Earth not that long ago. He just let it go and enjoyed this new feeling.

"Tony... Tony... Tony..."
There was this soft voice speaking to him now and he knew it not to be something he was imagining. To his best recollection it was the voice of a female, one that sounded very attractive and enticing. He turned, at least that is what he thought he had done, when he saw the figure in front of him. It was indeed a female; a very gorgeous one at that.

"Tony... I know this is all very strange to you, but you must believe me this is just a moment in your travels and soon you will be in a different reality to the one you came from."
Tony looks at the woman in front of him and listens to what she is saying to him. He would have to keep his mind focused on what she was telling him, even though it was hard to do as her beauty was taking him off guard.

"Where am I?"

He thought to ask as there was a pause in her speaking. She looked into his eyes and smiled.

"You are in Heaven Tony."

He had had that feeling that something was very different, and possibly he had finally died on the planet Earth after a very electrifying life. If it indeed was Heaven, he felt himself fortunate.

"Heaven you say, you're not bullshitting me are you?"

He had to know and was sure his bluntness would deliver him the right answers.

"Heaven as you know it Tony."

She replied as he just looked into his eyes. Tony reciprocated, but his gaze lowered as he took in the very beautiful woman in front of him.

"It is a Heaven you believe in Tony and you will have a short tour so as you fully understand how things work here. I know you will pick up on the subtleties of this space quickly; it is your nature Tony."

She looked again at his eyes as she spoke to him. He thought it now a good time to ask the question foremost on his mind.

"What is your name?"
He asked as he looked her straight in the eyes.
"Maria."
The name ripped through Tony's brain. He stared at her and the moment seemed to take forever.
"Maria."
He responded by repeating her name, more for himself as he wasn't sure he had heard her right the first time.

"Yes, Maria is my name and I am here to help you with your next step of the journey."
Tony looks at her with a puzzled look on his face as he tries once again to grasp the meaning of all that is taking place. His wife's name was Maria who was, as far as he knew still alive.
"If you will just follow me Tony, we will go to the first step of your induction."
He could see Maria turn and move in a direction, it was difficult to tell in which as the space around them both was void of anything.

She wasn't even walking, it was more like gliding. Tony looked down at his feet and he was moving in the same fashion as Maria. It was all so confusing to him, but he would do his best to grasp the concept of this place called Heaven.

It was a few moments later and Maria stopped as Tony glided up to her where he also stopped. He was not in control of his motor skills and assumed Maria was.
"This will do just fine Tony, I want you to look straight ahead as I project some of your past life in front of you. Most of it you should remember."

Maria looked right into Tony's eyes as she spoke. He then looked ahead as her head turned in the direction of what appeared to be a screen of some sort floating in mid air. On this screen a series of moving pictures started to form, Tony's attention was garnered as he watched. It appeared it was his childhood where he grew up in Italy, a small town where there were not too many inhabitants, but the ones that were there were good people. At least they had been good to him and his family.

The series of photos and videos took some time as Tony saw himself age into his teen years. At that point the screen disappeared and once again there was nothing.
"We must move on now Tony, just follow me please."
Maria says to him as they start to move in another direction. Tony was now getting used to this system and just thought to relax and enjoy the journey.

It was not long and Maria once again stopped the two of them. Another screen appeared in front of Tony and he watched the video footage, it was him when he was in his twenties and started in the family business. He watched closely and found it very interesting to say the least. He was starting to see how his upbringing had caused a lot of grief for many other families, but of course was very lucrative for his immediate family along with extended family. The video continued showing his life into his thirties, and the reality of his life was sinking in. He thought all along he had been doing the best he could for his family.

Truth be told, he had been doing the exact opposite now that it was unfolding in front of him on the video. Maria was silent as she had been through the last video, he was to watch in silence as his life unfolded before him. He found it hard to believe that his training as a hit man for the Mafia was actually now unfolding as something bad.

Tony had always thought his work was for the better of the family. He had killed more than twenty men connected to the Mafia. This in itself was not so bad as others had killed many more, it's just that his marks were high profile ones; people that were deemed a very real threat to the whole industry at the time.

He was not one of those that received pleasure from his killings; it was a job. A job that in his mind needed doing. The graphic videos started to get Tony feeling just a little bit uncomfortable; something he had virtually never felt before. It wasn't long and Maria signaled Tony to follow her once again in a different direction. He was starting to feel a little anxious not knowing what would be waiting for him at the next stop.

John P Gibson *High Tide*

It was a few moments again and they were in front of another video screen. This time Tony was viewing his life in more recent times. With his immediate family and friends. His wife, children, parents, and grandchildren. The reason he had lived his life the way he had was for these people. They were his priority in life.

"Can you see how your life unfolded Tony?"
Maria asked in a soft and concerned tone of voice. Tony was still looking at the video screen in front of him; it had now gone blank and was slowly disappearing in front of him and Maria. He remained silent as his thoughts roared through his mind.

"If not now, it should within a short amount of time become obvious to you Tony that your life was not one that involved the qualities that we here look for in a human."
Maria looked at Tony who now turned to look at her. He had tears welling up and it was easy to see that the images he had seen in the past while had proved their point.

"You must now follow me Tony to our last position."
Maria took the lead and Tony followed. It was a few moments later and they came to a stop in front of a large very beautifully carved wooden door. Tony just stared at it and of course wondered what could possibly be behind it.

He thought to himself it must be the entrance to Heaven. The place he could live for eternity in a state of bliss. With all of his schooling on his chosen religion, he knew it would be a generous reward for his devotion to his God. Maria was not making a move, and Tony just looked ahead at the door waiting for it to open.

The door finally started to open slowly and as it did a swoosh of warm air flowed out and surrounded the two of them. It was a bright light that caught Tony's attention as he started to move in the direction of the open doorway. He felt good inside and the warming air around him made him feel at ease with the entire situation.

"Tony… you must enter and accept what it is you will be given. It is your destiny and something you cannot change. You will learn the ways or continue to live in this place your kind refer to as Hell."

Tony turned to look at Maria with a look of terror in his eyes. It was not what he had expected at all.

The End
(Maybe)

Hell's Game

Tony moved on through the narrow passage as the heat increased. Again it was unfamiliar territory to him. He kept moving in a way similar to when he was with Maria. There were no obvious sights, just a strange yellow orangy glow surrounding him as he moved. It was now very hot and he wished he could do something about it. He could not take any clothes off for the simple reason he wasn't wearing any; he was comletely nude from head to toe. The narow passage seemed to be getting larger in size and the brightness was increasing along with the heat he was feeling. It wouldn't be long he thought and he would burst into flames where he was standing. His movement continued and all of a sudden his view opened up to a very large area in front of him.

It was indeed what his upbringing had taught him about hell would look like. It was a massive place with what looked like many thousands of fires burning and creating the orange glow in the sky above him. He just stood there in awe. There were also many more thousands of small figures in the distance moving about stoking the fires with something to keep them alight. At least that is what Tony thought them to be doing.

He was now getting even hotter and thought that he should be sweating buckets with the way the temperature had risen so much since entering the door some time back. All of a sudden he felt something close to him. He turned and saw a very crude and scary looking figure standing behind him. It had massive red horns protruding from it's forehead and a very large and scarred nose. The eyes were deep red and penetrating and ears that came to a point. The body was nearly naked and also looked to be scarred from head to toe just like the nose. There were some dark brown pants that came short of the ankles where no shoes could be seen.

All in all this creature was very ugly and was putting off more heat for Tony to deal with. The strange creature just stared at Tony and then with a very deep baritone voice it spoke.
"Tony, I would like if I may to show you about your new home."
If the creature could have smiled Tony was sure this would have been one of those moments. Tony just looked at him, of course assuming he was indeed a male of his species.

"I know this is all new to you and somewhat overwhelming, but it is my job to show the new tennents their new digs."
Tony thought it strange the way this man talked, and why was he assuming he was looking for a new place to live?
"You can call me 'Firewalker', that is what everyone else calls me."
Tony again was not sure as to what he should say or do while this oddity stood opposite him in this more than hot enough place. He kept his silence.

"At some point Tony you are going to have to speak, if not to me, then, the master himself. And trust me Tony, you do not want to have to talk with this man. He has been here far too long and even though there are no innocent bystanders here; Bick has continually expressed his innocence in everything."

Tony again looks at the absurdity standing before him that goes by the name of Firewalker. He figured he might as well start to converse so at least he could get more information on this place.
"New home? You call this place a home? It looks more like Hell than anything else."
There, he had put in his two cents worth for all it might do with this Firewalker character.

"You got that right Tony… this is Hell and you are now a part of it. Just to let you know, you and only a couple of others here are in the running for Chief."
Firewalker made it sound like this was a place anyone would want to rise to the top and control the masses. Tony took a closer look around just in case he spotted Donald Trump as being one of them.

"Are you one of them?"
Tony thought to ask Firewalker as he certainly semed to have the ego density of someone pursuing leadership. Firewalker just looked to Tony with his bright red eyes. It was difficult to see if he had a smile hidden within all of the wrinkly skin.

"No… unfortunatly I have not got the qualifications, something you will soon start to understand."
Firewalker still held no emmotion at all when he spoke. He did however look down at his ugly feet and kick at the red coloured dirt he was standing on. It was like watching a young child when upset with something an adult might have said to them. Tony just looked at the ugly man in front of him and thought for a moment. He somehow knew that he was now in a place that he could thrive in. Not unlike his life before when he was alive. He would get the lay of the land and get to know any and all of the individuals he would need to know to get his way.

"Bick?... Bick is the name of the leader of Hell?"
Tony finally gets his nerve up to find out more about the man that claims to be the leader of Hell

and what the hell Firewalker's job is here in this hell hole.
"Yes… that is his name. It was something to do with a human object that many used to light a fire with. At least so I was told by Bic himself."

Tony just shakes his head in disbelief as he heard Firewalker speak. It was now becoming quite apparent that most, if not all names here in Hell would have some reference to fire.
"You said I should not speak with this man, the leader of Hell whom we on Earth always called the Devil. Why shouldn't I do so?"
Tony had now taken a better stance as he was now starting to get accustomed to the raging heat surrounding him. Firewalker in front of him now looked at Tony in the eyes and thought for a moment. It was obvious he was collecting his thoughts before speaking back at Tony.

"Because of how the system works here, you will be in direct competition with Bick. Your previous life had groomed you to be a contender for the leadership here in Hell."

Tony once again had to sift through this information in his brain. He was completely confused about why *he* would be a contender for the Devil.

"Are you trying to tell me that I will be competing with the Devil for the leadership of Hell?"
Again Firewalker looked down to his ugly feet. Then slowly back up to Tony before he answered the question.
"We have been waiting for you for some years now, you are our only chance for a civilized existence here in Hell."

Tony had to digest this information, he at some point in his life had considered the fact he might very well end up here, but to have to deal with the devil himself for leadership of this place sounded utterly perposterous. How the hell was he going to defeat Bick for the role of Devil?

"And how do you propose I do this Firewalker?"
It was a simple and direct question, one that Tony would expect a clear and detailed answer. Looking at Firewalker however suggested something

different. He shuffled his ugly scared feet before looking to Tony with his response.

"Bick will approach you within a short while and propose a challenge to you, one you must accept or live for eternity doing very cruel work with virtually no end in sight. I am the second to Bick and am telling you now that it is in your best interest to take the challenge and fight for not only your freedom, but the freedom of millions of others here in this hell hole."

It all sounded all so strange to Tony as he had assumed that anyone and everyone living in Hell would not be there to have a good time of it. Of course he had many other questions and would do his best to have them answered before accepting this challenge, whatever it was he would have to do to be the Devil of Hell.

"So… what do I do now? Is there a place I can get some good Italian, and maybe a beer?"
Tony thought to be just a little cocky as he knew the worst that could come of it would be to possibly go to Hell? Firewalker just looked at him with his

creepy scarred eyes. It was obvious to Tony that this weird guy had no sense of humour.

"You and I will wait here a few moments more. I have been informed by my colleagues that Bick is on his way as I speak. I warn you though, you must at least feign that you respect and admire him; at least until the challenge starts."
Firewalker says as he then turns to look behind him as there was some sort of commotion with many of the slave workers.

It took another moment for Tony to realize the many workers around had now stopped and were circling Firewalker and himself. It was time. This he now knew. Off in the distance a loud howling could be heard as the masses of workers became silent. It was the howling of wolves, very large ones moving in formation in front of, and pulling a chariot of sorts in the direction of Firewalker and Tony.

If this wasn't something to remember, then nothing was. The wolves as large as cows had horns protruding from their foreheads as they towed this very ornate looking golden chariot with an absolute massive creature riding as sure as any king would. It was Bick, the Devil himself with a long flowing red cape and a very long tail which he wrapped up and over his lap as he was paraded through the masses and towards Firewalker and Tony.

Within a few feet of the two of them the chariot stopped along with the masses of followers. The flames rising in the background made for a very pituresque visual. Tony was at best ill prepared for anything like this, all he could do was look at the large figure now standing in the chariot and raising his gold pitchfork. It was obvious he was about to speak as everything became quiet. All Tony could do was watch the large figure in front of him and guess what it was he would hear from this formidable monster named Bick the Devil.

"You… Tony… will take the challenge I will present to you. If you decline the offer you will spend eternity as the others you see here are doing."
Tony again took the opportunity to look around at the thousands of burnt, scarred, and ugly beings in the background and surrounding the Devil himself who continued talking to Tony.

John P Gibson   *High Tide*

"The challenge will be a very difficult one for you, and if you should win; which is unlikely of course. You will become the leader of this hellish place."
Tony looked to Firewalker who at that moment turned to him and then shrugged his ugly shoulders. He was not about to get involved at this moment.

"My servents will now dress you accordingly for our scheduled event that will determine the final leader of Hell."
Bick said this with all the egotistacle fervor of a politician running for office. It was then that several ugly men came up to Tony with several bits of clothing and what appeared to be a helmet with horns on it not too dissimilar to that of Bick's. Only the one Tony was to wear had smaller horns.

It was still unclear to Tony as to what the two of them might be up to with this perceived important challenge. All he could do was wait for the moment to present itself. It was obvious Bick wanted to impress his followers by dragging out the lull in the otherwise noisy, loud, and sickening place this Hell was.

"It is now time for us to compete, and it will be in a game that I rather like and one that I have never been beaten at. You will not win this challenge Tony. This I assure you."

The Devil looked around at his minions who now started to cheer and move their arms as they looked to him and then to Tony. Firewalker just stood his ground looking at Tony hoping in his mind that this man could indeed beat the Devil. Something that had not been done for centuries. If any of the poor souls in this place were to get a break from their formidable leader, it would be now, and only if Tony was able to win the challenge.

"If you will look over your shoulder and to the right of you Tony you will see the place where you and I will compete for leadership of this Hellish place."

Tony did as he was told and looked over his shoulder to where he saw a large flat area with what looked like a lawn of sorts, brown in colour of course due to the heat in this place.

At this moment the Devil himself brought himself down from his chariot with the help of several minions groveling and drooling in anticipation of some reward for their effort. He made his way over to Tony and stood beside him; at least another four feet taller and then raised an ugly scarred arm to point in the direction of the area in front of them.

Many more of the slaves moved quickly bringing what appeared to Tony as large balls of some sort. With closer inspection it was obvious they were the heads of those who had perished here in Hell. Tony looked up to the Devil with a curious look on his face. The Devil picked up on it and leaned in close to Tony, their faces only inches apart.
"We will play the game Bocce, I have over the centuries become quite fond of the game and consider myself to be very proficient at the sport. Good luck to you Tony."

The Devil says in a voice that suggested he just might be as good as he thought he was. Tony however just let a smile come to his face. Being Italian, this sport of Bocce was something he grew up on in Italy. It would be a devastating day for Bick the Devil.

The End

Down Under Slither

It seems life is not always fair. Especially to a young woman named Wendy. Wendy Ackland. A very beautiful twenty year old with a fascination for adventure. Being smart as well as physically fit, she was drawn to the outdoors in a time when most would be nestled into their sofas with both arms frozen in front of them while their hands; especially their thumbs, working overtime while absorbing the latest shit on FaceBook. It was no wonder the planet was going down the toilet; and fast. Wendy however was one of those that did not need the daily fix of the internet, she needed the daily fix of the outdoors. Being physically fit and having a high IQ, Wendy understood the importance of activity outside of the brain.

Australia; it was a place Wendy had heard about ever since she was a young girl. Being born and brought up in a small town in Northern BC, Canada; she had been told of this place down under and was fascinated by what she had been told, and the pictures and video she had seen over the years.

Wendy was fortunate that in her years growing up she had landed some very profitable jobs. She was now in a position where-by she could sit back and enjoy life for the balance of her years on this planet. She had heard about Australia through friends that had visited there. To her it sounded like the only place on Earth that had not been fully explored.

It was all planned then, she had her flight tickets and the blessings from her family and friends. It would be a long flight to Sydney and this would give her time to research some of the places she wanted to visit. The books and brochures on her lap kind of gave it away to the older male passenger sitting beside her on her long flight. He seemed to be in his forties; or so she thought based on his looks and attire.

"Ever been to Australia before?"

The question was surely a valid one as he looked to Wendy's lap and at all of the paper work she had spread out and creeping over to his side.

"No, it's my first time. And you?"

Her curiosity took control.

"I actually live there. Have done now for more than thirty years."

He smiled at Wendy as he shuffled just a little closer to her as he spoke.

"Wow, how fortuitous for me. Can I ask you some questions about Australia? That is OK right?"

She asked as she put on one of many smiles that she was sure would do the trick.

"Of course it is, my name is Mike."

He says as he looks expectantly at Wendy. She again sports the smile she is sure will unlock Tony's friendly side.

"Hi Mike, my name is Wendy, pleasure to meet you."

She extends her hand for a shake which Mike accepts as he takes her hand which Wendy held onto to suggest she was definitely interested.

Mike smiles as does Wendy during the lengthy and now uncomfortable silence that took over. There was an obvious attraction that the both of them were taking advantage of to the fullest.
"Sooo... you want to know all about Australia do you?"
Mike breaks the silence as he still holds Wendy's hand.

"Yes... yes, it will be my first time there and I want to do some real back country hiking to see the real country that I have read about."
She holds up a few of the brochures and books she had on her lap to show Mike. He looked at them briefly then brought his gaze back up to meet Wendy's eyes once again.
"Well, you're in luck my friend, I just happen to be in the business."
Mike said with a smile as he awaited her response. It came quickly as Wendy shuffled in closer after unclipping her seatbelt.
"Really? You're like some kind of tour guide or something?"

"Yeah, something like that Wendy. I take tourists around to some very unique places. Something they can really impress their friends with once they return home."

Wendy's eyes light up as she again moves in closer to Mike.
"So… can I hire you for some of these excursions?"
"Of course you can. Here, take one of my cards and when you get settled in to wherever you're staying, give me a call so we can get together."
He hands the card to Wendy who takes it and looks it over on both sides, then looks back to Mike.

"Why thank you Mike, I will certainly do that."
Wendy continues to look at the card as Mike just looks at her. There is a loud crackle as the pilot comes over the PA system to alert the passengers that they are making the descent to the airport at Sydney.
"Well, it looks like we made it."
Wendy says to Mike as they both buckle up their seat belts and Wendy does her best to clean up the array of paper brochures on her lap.

"Sure does, how about we hook up after we get our luggage and have a coffee and discuss a possible time to get together so we can discuss a tour or two for you."

Mike says as there is the usual comotion of people putting things back in the overhead compartments, or taking things out.

"Sounds great Mike. I'm in no rush as I have my room booked at the Hilton."

Mike looked to her as she said Hilton. It was obvious she was not doing the Hostel thing.

"OK then, if we get separated, we'll meet at the luggage carousel… "

"No problem, we'll just stay close then."

Wendy smiles as the two of them ready themselves for the landing, which by the looks of the weather would be a smooth one.

As they taxied into the main terminal Wendy kept looking out the window at the new vista in front of her. The sun was shining and it all looked so new to her.

John P Gibson

High Tide

"Always nice when it's a safe landing."
Mike says as he unbuckles his seat belt before the plane had stopped which of course was against what the flight attendent had said over the PA system. Wendy as tough as she was normaly, was now clutching the armrests on either side of her and clenching her teeth. She was not the best flyer when it came to commercial planes.

"It sure is."
She quickly replied as she started to breath normal and look about at the other passengers. Some of which were doing what Mike had done, anticipating a quick start to getting their personal belongings from the storage above them. 'Why? She thought as they would not get off the plane any quicker.' They were eventually escorted off the plane and Mike and Wendy moved along with the others until finally they were separated. It took at least a half hour before Wendy made to the luggage carousel where she saw Mike standing looking at the line of bags and suitcases moving around.

"Hey you…"
Wendy says to Mike as she appraoches him while he is in a trance looking at the bags of luggage motor by him.
"Wendy, you made it through customs, way to go."
He says in gest as he finally notices his suitcase as he goes for it and with one hand pulls it off the conveyor belt and places it beside Wendy.

"Yeah, they sure ask a lot of questions don't they?"
She replies as she now starts to pay attention to the baggage carrousel. It wasn't long and her bright pink large back-pack tumbled onto the revolving carousel. She left Mike's side and retrieved it as did he; with one hand and of the proficiency of an expert.

"You must work out a lot, I wouldn't want to mess with you that's for sure."
Mike says as he smiles at Wendy as she slings the pack over and onto her shoulders. She smiles back.
"As a matter of fact I do work out Mike. Well, where do we go for this coffee you promised?"

Mike looks over his shoulder and then back to Wendy.

"Just over there, not the best coffee in the country but better than most. It's on me."

"Not literally though, right?"

Wendy throws her humour in now that the flight has finished and her tension has subsided. Mike smiles as he extends his luggage handle and pulls it along behind him as the two of them walked to the coffee shop.

"So the weather looks good."

Wendy thought to say as they approached a lone table with two chairs.

"Yeah, it's pretty much always like this, at least this part of the country; this time of the year."

They took the seats as a waitress made her way over to them. A couple of coffees were ordered along with a bit of food to offset the poor airline meals provided on their flight.

"I thought it might be best for you to take a couple of days at least to get over your jet lag before we make any plans for the first of your ventures out and about."

Mike says to Wendy as they devour their sandwiches.

"Sounds like a good idea, but I really want to experience what Australia has to offer in the way of excitement."

Mike looks at Wendy as she shoveled another mouthfull of sandwich in her mouth. He took a sip of his coffee then replied.

"You don't have to worry Wendy, the tours I take people on are some of the more dangerous and exciting ones offered here, I have some reviews I could show you if you'd like."

Wendy continues eating her sandwich as she now picks up the napkin to clear the bits that are falling out of her mouth as she gets ready to reply to Mike. He just waits.

"Sonds perfect Mike. I need thrills, danger; unpredictability is my second name."

She says with the confidence of a skilled hitman in an Italian movie.

"Well, let's get you to your hotel and in two days I will come and pick you up early in the morning for the adventure of your life. I will leave you with a list

of things you should get, such as clothing, certain food snacks, and of course a good sunscreen."
He looks at Wendy and her very white complexion. She is now turning a shade of pink as embarrassment takes over.

"Sounds good Mike, I am so looking forward to it."
Wendy replies as she gets her baggage and makes her way to the taxi cue with Mike right behind her.
"How about I share the cab with you, I need to go your way and I can explain more about what our tours are all about."
It was obvious now that Mike was taking an interest in Wendy and wanted to be near her as much as he could. The ride to the Hilton was a busy one with Wendy looking about as the car drove along the busy streets. Mike was in constant talking mode as he went over several options for wendy to consider when it came to some of the tours he was offering her.

"Well… we're here."
Wendy says with an exasperated tone as Mike had not shut up the entire way to the Hilton.
"I'll help you with you luggage."

Mike says as he adjusts in his seat.

"I think they will have someone do that for me Mike, but thanks for the offer. It is the Hilton after all."

Mike looks out the window at the two men approaching the cab. One to open the door for Wendy to exit from and the other to the rear of the cab in anticipation of some luggage.

"Here, don't forget this."

Mike says as he hands a few pieces of paper and another business card to her.

"Thanks Mike, I'll give you a call in a couple of days so we can get a tour together, looking forward to it and thanks for your company."

She says with a smile as she gets out from the cab with the assistance of the Porter.

"It was real nice to meet you Wendy, look forward to your call."

Mike says as he shuffles over on the seat and looks at Wendy through the open car door as she walks with the Porter into the hotel. Wendy turns back and waves to Mike before entering the hotel. Mike kept looking as the cabby was now looking over his shoulder with that look. The look that says 'Get your shit together man, I gotta make a living here.'

It was exactly two days later and Mike was standing at the front desk of the Hilton where Wendy was staying. He had requested the lady call Wendy to let her know he was waiting for her. It was six AM in the morning. It was the agreed time through their many phone calls. Mike just waited patiently for Wendy to exit the elevator that he was staring at while standing in front of it. Along with him he had a small carry bag and was dressed for a day of hiking and exploring. He continued to wait in front of the elevator as he looked to his watch to check the time. The elevator doors remained closed as he looked straight ahead.

"Oh hi Mike, you're right on time."
Wendy says as she walks towards Mike from the stairs off to his right. He turns to see Wendy dressed in appropriate gear for a serious hike around and carrying a small back-pack.
"Wendy, I was expecting you to come down in the elevator."

He says as he continues to look at Wendy who has about the fittest body he had ever seen on a woman.
"Well, you know, keep fit as one can. I always use the stairs, helps with staying in shape and you never know when one of these things will break down."

She replies while looking at the elevator that now had it's doors opening and people were exiting into the lounge. Most of them overweight.
"Well… you ready for the day ahead?"
He thought to ask as they both looked each other over dressed in their completely opposite attire. Mike in what would be considered the standard Australian look for any outdoorsman. Shorts with thick heavy belt with accessories. Heavy light coloured T-shirt with multi-pocketed vest the same colour as the shorts. Dark socks with very tough looking boots, a wide brimmed hat, and sunglasses.

Wendy on the other hand was wearing a tight fitting skimpy top, short shorts, sandals, and sunglasses. Mike could not take his eyes off her. It was obvious to anyone watching; especially Wendy.
"Well… shall we make a move then? The Land Rover is just outside and I thought we should do a

one day tour first, then if you like maybe do a longer one way out in the out-back. Sound good to you?"

Mike asks Wendy as she adjusts her very tight shorts. She then looks at him with a smile as she responds.
"You know Mike, we can do the full on tour starting today, I'm ready for an adventure."
She continues to smile as Mike picks up her bag and with his other hand directs Wendy to the front doors to exit and out to the Land Rover.

It was one of the larger models with an open back for about six clients with room for another three tour guides. Not unlike the vehicles Wendy had seen in Africa when there on safaries.
"Looks awfully big for the two of us."
She remarks as they approach the vehicle.
"We'll be picking up the others on route."
Mike replies as he puts the bag in the back then gestures to Wendy to take the front passenger seat.

Mike was true to his word as another couple were picked up at a hotel not too far from the Hilton. It was a young couple, and by their gestures it looked to Wendy like they had just been married and this was possibly their honeymoon adventure; or they were just a little too touchy-feely all of the time. An insecurity issue Wendy did not have. The drive out of the city and out to the back-country took a few hours and along the way Mike had stopped for a short break at an out of the way small café in the middle of nowhere. The couple were still far too clingy and if not for the engrossing conversation with Mike she would have been very unhappy with the whole situation.

It was soon after the café stop and Mike was heading into some very rough and dangerous looking territory, and it was obvious as the young couple now were clutching each other in a way that said they were just a little nervous and far out of their league. Wendy on the other hand was in her element.

"We'll be in the thick of it soon, be prepared to see some amazing sights."
Mike says in a voice that a salesman might use trying to sell something to a potential customer. The young couple just kept looking about as the male of

the two managed to get his cell phone out to take some selfies as the Land Rover started to slow down.

As the vehicle came to a stop several native animals could be seen off in the distance. There was a silence in the Land Rover as Mike shut it down and then made his move to the rear to bring the equipment necessary for the first nights camping. Wendy of course started to help as the other couple just continued to take selfies with all of the animals in the background.

"Looks exciting Mike, I'm not sure I recognize all of the animals I see looking around. We are safe aren't we?"
Wendy thought to ask just to assure herself this would indeed be a very safe and exciting tour.
"You could not be any safer and I will go over with you and the others about the animals out there once we get the camp set up."

Mike along with Wendy's help started to put up the tents; three in all. One for Mike, one for Wendy, and one for the young couple who to this point were still taking selfies on a continuos basis. It was starting to irritate Wendy and Mike to the point they were almost ignoring the couple. It took about an hour to get the camp just right, and Mike's finishing touch was the very upscale firepit, where he was now getting some chunks of wood he had brought engulfed in the flames the starter was putting forth. With the sun setting and the air cooling, it made for a very picturesque scene; which is exactly what the couple were still doing. It would be a busy time on FaceBook when they returned.

"We'll get an early start tomorrow morning of course after a good breakfast. I'll fill you in on what is expected of you, for safety reasons of course."
Mike looked around at the three of them with Wendy taking most of his attention. The young couple had now taken the time to put their cell phones away and pay attention to Mike. Afterall, it was getting dark.

"We will be safe right?"
The girl asks as she looks to Mike while clutching her boyfriend.

"Yes of course you will, I'll get the fire going just right and start cooking some dinner for us all."
He replies as he starts to rummage through a cooler he had taken from the Land Rover. Wendy was doing her best to relax and enjoy the relative quietness surrounding her. She was at peace as the only sounds were the crackling of the fire, the odd animal noise in the distance, and the giggling of the girl as she took selfies of her and her boyfriend.

It took about an hour for Mike to get the meal ready for everyone, and the smells were intoxicating to Wendy as she always enjoyed a man that could handle himself in the kitchen. The four of them ate their meals and talked for a while about the following days activities.
"We should get some sleep, it will be a very long day tomorrow and I want everyone in their finest. It is as usual supposed to be a hot day again. Be prepared."

The young couple nodded in agreement and made a hasty retreat to their tent.
"Well Wendy, if you have any problems through the night, don't hesitate to knock on my tent door. It

looks like it should be a peaceful night so we should all get a good nights sleep."
Mike says as he bundles up a few items and makes his way to the Land Rover.
"Oh… and don't forget to make sure your tent is zipped up as there are many critters that just love snuggling up to us humans."
He says as he opens the back door of the Land Rover and places some of the equipment in he had used to make dinner with.

Wendy looks over to Mike with a look of concern she had not expressed since they had met on the plane.
"You know Mike I will confess to you that I have no problem with any living species on this planet apart from snakes. I am deathly afraid of them; and some humans; who are not unlike snakes."
The look she gave Mike said it all, he had no answer for her and continued with his job at hand.

"I'll make sure you are all tucked in and the tent door is secured."

He said in a tone he hoped would satisfy her. He knew the snakes here could be lethal if contact was made.

"Thank you Mike, and you have a great sleep, see you early in the morning."

"Same to you Wendy, sleep tight, don't let the bed bugs bite."

He smiled as he zipped Wendy's tent door closed. She just gave him the evil look one does when sarcasm had been demonstrated.

It looked as though the night would go along just fine as everything was quiet and Wendy could only hear the light crackle of the fire as it slowly burnt out. There was of course the soft chatter of the young couple in their tent as it was obvious they were getting down to it in the sex department. The noise from their tent increased with every moment. Enough now to gurantee Wendy would not get any sleep.

It was nearly two in the morning when Wendy looked at her watch. The noise now from the young couples tent was louder, more intense, and getting on her nerves to the point where she desperately wanted to kill someone. She made the effort to get herself dressed and move cautiousley out of her tent to go and consult with Mike about the noise. Once out of her tent after inspecting for any creatures skulking about, she made her way to Mike's tent. She had noticed the young couples tent moving about as they nearly screamed in ecstasy. It must have been one hell of a romp in the sack she thought to herself as she approached Mike's tent and started to talk quietly at first.

"Mike... Mike... are you awake?"
He certainly should have been with all of the noise. Now Wendy could hear the tell tale sounds of a man deep in sleep. Snoring. The one thing she did not like when it came to men.
"Mike... get up, I need to talk with you."
She said this time with a little more volume, along with some rapping on the side of his tent with her hand.

"Heyy…. What's up?"
A groggy response came from the inside of his tent.
"How can you sleep with all of this noise going on?"
Wendy's reply came in a louder voice as the noise from the couples tent was now increasing along with the movement of the tent itself.

"Get your ass out here right now Mike, this has got to stop."
Wendy was now getting very aggitated and was not in the mood for anything but a solution to the problem.

Mike finally poked his head out from his tent and looked up to Wendy standing right in front, but not before looking over to the couples tent that was moving around so much it looked like it was going to take flight. Not to mention the horrific screams coming from inside.
"They're sure having a go at it, aren't they?"
Mike says to Wendy as he removes himself from the tent completely and looks at the scowl on her face.

"Hardly romantic the way the tents being thrashed about, and that screaming... sounds like they're both scared shitless."
Wendy's agravation had more than surfaced as she spoke. Or was nearly shouting over the noise from the more than animated tent.
"Well come on then lets get over there and give them some lessons on how to keep quiet so the rest of us can get some sleep."
Mike gestures with his arms and directs Wendy to lead the way, which she does with an aggressive stride.

The two of them get to the front of the tent and notice the front zipper is slightly up about a foot. Mike leans in and pulls the zipper up the full length of the doorway and now Wendy can see into the tent as Mike shines his flashlite onto the chaotic scene before them. He turned to see Wendy scream and then passout as she fell to the ground. The screams from inside the tent had subsided.

Mike was looking at a tent full of snakes that had not only bitten the young couple with their poisen fangs, but were now eating the two naked bodies in front of him. All he could do was drag Wendy away from the slaughter. It was obvious Wendy was afraid of snakes.

The End

John P Gibson — High Tide

McDougals

The line up was predictable as Donny cued up in line with the other cars. He was a medium build of a man in his forties. He had just recently purchased a new car, one that had the front seats of a four seater that heated up for the cold winter months. Something they always were in Canada. It was of course one of the coldest days he could remember. It was mid January and he was on his way to work as he was pretty sure the rest of the line up at McDougals were as well. The six-to-six grind he had been doing since finishing High school. If it wasn't for his first morning coffee before the commute to work, he would have committed suicide years ago. McDougals was one of his saving graces, the other his adoring partner Terri.

John P Gibson *High Tide*

"Good morning what can we get you this morning?"

The automated overly cheery mechanical voice asked through the intercom once Donny stopped in front of the menu board, speakerphone, and a somewhat pour imitation of an animated human face talking to him.
"I'll have a large dark roast coffee and a bacon bagal."
It was Donny's favourite and he had it every morning before heading into work.

He could tell by the smiles on the faces of the patrons through the window to the left of him that they too were having their favourite meal. If it wasn't for the automated robots doing all of the taking of orders, serving them, and the cleaning up of the restaurant, it would truly be the best place. Donny's work was of course in a large and very tall building where many thousands of people did consistant research on past history.

He had been doing this now for all of his years since finishing school when he was fifteen years old. He wasn't sure if he liked his job or not, it was just something one did. One always did what they were told to do. One thing Donny had discovered was that the past was certainly different than today. He did feel rather good though in his new Drone Car with the heated seats.

Of course the altitude of any vehicle other than the authorities was restricted to no more than 30 feet above ground. If one was caught cruising higher, or at an unsafe speed, their vehicle would be taken and that person would have to use the underground transit system. If they argued in any way they would then be sent to prison. Most who went there were never seen again.

Because of Donny's work he did, he had managed through a friend to get a restricted copy of a book called 1984. After reading it he was just that much more nervous. The book of course had to be handled and passed about to those one could trust. His mind was wandering and all he really wanted was his morning meal before getting to work where all there was was a slimey green drink that the authorities guranteed had your daily nutrients in it. This was given thrice daily while at work for the 16 hours. He now pulled up to the delivery window where the robotic arm passed the plastic package through the open window to Donny. It smelled delicious as he put the bag across and in the passenger seat as he drove away. The robot saying 'Thank you, come again to McDougals.'

Donny had been hearing the same message for many years now after he had changed from one of the other fast food outlets to McDougals. The smell was driving him carzy, he would do as he always did and pull over into a parking lot not too far from McDougals. Donny had always allowed time for this morning ritual.

As he stuffed the Bacon bagel into his mouth he let out a great sigh and just sat back in his seat to savor the moment before heading into work. He managed to watch the steady stream of workers walking or flying to their respective places of work. It was something he had witnessed for many years. The constant mass of workers doing what it was they were told. Because of his particular line of work, Donny sometimes wondered if the human race was actually doing the right thing. As he finished his breakfast as his large clock on the dashboard told

John P Gibson

High Tide

him, he only had ten minutes to get himself to work. Being late would put him in trouble with the authorities. Donny was always on time.

He put the large amount of wrapping paper for the bacon bagel and empty coffee cup into the bag it had all come in and placed it on the passenger seat that was now fully warm. He would dispense of it when he was at the right altitude leaving the large parking lot.

The building Donny worked at was straight ahead and one of the largest in the city of four hundred million. It rose high above all of the others and of course above the thick smog surrounding most cities around the world. He parked his car in the spot reserved for him and then made his way into the building and to the elevator that would take him and many others to their respective floors. Because of his staus within the corporation, Donny had managed to rise to one of the top floors where one could almost see over the heavy smog below. As he exited the elevator into a seemingly ever expanding plethora of small desks with a human seated at each, a young and attractive female approached him. She was in her thirties and Donny knew her well as their desks were beside each other.

"Hi Donny, on time as usual."
She stated as she looked at her large wrist watch that happened to be a pink colour. Donny just smiled as he looked up to the very large rectangular digital clock hanging high on the wall above them.
"Looks like you spilled something on your shirt Donny."
She says as she looks at him and points a finger at his shirt.

Donny looks down at his shirt and tie where a small splotch of red sauce from the bagel must have dripped onto it. Everyone was made to wear ties; even those that did not work had to wear them. Terri's was pink as all were that the females wore. Men's were green in colour. This made the red sauce stand out even more.
"Must have been good."
Terri continues as Donny does his best to clean the mess. It was forbidden for anyone to come to work without being clean and presentable.

"McDougals."

Donny replied as he continued with his clean up. He had over the years done his best to try and impress Terri with what ever he could do or say to her. He felt like a bit of a knob right at the moment.

"Yeah, it's my favourite place, their bacon bagels are to die for."

Terri says as she moves in to help Donny with his challenge.

"Yeah the bacon is sooo… good. I could eat them all day long."

Donny replies as he looks around to make sure there is no supervisor or android paying any attention to them. It was now time for everyone to be at their desk doing their work for the day.

"We better get to our desks, I'll see you at break number one.

Terri says as she gives Donny a wink and then turns to go to her desk which was a couple down from Donny's. All he could do was watch her walk away, and himself get to his desk before any authority person came asking questions as to why he was standing where he was and with a dirty tie to boot.

John P Gibson

High Tide

Rules had to be obeyed or else. Donny sat at his chair at his desk piled high with stacks of paper and books. It always was this way, for all the years he had been working for the Government. He thought he must have been doing a good job as he always got his meagre pay on time and to this date no questions asked of his work.

Terri managed a quick look his way with a wink, he quickly looked about to see if anyone was watching. A slight smile came across his face as he delved into his daily routine. The many security cameras around the large room would relay video to an equally large room full with uniformed men and women continually watching the workers.

All Donny could think about was the bacon bagel he had had for breakfast and how he wanted one for lunch, his afternoon coffee break, dinner, and as many snacks as he was permitted to have through the day. MacDougals was without a doubt the best place to eat on the planet. The food chain had fifty-five million outlets around the globe.

John P Gibson *High Tide*

Donny often wonderd about all the pigs required for everyones favourite meal the bacon bagel. It was pretty much all he ate and all his few friends ever ate, not to mention everyone else he saw in any given day. In his research throughout the day Donny would sometimes come across diet related material; anytime he did he was supposed to notify his superior and it would then be sent to the right department for further research.

His duties were strictly defined, as everyone in this building and the many millions of buildings like it around the world. Donny didn't care as long as he was able to indulge in the bacon bagels and he could fantasize about Terri and himself. He had read somewhere long ago about sex between a man and a woman. It had got him thinking about how things must have been on this planet many years ago. He did have to be careful even with his thinking as the new class of surveilance monitors had the ability to detect energy wave lengths the brain produced in certain situations. Donny made a conscious effort to think of something else, like the work load in front of him on his desk.

It was a simple process; just take the top book or stapled pieces of paper and start to read through them with marker pen handy for places that might be of concern to the powers that be. For the most part it was very boring. It was normal for Donny to start thinking about the bacon bagel he would have for his first of four breaks in the sixteen hour day.

He sometimes wondered how any human being could survive on only bacon bagels, then he remembered once a day upon waking up at five am he took one of the green pills. The powers that be told everyone that this tablet would provide them with the required nutrients for the day. Donny always felt fine at work and on his half day off every month.

He now absorbed himself in his work and started to review the papers and books stacked in front of him on his desk. Most days it was pretty much the same; a quick scan of the papers or the book and then place them in their appropriate bins. Of course there was the odd ocassion where something caught Donny's interest. Such as this moment right now.

John P Gibson — *High Tide*

It was something frowned upon; anyone expressing an interest in anything they were researching. If the cameras picked up on anything out of the norm, such as a strange facial expression, weird facial tick, unauthorized body movement, an officer would come in from the door painted red and make their way over to the offender. Usually these people were never seen again.

Donny did not do too much thinking on this topic and just did his job. He had done so now for more than thirty-five years. What he saw attached to one of the pieces of paper was a torn and weathered looking small square of paper. On it were some words that had hastely been written down; when? Donny had no idea.

It was an address that sounded familiar to him. The street he knew of, and the building; although now an empty shell had its history within the city. The note also in smaller letters said to meet at this address tomorrow night at midnight. It seemed strange and Donny did his best to keep the straight face he had practised for so many years.

McDougals. It kept coming back to Donny as he rifled through his large stack of papers on his desk. He was never sure if it was just him, or everyone that was addicted to McDougals; especially their bacon bagel. This little distraction helped he was sure, with his body language after reading the short note.

The addresss to which the note stated was close to where Donny lived so it would not be a problem for him as he could go there right after his shift at work. It would be a little difficult to explain to authorities if he were asked why his car had been parked there at a strange hour of the day. He was now wondering who it was that was making sure this note had been in *his* pile, on *his* desk.

As he thought about it he quickly grabbed the small note and made it disappear through the paper shredder next to his desk. If he were to be caught with something like that on his person he would have been dealt with by the personnel behind the red door. This is something Donny would not wish on anyone.

He would remember however the exact details and be present at the time and place written on the small piece of paper. His gut was now letting him know it was time for another bacon bagel and his short break would give him just enough time to do so.
"Terri… would you like a bacon bagel from McDougals? I'm heading there right now."
He says as he walks by her desk.

"Yes, that would be great Donny."
She replies as she fumbles in her slim and small purse on her desk.
"Don't worry about it Terri, I'll get this one, they're on special today… only $5,000 dollars each."
"WOW!... that is a good deal, nearly half price. Thanks Donny, it'll be my turn next time."
She smiles at him as he walked on. He was sure he had made the right move by offering to buy her a bacon bagel. This would however cut into his savings in a big way. He would have to scale back in some way to recuperate his finances. He made his way quickly to his hover car and started towards McDougals.

Donny had it timed perfect, he had a ten minute break and because he had the route down perfect he could get to McDougals, pick up his bacon bagel, and then get back to his desk with usually ten seconds to spare. These he would use up in the devouring of the bagel as he watched Terri do the same as he had passed hers to her and she quickly unwrapped it.

"Good?"
Donny mumbled to Terri through a full mouth of his favourite food as she did the same. All she could do was nod her head in a dramatic way while bits and pieces of the bagel fell to her napkined chest. Donny thought this to be somewhat sexy in his limited way of knowing anything about the subject. It was just the way it was; no one except those chosen were to know anything about the banned topic of sex. He resumed to his finishing of his bacon bagel and making sure he was nice and tidy so he could start into work once again. The thoughts running through his mind now were on this exciting rendezvous the following night.

John P Gibson *High Tide*

Who could possibly want him to meet at this location? And what the hell was it all about? These questions and more raced through his mind as he continued with the sorting of the papers in front of him. It would feel like a longer day than usual for Donny now with this new twist and the nagging thoughts in his brain about his next meal at McDougals.

"Well that was a good day."
Terri says to Donny as they prepare to leave, he thought maybe this would be a good time to say what was on his mind all day.
"Want to join me at McDougals for a bacon bagel and coffee?"
He thought this to be a somewhat advancing question that should tell Terri that he was somewhat interested in her.
"I would love to Donny, but I have to catch my bus in five minutes."
"No problem, I'll give you a ride home after, I have a new hover car, the seats heat up."
This seemed the perfect thing to say as it was still cold outside.

Donny hoped he wasn't coming on too strong, he did not want Terri to feel uncomfortable.
"Really? They get hot?"
All Donny could do was nod his head in agreement and in a small way start to blush.
"OK… Show me this new car of yours."
Terri continued as she gestured with her arm in the direction to the car sortment tower.

It was a short trip to McDougals and the line of cars was a long one. This Donny thought a perfect opportunity to get to know Terri somewhat better. Their conversation was all over the place with Terri on the more than odd occasion yelling out at the line of cars in front of them. At least they could not hear her. Once they had bacon bagels in hand Donny moved his car out to a secluded place in the vast parking lot so they could enjoy their meal.

"You were lucky to find a spot so close. You must know the routine well Donny."
Terri states as she takes a big bite of her bacon bagel. Donny would have answered right away, but he too had a mouthful of the favourite food.

"Well… if I do say so myself I am probably an expert on the topic."

He smiled at Terri as she smiled back and with some awkwardness pointed at Donny's tie. He looked down and realized there was a large red blob on it that had spilled from his bacon bagel.

"Oh shit! Not again. If the sauce didn't taste so good I would probably ask them to not put it on."

After trying carefully to take the blob of ketchup off his tie he finally gave up and just smudged it in.

"I think I have enough money in my account to buy a new one."

He says as he looks to Terri who has now finished her bacon bagel. She puts her hand up to her mouth to stifle a laugh.

The evening continued with Donny giving Terri a ride home and finding out how close she lived to the exact spot he would be visiting the following night. He turned to look at the old and decomposing building off to his left. As they were high enough for him to get a good look at it. A shiver of angst rushed through him. He was now more nervous about what it possibly might be about; the meeting tomorrow night.

After their somewhat short goodbye's, Donny was on his way home. He would not get much sleep this night with Terri and this meeting on his mind. As he had thought, his headache and brain fog from lack of sleep had taken its toll as he reached to quiet the noise of the alarm clock. He would have to get a move on if he were to get to work on time. The hard part would be finding his other tie.

On his ride to work he noticed the weather had changed to dreary as well as dark. He wished he could have had his day off on this one, then he would have just stayed at home watching the vid screen all day while ordering in McDougals bacon bagels. It was his dream for his retirement. That and possible sex if he was permitted to.

Of course Donny smiled at everyone he ever did when entering his place of work; of course not until after he had checked his tie for any ketchup stains from his McDougals bacon bagel; the one he wolfed down as he was running just a little behind schedule. If he was caught, it would mean ten-thousand dollars off his monthly payment.

He sat at his desk looking at the mass of paper and books. He had given a secret signal to Terri as he walked by; it was something they had agreed upon the night before. Something else they had agreed on; Terri would accompany Donny to the rendezvous place after work this night.

He knew it was risky. Very risky, but he and Terri had talked about it and she demanded to be part of it. Donny was having a difficult time focusing on his work, and the rare occasion to look over to Terri was taken. The strangest thing was that he was not hungry... not even a McDougals bacon bagel.

"You OK?"
It was the first thing Terri said as the two of them sat down for a quick coffee on one of their breaks.
"Yeah... yeah... I think so."
"You look like you're in deep thought about something, just be careful of the vid cams, just saying Donny."

Terri showed a quick look of concern for Donny, then returned to her very practised calm and non-committal look she used most of the day and every day she worked.

Terri was not stupid. She had learned a long time ago like Donny that they had been used all of their lives. This meeting later tonight might just be the opportunity the two of them had been hoping for. A chance to experience life the way they thought it should be lived. At least the way they had read about it in so many reports and books they had gone through.

It was now the last break before Terri and Donny would finish their shift and could make their way to the designated meeting place. Donny had finally become hungry and would make a quick stop at McDougals for his favourite bacon bagel. They were open 24 hours per day. Instead of parking somewhere to eat the bagel he just stuffed it into his mouth; of course not before offering Terri some.

The drive took less time than Donny figured and found a place to park where the two of them could get a good view of the front door where they were supposed to meet someone. This person or persons he had no idea of whom they might be.

It was almost at the alloted time when Terri and Donny noticed a faint light approaching the meeting spot. There were two people dressed in dark clothing and wearing hoods, which was highly illegal. The light quickly shone in Donny and Terri's direction. The code was acknowledged when Donny turned his right turn signal on three times.

It was now time to get out of the Hover car and quickly get to where the two individuals were.
"Hi… I'm Donny and this is Terri."
Donny says to the taller of the two.
"Yes… we know. Follow us and do so quickly."
Donny wanted to see this person under better lighting to see if he recognized this man whose voice gave it away. The two of them followed the dark figures in front of them. After going through a single metal door they were now in what appeared to be a very large room. The two hooded figures stopped

and slowly removed their hoods. Donny did not recognize either of them, and it appeared Terri did not either. All the two of them could do was stand and wait for one of them to explain the situation.

"You did keep silent about tonight, right?"
The man that had spoken first asks. The other who now without her hood was obviously a woman.
"Yes… it's just the two of us. What is this all about?" Donny asks as he needed to know.
"We'll fill you in more in a minute, for now just follow us and keep the noise down."

That wouldn't be difficult as Donny and Terri had been trained this way all of their lives. As they followed the two darks figures, it was obvious they were in the large warehouse structure. It appeared to have been once upon a time a meat processing facility. Donny figured this from all of the research he had been doing all these years.

It did not take too long and they were all in front of another door which appeared to have some soft lighting in behind the blocked window. It opened slowly as the first man keyed a lock then opened the heavy door. All Terri could do was look over to Donny who had not a clue as to what was happening.

All he knew was his heart rate was racing. There were a few other dark hooded people in the room and they all looked to Donny and Terri without expression. It was an awkward moment at best. The conversation that ensued was about something Donny and Terri could hardly comprehend.

It was about the manufacturing plants for the food that all humans consumed on a daily basis. It was not only enlightening, but it was also frightening to the both of them. It was also explained on more than one occasion that if anyone was caught in this place, or have any information as to what they were talking about. They would be arrested and never seen again.

Donny's mind seemed to drift and when the bright lights surrounded them it was if he was under some other influence. He could not explain it, the loud voices, the bright lights, the rough handling of his frail body. This was something Donny was not expecting. He thought about Terri but could not see her or hear her. He just drifted off.

*****

The loud buzzing beside his ear was familiar as Donny looked over to the clock that was saying to him 'Get up... time to go to work.' And that time was four AM in the morning. He dressed, then made his way to a common area for one of his two meals per day. They were a bowl of some kind of soup. At least this is what he thought it was.

After eating he followed the others in line and through the open doorway to the very large factory floor. Off in the distance Donny could see thousands of lines of workers enter the building at the same time thousands of lines were leaving. There was nothing he could say or think that might bring him back to some sort of sane reality.

As he stood at his station the loud horn blasted telling all the workers to start their machines and get to work. As Donny started his machine and watched the carcass's rumble through the plastic pieces in the opening he involuntarily started to heave the contents of his stomach onto the conveyor belt in front of him.

He now knew where the meat came from for the McDougals bacon bagel. It was the never-ending line of humans that had passed away that day. It was a waste-not-want-not mantra that the foremen constantly drilled into the heads of those taken away and never to be seen again. He never saw Terri again.

The End

John P Gibson

High Tide

Wine Not

The light was fading as the late afternoon approached. Jose had arrived early as was his fate through life. Always being punctual, or at least a few minutes early. This particular day though it was an important one; he had been asked if he could help out with the setting up for a birthday celebration for several locals. It was a small public building that people could rent out for special events. It would hold about one-hundred people at best with a full kitchen and bathrooms of course. He had been asked by Shona one of the lead organizers to help put tables and chairs in place and help set up a bar for those that might want a drink. It would not take long and it would give Jose a chance to catch up on some of the local gossip. He had been away for awhile now.

The building looked derelict and run down with the odd roof shingle missing. As he approached the front doors he noticed a single torn sheet of paper tacked to the front of it. He carefully read the note without knocking it from it's precarious place by the door-handle.
'Will be later than expected Jose, sorry. Vern.'

Vern was the other person organizing the party. Jose thought to wander around the forest in behind the building. At least it would kill time and he might even spot a local ferret, squirel, frog, or cougar. He hoped not the latter. The afternoon was calm with low lying clouds and the threat of rain. A normal winter here on Vancouver Island.

Vern also celebrating his birthday along with Shona and several others. Jose suspected he might again be one of them as his birthday was just a few months previous. For the birthday card and small gift helping to set up was the least he could do. The rules were that anyone coming for the festivities would pay ten dollars for the food and music supplied by a young and up-coming duo.

The food was prepared by Shona and was always spectacular with far too much of it and having many of the guests taking some home with them. There was even a bartender hired for the evening. All drinks were three dollars each and the variety somewhat small. Jose was used to this sort of thing and would probably not consume too much. Maybe a glass or two of red wine only.

After doing the loop through the forest Jose arrived back at the community hall. He felt fortunate that he did not run into a cougar. It wasn't that he was afraid of cougars... he was afraid of most all animals. He took a seat on a bench close to the front door of the hall and thought to try and get a short nap. He knew he would be up late this night as he would of course help put everything away with some of the others.

John P Gibson *High Tide*

It could not have been any longer than about five minutes and Jose was jostled awake by the sound of a car engine that seriously required a new muffler. He looked up with a yawn and saw Shona drive up along with her sister Pam in the passenger seat.

A quick honk of the horn and Jose was up and making his way over to the car reversing to the door of the hall. The drivers side door opened and Shona extricated herself from the car.
"What the hell are doing standing there? Get your ass over here for a hug... you know how long it's been?"

One thing Jose knew about Shona... always do what she says. After the hugs and brief chatter about what everyone had been up to over the past couple of years it was time for another word from Shona.
"Well we better get our asses in gear and get this stuff inside before it starts to rain."
She commanded like a general with his troops.

"Jose make sure that all of the cold stuff goes right into the fridge, and stay away from the chocolate cake."

Jose just looked at her and smiled, he knew the rules and it would not be long and they would change. Usually for the better.

As the three of them started to bring the many boxes and bags into the hall, another vehicle pulled up; it was Vern.
"Hey... Jose, get over here and help with this booze will ya!"
Vern says in a loud voice followed by a large smile as he approached Jose with arm extended for a hand shake.

"Hey it's been awhile Jose... how are your travels going?"
"Just great Vern, and good to see you. Got enough booze for tonight?"
The two of them look to the trunk of Verns car. It was loaded with cans of beer and boxes of wine, and a few hard spirits.

"Where's the bartender to help with this.?"
Jose asks as he figured it should be part of the bartenders job to get the booze into the hall and

organized while the others set up the tables and chairs. Only seemed fair he thought.
"He called me a while back and said he was running late."
"Hey you guys quite sluffing off over there, we've got work to do. We'll have a small glass to celebrate when were done this work… OK?"

Shona says in a more than loud enough voice as Pam and her continue to bring boxes of food into the hall. It wasn't long and more vehicles started to arrive. A tall fellow got out of one of them and walked towards the crew working. Vern looks up to greet him.
"Hey Rick, good to see you, glad you could make it."
"Hi Vern, where's the wine?"

Quick and to the point thought Jose as he approached Rick for a handshake, but only after he had put the box down he was carrying.
"Hey Rick how are you doin?"
Jose says as they both shake hands.
"Better once I get a glass of wine in my hand."

Rick says with a chuckle as the others start to laugh. Now there was an urgency in getting things ready for the party, especially so Rick could get his glass of wine sooner than later.

It wasn't too long and Vern and a few others had the boxes of booze set up for when the bartender showed up. Rick was next to one of the three boxes of wine pouring a generous amount into a small plastic wine glass.
"Merlot Jose?"
He asks in a generous tone. Jose looks at the boxes and and thought maybe to try the other red wine, Shiraz.

"Maybe I'll try the Shiraz Rick, not really a Merlot fan."
Rick just gives him a look and pours a glass of the Shiraz for Jose and passes it to him.
"Here ya go, don't drink it too fast now."
Rick says with a smile. Jose takes the glass and takes a small sip to test it first. He almost gags as Rick quickly backs up and away from Jose.

"Must be good stuff Jose, did you manage to keep any of it in? I'm sure glad I decided on the Merlot."
Rick then takes a drink of his wine and does almost the same as Jose as he goes over to the sink and spits out the mouthful of red wine.

"I don't believe this shit, and they want us to pay a whole three dollars a glass for this crap?"
Rick just looks at his glass and then to Jose who is trying his hardest to control the smirk behind his hand.
"Well if this is the only choice of wine tonight, I think it might be a short one."
Rick continues on as he looks around at more people entering the hall.

Something caught his attention as it did Jose, Shona, Pam, and Vern and some of the others strolling in to the hall. It was a larger man with a very expensive three piece suit and tie. No one was really sure who this man in his mid fifties might be. Everyone else was dressed very casual. It was the norm for this group.
"Who the hell is this guy?"

Doug asks as he settles in with the rest as he had just come into the hall shaking hands as he walked in closer to where the kitchen was and the three boxes of shit wine.

There are some general polite 'How-do-you-do's' then the attention went back to the over dressed man.
"He's our bartender."
Vern says in a loud voice so not only those standing around him could hear, but also the man who would be the bartender for the evening.
"Everyone this is Joe, he'll be looking after your drink orders for the night."

Everyone sort of nodded their heads with a few vocalizing their acknowledgement. Joe went right over to where the booze was stacked and the three boxes of shit wine and started to organize things with out any reply to his introduction to the group. There was an uncomfortable silence as everyone looked at Joe and his obsessive compulsion to organize the small bar in front of him. Then it came.
"If you would just line up here in front of the bar I'll start taking your orders."

Joe says with some authority without looking up to anyone.

As he starts to organize the cash tray and tip jar in front of him a line of people start to line up excluding Rick and Jose as they still have nearly a full glass of wine in their glasses. Nothing was happening as the line grew and Joe continued to count out the cash in his tray.It was strange at best to see this. He was not becoming popular as most bartenders always did.

As things calmed down Doug came over and and stood along with Rick and Jose. The three of them just staring at the line and then Joe counting out his cash.
"Hey... you guys want some good wine?"
Doug says as he turns to Rick and Jose. He has no expression on his face as the two look to each other then Rick speaks first.

"You mean better than this shit?"
Rick asks as he puts his glass up and Jose follows suit as he looks to Rick.

"Well I would think so. I have some special bottles in the trunk of my car. We could take a little stroll outside if you know what I mean."
There was a short silence as the three of them looked at the line waiting to get their shitty drinks.
"Wine not."
Rick says with a smile coming across his face. Jose looked confused as he looked at Rick, then Doug.
"Wine not."
He reciprocated by raising his glass in the air.

Doug just looked at the two of them and shook his head. He then looked around the room and especially at Joe the bartender before taking the lead and walking towards the entrance to the hall. Rick and Jose fell in line and followed him. After passing a few people coming in and of course making the small talk; Doug brought the two over to the back of a sleak black sedan. He keyed the trunk, but only after looking over his shoulders several times. He looked at Rick Jose.
"Never know when the cops might be about."
He again looked over his shoulder towards the main road.

Now Jose and Rick were looking around as Doug pulled a bottle out of a box in the trunk of his car. It was a screw top cap so getting into it was a breeze.

"Your glasses gentlemen please."

Doug held the bottle up as Rick was first to empty the contents of his glass onto the ground; Jose followed his lead.

Then the two of them put forth their glasses for a fill up of what they anticipated to be much better wine than they had experienced in the hall.

"Looks red enough."

Rick says in his humorous way. This prompts Jose to lift his glass to look at his wine.

"Keep em down boys…you just never know."

Doug says as he again looks over his shoulders to see if the authorities are anywhere close by.

"I think you're being just a bit paranoid Doug, don't you remember the good old days growing up here?"

Rick started off just after he had taken a drink of the wine.

Jose of course was well into his drink and enjoying it.

"Easy for you to say Rick its not your car is it?"

Everyone starts to laugh as they all now have a full glass of wine.

"This is really good wine Doug, how much you want for a glass?"

Doug just looked at Jose with a dumbfounded look on his face.

"Don't be silly, just enjoy it. All that I ask is that you make sure you come out with a full glass to get some of this wine. Don't want Vern getting suspicious."

Jose thought through this statement for a moment while taking another drink of his wine.

"So I guess the best thing to do would be to go up to the bar and buy a glass of the shit wine and then walk out here like we're going for a smoke, empty the wine onto the ground and then partake in the good stuff you brought with you. Right?"

"Good one Jose, now your thinking."
Rick pipes up as he takes another drink of his wine.
"What I suggest we do is make the excuse to go outside for a cigarette when we want another glass of wine. This should keep Vern from thinking otherwise."
"But none of us smoke."
Jose interupted.

"I don't think Vern will clue in Jose, anyway, there will be enough people going outside to light up regardless."
Doug says as he corks the wine bottle and replaces it into the trunk and closes it.
"I guess we should get back in before Vern or Shona figure something is up."
Doug gestures with his arm towards the door of the hall.

Everyone entered to a somewhat quiet room with the line-up still at the bar. Doug, Rick, and Jose took a seat near the rear of the hall where Doug figured it would be easier to duck out for another refill when the opportunity presented itself. It took about another fifteen minutes before Joe had his bar set up the way he wanted. The frustrated line of customers had dwindled somewhat as some decided to dig into the food presented on the tables.

"If I could please get everyones attention... please everyone..."
Vern was now up at the mic where the musicians had set up their gear. He had a piece of paper in his hand and was doing his best to quieten the group in the hall.
"Our main goal here is to make sure everyone has a good time. The music, the food, all you can eat, and the bar where drinks are three dollars each from Joe. If we could have a great hand for Shona who has put all the food together again, and any leftovers will be sent home with you."

There was a roar of applause as Vern finished up and the music then started in earnest. The table at the back with Rick, Jose, and Doug now started to grow as those that were curious about the trio exiting for a cigarette when none of them smoked drew their attention. After finding out the routine, more of the group started to exit the building but only after purchasing a glass of shit wine from Joe.

On one of these excursions Doug seemed just a little nervouse as the group huddled around his car awaiting their glass of wine after they had emptied it on the ground. It was a police car with lights flashing as it had pulled a car over on the main road. He had to keep telling people to keep their glasses down and out of sight.

"Pat... c'mon, keep your glass out of sight like I told you. Judy... make sure he listens eh?"
One could tell he was getting just a little frustrated as he filled the glasses. He must have had a full trunk of this wine.
"You like the wine Cindy?"
He asks as he pours a glass for her and her partner Andy. Both had smiles across their face.

"You bet Vern, haven't had a glass of wine this good for a long while. You Andy?"
She turned to Andy with her question to which he just nodded his head as he was involved in a rather large gulp of the wine.

It did not take long and Vern made his way through the crowd outside and towards Doug. It was obvious he was not thrilled as he strolled past Shona and Pam who both had a glass of wine in their hand.
"What the hell is going on out here? I know most of you don't smoke so why would you keep coming out in the cold and rain?"

His question was directed more at Doug who was continuing to look over at the patrol car with its red and blue flashing lights.
"Sorry Vern, just talking with a few friends I haven't seen in a long time."
Both Vern and Doug looked around at everyone and in turn most of them returned a look of acknowledgment. A few now started to return to the hall.
"Hey... I know what you're doing Doug and I'm OK with it. Joe says were just about sold out of the wine at the bar. How about you?"

Doug just looks at Vern, he knows what he is fishing for and decides to play dumb on the whole matter.
"I'm having a great time, think I'll head in and listen to the music."

He replies as he takes his full wine glass with him as he turns to follow a couple in through the doorway to the hall.

"Hey great night Doug and great wine… thanks."
A blonde woman standing with a fellow wearing glasses.
"Yeah, it is a good night Janet, and make sure you and Dave keep it quiet about the wine, don't want Vern to find out."
Doug replied while putting his finger up to his lips and doing the Shhhh…… posture.

It took a few minutes for everyone to get back into the hall where Vern was now in front of the mic once again along with Shona who had some envelopes and other odds and ends in her hands. It was time to give out a few gifts to those that had had a birthday within the last few months. As the individuals approached and accepted the cards and such, applause broke out each time.

"I would just like to thank Shona for all her work getting this party organized and for all of you coming out to celebrate. The band for their music, and Joe for his great ability to sell all of the red wine tonight. Stick around for some more music and fun." Vern wraps it up by raising his glass of water for a toast. Everyone reciprocates with their glass and a loud cheer fills the hall.

It did not take long for most of the people to go to the bar to get another glass of shit wine so they could go outside to see Doug who had snuck out quietly. It wasn't long and there was no one except Vern, Joe, and the band in the hall. He started to make his way to the entrance of the hall and on his way he caught up to Chris, Sharon, and Verle who were on their way outside. Once through the doors he had to make his way through Diana and Stewart who were talking with Doug and Sandy.

Everyone was now outside and doing their best to move towards the open trunk of Doug's car. The police car was still there with it's flashing red and blue lights; this time however the patrol car was right behind Doug's car and the open trunk as he pulled out another bottle of red wine out the police officers stepped in and handcuffed Doug. The party would now be officially over. Everyone stayed put as they emptied their wine glasses onto the pavement below.

The End

Beach Impressions

It wasn't Randy's favourite passtime, but when it came to a beautiful woman he would do almost anything she wanted him to. This time it happened to be a leisurely stroll along an unfamiliar beach in Mexico. Randy had been to Mexico once before a few years back, but had mostly spent his two weeks spaced out in a lounger at the pool close to the smorgasboard of food and beer in hand. Afterall, it *was* all inclusive. Nothing better than a two-week holiday in paradise with everything you wanted, all for five-hundred bucks. Even the flight was included. As before, Randy was just settling in to his routine when a young female caught his attention.

Her name was Adriana, the name came fast as Randy was a professional when it came to courting the opposite sex.

It was only a day or so and Adriana was itching for something different. (Not literally, afterall it was the coast of Mexico.) She thought a walk along the beach, as it was a very long one with possible surprises along the way once they turned the corner at the one end of the beach. Randy was not so enthused.

"Are you sure? You don't just wanna stay around the pool all day?"
Randy says as he tips back a beer as they discuss the days itinerary. It was afterall after nine in the morning. He just wanted something simple for his holiday in Mexico and trudging along a beach was not something he had even considered; ever.

"C'mon Randy, a nice walk tip-toeing through the surf, hand-in-hand and maybe just around a corner a secluded spot to watch the ocean."
Adriana gave Randy the sexy look. He finished his bottle of beer, let out a loud belch before replying to her. He did not want to make the wrong decision. It

did however sound to him that she was interested in some fooling around for just the two of them, providing the place was secluded.

Randy thought about it for a moment and of course was never concerned about seclusion, ever, when it came to women and the possibility of bodily closeness.
"OK… lets get a move on then… maybe there might be a spot to get a refreshment along the way?"
Randy was of course thinking of a beer spot of course.

"I'm looking forward to it Randy. We better make sure we bring along a beach towel and some sunscreen."
Adriana looked at Randy who was always a dark brown no matter where he was. She however was a very fragile white, a very smooth white, one that Randy could not keep his eyes off of. This she would need the sunscreen for and Randy hoped he would be the one to apply it. It took them a little while to get ready as Adriana made sure she had a couple of small snacks and a couple bottles of drinking water. Randy of course had a couple of beer with him. They

would not last too long in the heat as the first was already open and he was consuming.

They were off and in a direction the bartender by the pool suggested as it would come out to a public transit location so the two of them could return no problem. The sun was getting higher in the sky and without a breeze it was getting hot quickly. Not like sitting around the poolside with the fans and water mist systems.

"You sure you know where we're going?"
Randy thought to ask as he deposited the first empty beer bottle into a garbage bin as they walked.
"The bartender seemed to think this was the best direction to go in. He said if we were to get lost at least there was a small restaurant along the beach a ways."

Adriana replies as she hefts her large bag over her shoulder. Randy often wondered what women carried in such large bags. His wallet seemed to manage everything he ever needed when out and about. They were now side by side and strolling along the sand with the water about ten feet off to their right side. It was a very idyllic setting and Randy felt it was time to open his second beer.

There was little conversation as the two of them walked towards the end of the beach. Randy finished his beer and thought about asking Adriana if she needed some help applying her sunscreen lotion. It was just about when they reached the first rock bluff they would have to go around when Adriana speaks out.

"Randy… Randy… quick, look at this will you?"
She says in a rather loud voice as she moves quickly ahead and then kneels to the sand. Randy follows up and looks over her shoulder at what she was pointing at. A simple impression of a flip-flop. Then he looked closer at it.
"Holy Shit! Do you see what I see?"

He says to Adriana as she looks a little further from the first imprint to another. The first one had the imprint of a couple of words… 'Follow me.' It read and as one looked further on to the second imprint it read 'and bring beer.' The two of them looked at each other and smiled then broke out in a small laugh as they sat down onto the sandy beach.

"Crazy… I need to get me some of those."
Randy says as he looks at his empty bottle of beer.
"Well, we don't have any beer, but let's follow those flip-flop messages."
Adriana says as she gets up pulling Randy with her. They start to walk in the direction of the flip-flops around the big rock bluff.

Randy was still carrying his empty beer bottle and keeping an eye out for a garbage bin close by. He wasn't all that into nature but he would never litter. Adriana seemed to like taking the lead as she was several steps in front of Randy as they moved into a cluster of large boulders and cliffs to the left of them.

There was nowhere to go but around them, and of course hoping the tide was not coming in on them or they would be stranded.
"Wow! Look at this Randy, I can't believe it."
Randy came up to her side and looked in the direction she was looking, which was down into the sand and there before him were more imprints.

Randy had to re-focus but finally the words appeared to him. 'Just, Just' and the next step said 'Around the corner' More flip-flop messages in the sand.

"Can you believe it? More flip-flop notes to us. This is really great."

Adriana says as she looks up to Randy with a smile. All he could do was return a smile the best he could. He thought this whole thing was just a little creepy.

"Maybe we should turn around and head back, I don't see any garbage bins close by."

Randy thought to say as he thought this their best course of action and he needed a beer. His excuse for a garbage bin sounded legit to him. He did not want to appear like a wimp to Adriana.

"I think this is the adventure we were looking for Randy. Let's keep forging ahead and see what's around the corner."

Randy looked at Adriana and then to where they would have to walk to get around the large rock bluff. He was unsure at best.

"You don't think the tide might get us stranded?" Randy was working hard now to get things moving in the right direction. The direction he wanted, which was to return to the poolside and get another beer.

"I think you're just being a wuss Randy, c'mon give me your hand. We're going to get to the bottom of this adventure. Got it?"

Adriana said with enough confidence Randy just nodded his head in agreement and took her hand as they moved around the large rock. The tide appeared to be coming in as it lapped the feet of both of them as they walked. Because of this any imprints from a flip-flop would be erased away with just one surge of the water streaming in.

As they came around the large rock Adriana bolted ahead leaving Randy to walk towards where she had stopped, and was looking down at the sand. Randy could only guess that she had found the next flip-flop message. He did have time however to look around and now could see a small beach ahead of them before coming to another rock bluff.

John P Gibson *High Tide*

"See what it says Randy? This is awesome, no one's going to believe us when we tell them."
She sounded excited and now looked to Randy and then down the beach.
"C'mon Randy... lets get a move on."
Randy got himself together but not before reading what the next two flip-flops had to say.
'A few steps.' 'Feel it?'
He resumed a fast pace to catch up to Adriana.

"All I feel like is another beer and maybe something to eat."
Randy thought to say as he once again came up behind Adriana who was looking down at the new flip-flop message in the sand. He looked down expecting of course something along the same lines as the other messages in the sand. 'Thirsty... Getting close.' Randy looked up from the imprints in the sand and along the beach hoping to see whom it might be leaving these foot prints. He saw no one, but he did see off in the distance what looked to be a small café or restaurant on the high tide line of the secluded beach. There would have to be a bin there as well as a refreshment of sorts.

Beer. It was now the only thing on his mind. Randy's feet were starting to ache and the way Adriana was moving ahead, he saw no respite in the near future.

"Hey, Adriana… Adriana… why don't we head up to that café? At least I can rid of this empty beer bottle and maybe we could get something to eat."

Adriana was on a mission, she was ignoring anything from Randy unless it concerned the discovery of another flip-flop message. Which she just happened to find just below where the café was. She was in deep thought as she looked up at the café, then down to the sand, then up to the café again, and then over to Randy who had now caught up to her. He looked down to the sand.

'Take a break… Look up.' Perfect he thought to himself, if this wasn't karma, what was? All he could do was look up at the café and think about the beer and some food he could get. He only hoped Adriana was on the same program he was.

"Well… looks like you'll get your wish Randy."

John P Gibson *High Tide*

Adriana says as she points up in the direction of the café. All he could do was watch her hustle up to the terrace of the somewhat quiet café. Randy watched her lithe body find its way to a lone table overlooking the beach and the ocean beyond. He now not only thought about the beer he could have, but also getting more involved with Adriana on a personal level. Something they had not had a chance to do once finding the flip-flop prints in the sand.

As he deposited the empty beer bottle into a bin on the way up the stairs to the terrace, Randy started to think about how maybe Adriana and he could get more involved. His mind was racing. He was hungry and thirsty for a beer, but also was thinking of how he could impress Adriana and distract her from this attraction to the flip-flop messages in the sand. His curiosity only concerned the possibility of a mutual bonding between the two of them. The well done burger and a beer would surely help with his energy and possible lean in that direction; he could only hope so as this walk was now turning into a very big test of his physical prowess.

"Hi, can I get you something to drink? Perhaps something to eat?"

A small attractive female waitress asks as Adriana and Randy get organized at the table near the front of the terrace facing the beach. Randy looks to Adriana as he passes her a small menu and opens one for himself. He looks at the waitress and notices her name is Maria, according to the name tag pinned to her left breast pocket.

Randy thought to be somewhat funny and ask her what the name of her other breast was and then made a mental note not to be so stupid. He would just respond in a polite way.

"I'll have a beer, how about you Adriana?"

She was engrossed in her menu as there was an uncomfortable silent pause. She finally looks up to Randy and then to Maria.

"I'll have a Margarita please, I haven't decided on anything to eat just yet, you go ahead Randy, I know you're hungry."

She couldn't have responded any better thought Randy as he opened his menu and pointed to his favourite.

"I'll have the burger please with the chips and salsa dip. Thankyou. Oh, and you did get the beer, right?" Maria looked at Randy and gave him a smile as she responded.
"Si senor."
Randy assumed that meant yes. His Spanish was weak at best.

Maria writes on her pad and then looks to Adriana with a smile. Adriana finally looks up from her read of the menu.
"I'll just have a salad please."
She says as she closes the menu and passes it back to maria with a smile of her own. Randy gives her a strange look as he could never figure out how any human could survive eating salads. He had tried one once when he was a young boy and never ventured there again. Adriana smiled at him as Maria wrote down the last of the order and looked at Randy before smiling and moving off towards the open doorway and back to the kitchen. Randy was now at a loss for words as all he could think about was the beer and burger he was about to devour.

"Well, this is nice and cozy. I hope the flip-flop trail continues, I'm really curious as to how it will all end."
Adriana says to Randy as she looks at him and gives him one of those special looks only a woman can. Randy now started to flush just a bit as he played with his napkin until the beer showed up. Luckily for him it was right away as Maria came over to the table with a tray and on it were the very large Margarita and the beer, which was a very large one as well.

After placing them on the table in the corresponding places, she smiled and made her way over to another table where a few people had seated themselves. It was a millisecond and Randy's hand was on the beer. He was just about to take a big gulp of it when Adriana raised her Margarita for a toast.
"Here's to you and I Randy and hopefully finding the end of the flip-flop trail and also becoming good friends."

They clinked their bottle and glass together and Randy was thinking of a response as they took a sip of their drinks, Randy of course taking a large gulp of his beer.
"I was thinking the same thing Adriana. Here's to hopefully seeing more of you."
Randy replies with a genuine smile on his face. More so probably from the beer in hand.

The moment actually went longer than expected as the two of them had now really struck it off. They were at the least becoming good friends. In Randy's mind he was hoping considerably more of course. The meal and three beer Randy had, compared to the one Margarita and two glasses of water Adriana had ended with another clink of the glasses as Maria appeared with the bill.

Randy of course paid for it as he was still doing his best to impress Adriana. She had of course expressed an urgency to get back on the trail of the illusive flip-flop person leaving all of the messages for them to discover. Randy would have been content just to return to the hotel.

Once on the beach again it was off at a quick pace in the direction they had been on before their break. It would take them to another rocky point off in the distance. Adriana was looking down at the sand of course, this time however she would not get ahead of Randy as they were holding hands.

"THERE!... Over there Randy!"
Adriana exclaims. He could see her pointing with ther free hand in the direction they had been walking. Randy could just make out the impression in the sand, the one Adriana was pointing to. As they got closer Randy could now read what the flip-flops were saying. 'Seeing.' And then a few feet along the second one read. 'Is Believing.' Randy did an obligatory look around him as though he had been instructed by some unseen force. He returned his gaze to the prints in the sand below him.

"That's a good one Randy, seeing is believing. I guess we have to believe… right?"
She looks at Randy who smiles back. He felt good now that the beer had kicked in.

"I guess so Adriana. Is that it then, we saw, so we believe?"

Randy thought just maybe she had had enough and would want to go back to the hotel and possibly fool around a bit. Randy even thought this strange after only a few beer. He was however on holiday and the beer here was new to him.

"I think we should continue on. I am really curious Randy, I need to know what's at the end of this. Aren't you just a little curious too?"

The smile on her face told Randy he had better do what it is she wants if he was ever to get what it was *he* wanted.

"OK then lets get a move on."

Randy replied with his best and sexy voice. He followed Adriana's lead and it was not long and they were upon the next set of imprints. This time it read, 'Thirsty?... Getting close.' Randy indeed was getting thirsty as the beer at the café had only spurred on his need for more.

"There, you see Randy, it should all be over soon... we're getting close."
She smiled at Randy and then cupped his face with her hands and gave him a kiss. This threw Randy off slightly but soon rebounded and was ready to dive in for the full on sex he had been dreaming of. It was not to happen as Adriana now quickened her pace to find the next imprint.

At least he assumed there would be beer at the end of the trail based on what this last message had said. It was a little further along before the next imprint made itself obvious. Adriana of course was there first kneeling down on the sand and looking intensively at it. Randy followed suit. 'Time... Is short.' The message seemed to get right to the point.

This thought had been on Randy's mind almost from the first step they took on the sandy beach earlier that day. He looked around and there was no one about; not even a fisherman, a person one would see all the time along the coast with his rod in the surf. It was an eerie silence and with the afternoon sun starting to descend in the west, it seemed forboding.

"I wonder what it could mean? Seems strange Randy, whose time?"
Adriana says as she looks at the prints in the sand and then to Randy.
"Not sure Adriana, maybe we should turn around and head back. It will likely be dark by the time we get there."
He replies hoping Adriana will agree and they could get a move on back to the hotel.

"No way Randy, I have to know what this is all about. Aren't you the slightest bit interested as to whom might be instigating all of this?"
Randy just looked at her and gave her the look that said he really couldn't give a shit.
"OK then, lets get a move on."
He said as he stepped in line behind Adriana as she walked towards an outcropping of large rocks ahead of them. Randy could only hope that he would be granted his freedom from this excruciating walk that so far was taking the two of them into uncharted territory. He thought that if they got lost they would be in for one hell of a night.

"C'mon Randy, get your shit together, I have a feeling what we've been looking for will be just around this rock bluff."
Adriana moved at a quicker pace and was leaving Randy behind as he followed her up to the rock as she started around it. He was praying she was right and this would be the end of it.

The next thing Randy knew was that Adriana had disappeared around the far side of the rock and it was her shrill scream that got his attention the most. He now started to run as fast as he could, thinking that possibly she had been swept out to sea by a rogue wave. It was not so; as he came around the rock he saw Adriana standing as she held her hands over her mouth. There was a short statured man obviously of Mexican ancestry. He stood there without a stitch of clothing on and in front of a stack of flip-flops. Obviously the ones that had been used to put the messages into the sand. He also had what appeared to be a cooler full of beer. Randy gravitated over to the man and the cooler. He looked over to Adriana.

"It's OK Adriana, it looks as though he just wants us to quench our thirst. I'm sure it would be an insult to refuse his invitation."

The End

John P Gibson

High Tide

John P Gibson *High Tide*

A Moving Experience

It was a typically hot day in a resort town along the Algarve in Portugal. Albufeira was it's name boasting itself as one of the busiest resorts along the coast. It so happened a young English man had the opportunity to get a place close to the marina with a spectacular view that he would open as a restaurant. It had been a restaurant before but with some issues that were never rectified. The mans name was Pauz. A fit man in his early forties and a likable smile with a full set of pearly white teeth. He had extensive experience in the restaurant game. On this day he would be interviewing staff for the large restaurant. He would need a chef of course, a chef's helper, dishwasher, bartender, and four waitstaff with himself filling in where needed. It would be a long and difficult day.

Because the restaurant had an upstairs roof terrace there was of course the opportunity to make it into a lounge area where patrons could have a drink and enjoy the ocean view. The only problem being, there was nothing up there at the moment, and it would take considerable investment and time to fascilitate it.

Pauz felt that once he got the restaurant up and running, then he could tackle the posibility of the rooftop lounge. His day however on this Saturday would be taken up with interviews for possible staff for the restaurant. Pauz had decided to keep the name of the restaurant, 'Castelo do Mar'. Which in English was Castle by the Sea.

"Hi, how are you? Jerry is the name right?"
Pauz asks as the large gentleman with a shaven scalp and a large tattoo emblazoned on it sat down. He started to nod his head in agreement.

"Yes... yes, I'm Jerry, Jerry Atric, pleased to meet you..."
He paused for a moment as he extended his hand across the table for a shake.

"Pauz Alder, please take a seat."
He gestured to Jerry to sit in the chair as he shuffled through some papers of Jerry's CV, his resume of sorts.
"So... you used to work at a Michelin Star restaurant back in England. Is that correct?"
Pauz asked the question without looking up from his reading of Jerry's resume.

"Yes it was a four star restaurant, still doing well. My wife and I just needed a change... especially with the weather."
Jerry stated without any emotion and almost as if it was a given he should work in such a place.
"Well that certainly sounds good and looking at your CV it tells me you are one of the best. When can you start?"
Pauz was in a hurry as he knew it took a few weeks for new staff to get used to each other so time was an issue when it came to hiring the chef, the king-

pin of the business; any restaurant that is. He was hoping he would hear the answer he wanted which was 'Right away' At least he hoped so based on the forced smile he was putting on.

"I can start right away on one condition though."
Jerry replied looking at Pauz with a stern look.
"Shouldn't be a problem… and what might that condition be?"
Pauz just hated it when people left the important bits out of any statement made. He did however keep his smile.

"My brother has been my assistant since I started this career of mine and I will not work without him."
Jerry's look was pensive at best.
"That shouldn't be a problem Jerry, as you know I am hiring complete new staff and I always take recommendations from the chef of course."
Jerry's look improved as a slight smile came across his face.
"What's his name? And is he available right away?"
Pauz asks hoping the answer will be he can start at the same time as his brother.

"Petey is his name, similar to yours but he only goes by Petey."

Pauz thought this strange as he ran the names through his mind; Jerry Atrics, and Petey Atrics. He would leave it alone for now.
"Great then, why don't the two of you come in tomorrow about ten AM and take stock of what's available and what we might need. I can meet your brother then."
"OK, we'll see you tomorrow and thank you very much. Once my brother and I go through the kitchen we can go over the contracts and everything else. It was nice to meet you, and thank you again."

Jerry stood up as did Pauz and they shook hands as Jerry turned and made his exit. Pauz now had a chef and assistant, next was a young woman applying for one of the wait staff jobs. He went over to the outside terrace as the weather was sunny and warm of course. There were a few people waiting for an interview. He looked at his list and then up to the group of people in front of him.
"Melony… Melony Anoma."

He looked at a young blonde woman rise from her chair.

"Yes that's me… everyone just calls me Mel."

She replied as she walked over to Pauz to shake his hand. Pauz quickly thought to himself the name he had just heard. 'Mel Anoma'. He would leave this one alone as well.

"Just come with me Mel and we'll have a little chat and find out more about you and what it is you are looking for."

*****

The day went well and Pauz more or less had his new staff in order; another waitress by the name of Axie Dent. A bartender with the name Hugh J. Arms, another waiter named Jim Nastics, a dishwasher Ann Orexic, and his last waiter Dick Tator. As he wrote the names down he had to shake his head and laugh out loud just a little. The important thing was he could now devote more of his time to the rooftop terrace project he had planned. He had a feeling this would be the year to make things work for the restaurant.

John P Gibson *High Tide*

Pauz's new staff started working well together and he was happy with all of the Trip Advisor reviews he was getting. Castelo do Mar was becoming a popular destination for those that expected a decent, if not great meal. The chef was doing fantastic things in the kitchen along with his brother, and the front of house staff were more than capable in their respective jobs.

Pauz one evening decided to venture up to the rooftop terrace and start to draw up plans for his new project. He had a pretty good idea on what he would have to do. As he walked along and to the front of the building; where the best view of the ocean was; he walked past a couple of stone statues that had been there since he started the restaurant.

He had been told they had been there from the start when the restaurant was actually a castle. They looked eerie to say the least and for a short moment thought that maybe he should have them removed. Then another thought came to him; why not have the old statues as a theme for the rooftop. He would look into getting more statues of the same height, (about as tall as he was, nearly six feet) and placing them in strategic spots.

After a few hours of making some quick drawings and taking some measurements, Pauz thought he had a handle on how this large space could be transformed. It would be a fair investment but he thought it would be worth it once all was finished. Starting this project early in the season should allow him time to finish it for the peak of the season in just a few months.

On his way through the large main door to the stairs that would take him down to the main restaurant he thought he heard something. He turned to look around. All he could see were the two statues and a lone pigeon resting on top of the head of one of them. Pauz continued down the stairs to do further work on his drawings and see how the staff were doing as dinner service was coming up fast and the reservation book told him they would be turning customers away on this night. That was something he could certainly get used to. His new staff were working out well together, and his new chef was better than he could have dreamed of. Apart from his full name of course.

He did however retain the services of a young front-end man to keep things working smoothly. His name was Joe Hahn. He would be responsible for the everyday operations of the restaurant so Pauz could put his time and efforts into the creation upstairs. It was suggested by Joe that they also employ the services of a Tout. Someone to help get people into the restaurant, and also to turn them away when they were full to capacity.

Pauz thought this a good idea and within a few days they had the right man for the job, his name was Herb Garden. Herb was in his late fifties, tall, and dressed impeccably with suit and tie. With a greying beard and stoic posture, he managed the job well. Not that getting people into the restaurant was an issue, but scheduling them in for another night would be. Pauz also thought to use him in getting the upstairs lounge constructed. He had expressed some experience in building things. All was set and Pauz was feeling positive about the new project on the rooftop. The customers after having their dinners were more than happy with their meals and the service.

"Pauz, Herb was telling me he was doing some work on the rooftop terrace when he felt something strange."
Joe said as he came into the office where Pauz was doing some book work. He looked up to Joe with a look that suggested he should leave so he could continue with his work.

"No, seriously Pauz, I believe him as he said one of the statues did something while he wasn't looking."
Pauz had to look at Joe and give him one of those looks to suggest that maybe he and Herb were just a little crazy.
"I'm serious, he said he was putting some plants into a bowl that one of the statues was holding… you know, the female statue, and after a few minutes of doing something else he returned to find the flowers spread around on the floor below her."
Now Joe had Pauz attention as he put down the paperwork he had in his hand and paid closer attention to what Joe was telling him.

"Well you're going to have to elaborate a little more Joe, it sounds just a bit weird if you know what I mean."
"Yeah, I know, but Herb is one of those guys that you know is not crazy and I believe him when he tells me something."
Pauz continued to listen and was taking it all in.

"Well OK then lets go talk with Herb so I can hear first hand from him. I'm sure he just forgot he had done something. Anyway, its time for a break, we'll get ourselves a coffee and go upstairs and deal with this."
Joe looked at Pauz and nodded his head as the two of them made their way to the coffee machine where Mel was cleaning glasses.

"How about a couple of Bica's Mel, thank you very much."
Pauz asks her as she smiles and puts down the glass she was cleaning. While they waited the two of them just sat at the bar in silence as the espresso machine whined and whirred and then pouring the small amount of coffee into the small cups.

"Here you go gentlemen."
Mel said with a smile once again as she pushed the small cups across the bartop towards Pauz and Joe. It took them but a moment to add the sugar and milk, then knock back the volatile mixture. The first to clunk the cup on the bartop was the winner. The loser would have to buy the winner a reasonably good bottle of wine.

"OK, lets go check Herb out and see how far along he has come with the work upstairs."
Pauz says to Joe as they make their way to the stairs that would take them to the rooftop terrace. As they walked through the door they could see Herb sitting on a bench with his head in his hands, not moving.

"Hey, Herb... you alright?"
Pauz asks as Joe and him walk and stand in front of Herb. He does not move. Just sitting there without even acknowledging Pauz and Joe. It seemed to go on forever until Joe spoke up.
"C'mon Herb, you alive or what?"

John P Gibson *High Tide*

Putting a bit of humour in Joe thought this would bring Herb around and respond to the questions being asked. He slowly lifted his head and Pauz and Joe could see the fright he was obviously experiencing. Pauz paused for a moment before asking an obvious question.

"What the hell happened to you Herb?"
He asked as he looked to Herb, then to Joe for some kind of confirmation that his question was appropriate. Herb slowly looked around and then up to Pauz and Joe.
"That statue over there... she moved... I swear it, she moved at least two feet from where she was originally. I think it happened after I put the roses into the bowl she is holding."

Of course Pauz and Joe just looked at him with a blank expression, thinking maybe hiring him just might have been the wrong decision. These days it was more often than not that one would run into a crazy person. Pauz decided to take a closer look at the statue, and true to his word the statue was in a different place.

Knowing the weight of these statues he knew Herb could not have moved it by himself. Now there was some serious thinking going on in his mind.

"Oh come on Herb, how the hell could that statue move on its own? Really? You haven't been drinking have you?"

The questions from Joe just made Herb and Pauz look at him like *he* was the crazy one. It wasn't a moment later and Hugh came through the door and over to the group of them off in the corner.

"Excuse me Joe, it's starting to get a little busy downstairs."

His statement of course implied that Joe should go downstairs to help. Possibly even Pauz by the way he was looking at the two of them. Herb just sat there with his hands cupped around his face.

"Yeah… yeah… I'll be right there."

Joe replies as he looks to Pauz and then to Herb before making his way in behind Hugh as he exited through the door to the stairs. Now Pauz started over to the Statue to have a closer look at her. Even though he did not totally believe what Herb had told him, he kept his pace slow.

The statue looked the same as it always had, and the flowers were still in the bowl she was holding. Everything appeared normal to him. He turned back to Herb.

"Herb, why don't you take some time off and come back when you feel better. I think it might just be some stress your feeling."

Pauz says as he puts his hand on Herb's shoulder who is now looking up at Pauz with an ocassional glance over to the statue.

"Yeah, no problem Pauz. I'll take a break... probably just me and all. It's just that I was sure Sally had moved on her own."

Pauz gave Herb an awkward look when he said Sally. It was obvious he had named the statue. He would leave that one alone and get back to his work in his office. He gestured for Herb to stand and walk with him down the stairs where they could both take a break and then resume the work needed to get things ready for customers upstairs. Pauz only hoped Herb would drop his insistance that the statue was moving on its own.

The rest of the day went well. The restaurant was busy once again and most of Herbs help was utilized in the busing of tables and helping with kitchen duties. Dick had proven to be an asset to the team as well as the others. Pauz was happy with his selection of staff.

Jerry was doing magic in the kitchen and if it hadn't have been for a thunderous loud noise up on the terrace, it would have been a perfect night for all. The noise was so loud the entire room of customers and employees went completely silent. Pauz was behind the bar helping with Hugh when he heard the noise.

It was so loud it was as if a bomb had gone off. Pauz was off and running up the stairs followed by Herb who was coming out the kitchen doors and almost ran into Pauz as they bounded up the stairs to the rooftop terrace. As they rounded the corner Pauz being the first there could see stacks of furniture piled and broken and twisted like a huricane had gone through.

It was not far fetched as this region of the Algarve could have on ocassion small tornados coming off the ocean. Pauz looked around with eyes the size of saucers; Herb was not too different in his expression.
"What the fuck happened here!"
Pauz says as he moves in for a closer inspection of the damage.

"Looks like a tornado came through."
Herb expressing the obvious. He kept his distance staying close to the doorway just in case another storm rolled through he could make his escape down the stairs.
"It doesn't make any sense Herb. It was a clear evening with no wind and it is the same now. Just doesn't make sense at all."
Pauz was trying his best to figure out how the destruction had happened. Most of the furniture and all of the work Herb had done was destroyed. The statues however were fine. It looked as though they had not been touched at all by whatever had done this damage. Pauz started slowly over to where Sally was, which was a different place than the last time he had seen her.

"What the fuck is happening here Herb? You tried to convince me earlier about what Sally was doing up here, now I can't for the life of me figure this out."
Pauz found a place to sit down next to some broken timbers the storm had obviously thrown about.

The two of them sat there with their faces cupped in their hands. It was quiet as Joe made his way up the stairs to see what was going on. What he saw made him gasp as he looked around. His eyes finally settled on Pauz and Herb sitting side-by-side on the broken furniture.

"You guys OK? I can't believe what's happened up here. If you guys *are* OK, we can use some help downstairs as it is getting busy now that Jackson is playing."
Jackson Rivers was the entertainment once a week to keep the guests entertained. He was one of the better musicians in town.

"Yeah… we're OK, just trying to figure out what the hell happened here. It was like a tornado went through Joe. Crazy. Just crazy."

Just then there was the obvious sound of someone farting. All three men looked at each other as they held back a chuckle. Then it started.

"It wasn't me."

Herb said as both Pauz and Joe were looking at him.

"Well it sure the hell wasn't me."

Pauz interjected as he and Herb looked to Joe.

"Oh c'mon you guys, you know it wasn't me, I work front of house, I have a lot better control than most when it comes to stinky farts."

Now the three of them looked to Sally who for some reason appeared to have a slight smile on her stone face. It was getting creepier as the three of them now were all standing and moving slowly towards the stairs.

"OK, let's get to work here. We'll figure all of this out later when the customers have left. Herb, if you get a chance can you check to see if a tornado or cyclone, or something like that went through."

Herb just nodded as they rushed towards the door and down the stairs to the main restaurant. The rest of the patrons had now started to resume their meals; that is the ones that were left. Some had made a hasty retreat after the loud noises. Herb made his way into the kitchen while Pauz and Joe resumed dealing with clearing tables and answering obvious questions from diners.

The rest of the staff were busy as usual and now that the commotion was over, Jackson was back to his repertoire. If it hadn't been for the loud noises heard up on the roof, it would just have been another good night at the restaurant. It was however obvious that Pauz, Herb and Joe were not their regular selves. It became clear to Pauz that he would have to deal with the situation upstairs and would get himself some security cameras the next day to place around in strategic spots on the roof terrace. This he was sure would solve the problem of whatever was causing the problems upstairs. He just hoped Herb would be able to resume his work and obviously do some major repair work.

After closing the restaurant that night Pauz started to make his list for the shopping the next day with the cameras of course at the top of the list. He was determined to get to the bottom of this fiasco. It would be a good idea anyway to have security cameras throughout the restaurant; just for peace of mind if nothing else.

It did not take Herb and Pauz long to get the cameras in strategic places up on the rooftop terrace. Herb had done a great job getting things cleaned up. Mind you he was somewhat cautious as he worked throughout the day.

"Hey Pauz, I think everything is ready to go upstairs. You got your computer turned on right?" Herb asks as he enters the small office where Pauz was busy with some paperwork in front of him on his desk. He looks up with a confused look on his face as he puts the papers aside.
"Yeah I do, but what does that have to do with anything?"
"You can view what the cameras are picking up if you go to the program I downloaded for you. Remember?"

Pauz paused for a moment as he looked at his computer screen then up to Herb who was waiting patiently for him to do something. He pushed a bunch of keys with his fingers then stopped as his expression changed.

"There... I think I have it. Come around and have a look Herb."

He says motioning for him to come to his side as he points at the screen.

"See... right there. That's the camera close to the bar. We can see most everything with just this one camera. With the other three there isn't a spot up there we can't monitor."

The two of them continue to look at the screen where they can see the clean up process Herb was doing and the statues in their respective places. That is all of them except Sally. She was not where she was supposed to be. Pauz clicked a few keys on his computer and another camera view came up on the screen. Still no Sally. Pauz finally brought up the view of all the cameras at the same time.

"There she is."

Herb blurts out as the two of them see Sally moving in the direction of one of the newly placed cameras. Pauz clicked a key and the view changed to the camera she was heading for. They could see her

getting closer to the camera and when she was just in front, her arm raised up and she grabbed the camera in her hand and tour it off. The screen went blank. Both Pauz and Herb just looked at each other, then Pauz spoke.
"Quick…get up and lock the fucking door to the rooftop terrace."

The End

John P Gibson

High Tide

Slide Rule

Derrick rustled himself out of bed as the alarm on his cell phone continued the abnoxious tune of the Simpsons. He managed to get the alarm turned off, but then dropped the phone onto the floor. It put another crack on the screen. This exact thing had happened many times before. It was nearly impossible to even see what was on the screen at any time. It was Saturday; Derrick's day off. He had promised himself that this day would be put aside to plan his holiday. It would be a short one as usual. One week, as that was what his contract had allowed him per year. Derrick a thirty one year old single, short and fat male had been working for

'Trivial Terms', an up and coming financial institution in New York. He had been with them for three years and planned of course to work for them till retirement at the age of seventy-five.

He was getting excited as his holidays would start the following week on a Tuesday. He had done extensive research on his computer and found a place practically a stones throw from New York. It was an all-inclusive resort; they *all* were these days.
It was a very large enclosed piece of real estate the size of a large county.

This was the growing trend now that the population of the planet had reached fifty-billion. This particular all-inclusive however had the worlds largest and most popular water-slide. Not real water of course as there was no water as such on the planet anymore. It was more of a blue coloured liquid derived from the bones of animal carcasses.

Derrick would spend the rest of the week with his downtime getting ready for the one week holiday he had been thinking about all year. Being a single male he could afford to splurge on himself more so than his friends that were married. He of course would take many photos to tease them with.

The rest of the week seemed to drag by as he every once in a while went through the same photos of the resort he would soon be arriving at. Derrick had been to many all-inclusive resorts over the years working for 'Trivial Terms'. He was what some of his co-workers would call an expert when it came to the idiosyncracies involved when staying at one of these places.

The day had finally arrived and the taxi to the bus station arrived a few minutes late. It was early… three in the morning so he could catch a five AM bus out of the city and to the 'Baretall' resort. Normally he would be getting up about six to go to work so with the excitement, this was not too bad for Derrick.

"Where to buddy?"
The short balding spectacle wearing cabby abruptly asked Derrick as he got in the back seat of the cab with his one piece of luggage. It took a moment to struggle with the large bag that was filled with

things such as minimal clothing, bathroom accessories, sunscreen, snacks, that sort of thing.

"To the bus station... catching a bus to 'Baretall' resort."
Derrick thought this voluntary information should arrouse some interest with the cabby. Afterall, it was the premier resort in the country. The cab driver seemed uninterested at best. He put the car in gear but only after engaging the meter.

The cab ride was a quick one, and one that Derrick could afford. It was probably the quietest one he had ever taken as the driver seemed pre-occupied with his driving; which was a good thing Derrick thought.

After paying the somewhat grumpy cabby, Derrick made his way to the correct departure bay where he could see emblazoned across the sides of the bus the more than fantastic pictures of the resort he would soon be off to. The entire journey would take about two hours depending of course on traffic. He was sitting beside an older lady who had almost instantly gone to sleep once she sat down. Derrick would put up with her snoring.

The bus journey was as expected. Boring, crowded, smelly, and something Derrick always told himself; he would never take a bus again. He had read a story a long time ago about a man taking a bus trip in Canada that made for one hell of a story to say the least.

Once he was let off at the main entrance to the resort he shuffled himself and his luggage to the front desk to sign in for his room. The place was crowded and it looked as though all of the staff were busy with others at the check-in. He would put up with the wait as he knew once he was settled into his room he could then get ready for his first adventure here at 'Baretall'.

It would of course be the lavish buffet that was set out virtually twenty-four hours a day. He could pig out and then go for the tour of the resort before again indulging in the buffet. It would also be time for him to start his consumption of beer, his favourite libation. He knew he would have to be careful with how much he drank as there were rules to abide by at this resort; as loose as they might be.

What Derrick loved about the all-inclusive lifestyle was the fact he had already paid up front and would never have to dig into his pocket for money. Of course at the end of his stay it would be customary to include a somewhat generous tip to the hard working staff of 'Baretall'.

Being his first time at this resort he would have to do some investigation to see how it was run. Every place had it's own rules that one would have to abide by. Derrick could see no problem with this as most of his stay would be in front of the large pool drinking the cheap beer and nibbling on the constant array of snack food.

"Hi, my names Jayne."
All of a sudden this female voice rang in Derricks ear as he stuffed his face with another snack. He turned to see a somewhat sexy looking female settling in to the lounger beside him. He did his best to swallow the cheese covered popcorn he had in his

mouth. He thought a chug of the beer might wash it down so he could respond to the lady.

"Hi… hi… how do you do? My name's Derrick… pleased to meet you."
He replies with some discomfort as he brushes away some cheese that fell to his bare chest. His face now turns a rare shade of pink as he was somewhat embarrassed to say the least.
"This is my first time here, how about you Derrick?"

The very beautiful lady named Jayne asks as she moves her lounger closer to Derrick. He had a difficult time trying to find a place to settle his vision on; she was naked from the top up and had a very nice body. There were a few around the resort that were similar, but Jayne was the first to talk with him. In fact it was very unusual for any female to talk to him.

"Yes… yes… this is my first time."
He was now turning different shades of pink and it was not from the sun above them, how could it be? It was an imitation of the sun. It was years previous

that the pollution in the city had blocked it out. Even at night one could never see the moon or the stars.

"I thought this would be a good place to take my holiday break as all of the reviews on 'All Inclusive Advisor' said it was the best."
Derrick was getting just a little more comfortable and would do his best to impress this beatiful lady beside him.
"Yes... yes... me too. I thought to give it a try. How long are you here for?"

He thought to ask as nothing else came to mind for him.
"They apparently boast the largest water slide in the world. I mean blue stuff slide, I keep forgetting there is no water anymore."
Jayne says as she smiles at Derrick. He always had to think of a time way back when he actually had tried drinking water. It had beem bland and very plain. He could understand why it was no more. There was a lull in their conversation as a very large couple waddled past them with one of them nearly falling into the pool. Derrick could see Jayne holding

back a laugh as he was also. It was now becoming obvious the two of them would get along.

Having a similar appreciation for humour was one of Derrick's saving grace's.
"Yeah, I can hardly wait to try it."
Derrick replies as he takes a drink of his beer. He then thought to be polite to Jayne.
"Could I get you a beer... or something else to drink?"
He asked as he showed off his beer in his hand as he looked to her.

"No thanks Derrick, I'm more of a wine person. I really like their orange wine, I mean the colour of it. It tastes pretty good."
Derrick could not think of a reasonable response as he never liked wine; especially the newer stuff with all of the weird colours, orange just being one of many.
"No problem."
Derrick says as he puts up a hand and his index finger to get the attention of one of the many servers walking around the pool.

He got the attention of one of them and as the weird dressed waiter approached it was all Derrick could do to hold back a laugh. He looked over to Jayne and she was in the same pose. The costume was minimal, and every once in a while his private parts could be observed swinging back and forth. Derrick noticed Jayne keeping a watchful eye.

"Yes… may I help you?"
The question was standard for these employees as they would repeat it hundreds of times per day.
"Yes you can, we would like one of your orange wines and a beer for me please."
Derrick smiled as he thought his politeness was far more generous than most of the tourists would offer here.

"Yes sir, I will get those for you. It should only be a few minutes."
Again a line often used. There was no smile, but Jayne seemed impressed with the funny dressed man as he moved away towards the bar with his balls swaying to and fro as he walked. For Derrick it was not a pretty sight.

He looked over to Jayne and of course she had her gaze fixed on the man's family jewels. She turned to Derrick with a smile on her face.
"I've never seen anything so funny in all my life."
She says as she puts her hand to her mouth to cover it. Derrick now smiled back to her and thought this was going to be a very interesting day.

"Well… I thought maybe a little something to eat and then maybe give this world class waterslide a go."
Derrick says as he hopes Jayne would respond positively. He could see the two of them spending the rest of the week together providing she thought he was at least somewhat attractive in someway.

"Yeah, it sounds like a real adventure that's for sure. I read somewhere that it is not only the longest slide in the world, but also the fastest."
Jayne offers up some information that Derrick already knew of course. He always did his due diligence when it came to things such as this.

"It certainly is and they have a shit load of rules you have to follow so as there are no possible injuries."
He took a sip of his beer as he smiled at Jayne who was nursing her glass of orange wine.
"Like what kind of rules?"
Now Jayne's curiosity was piqued.

"You can't have any jewelry on of any kind, no rings, glasses, that sort of thing."
He did a cursory look over Jaynes body to see if she was wearing any… there was none that he noticed.
"No problem for me Derrick, I'm used to hardly wearing anything at all."

Derrick looked at her with a look of uncertainty. She had a smirk on her face that he was not totally sure of. He hoped it was her way of saying she just might be interested in him. Even if it was in the smallest way ever. He thought to smile back at her before taking another drink of his beer. It was the right thing as she now smiled back and leaned over to touch his arm.

"I think we'll both be OK to go on the slide. We meet the age requirement, the weight, no accessory rule, and I'm sure we are both good looking enough."
She says as she gives Derrick a wink and grabs a little stronger on his arm. Strong enough he almost pulled away from her.

Derrick wasn't used to dealing with the opposite sex. Not that he didn't want to, it was just that he had had no experience with them. He wasn't sure what Jayne meant by her affection to him. He thought to himself that he would have to learn. After all, here was a good looking woman who seemed to like him.

He knew he wasn't the best looking man around and this obviousley had something to do with his apprehention to Jaynes advances towards him. It was comforting however that she seemed to like him; at least he hoped so, and it wasn't because she was drunk or something like that. They finally got their stuff together and made a move to the main area where the slide made it's start.

It took them about ten minutes to get there with the dodging of drunk holidayers staggering around the complex. There were many thousands of them walking with drinks in hand, and there it was the long line of people waiting to get onto the lift that would take them to the highest point of the massive water slide.

It was impressive and Derrick had to take his phone out to take a picture of the goliath of a marvel of human ingenuity. Jayne was just standing beside him looking in awe as were most of the other people in line.

As they moved to the front of the line they were given a piece of paper each and told to read through it thoroughly. As the line was so long and slow it would not be a problem with getting through the five pages they both held in their hands. Derrick looked around to see how other people were dealing with the process. Some were too drunk and just signed the bottom where a signature was required if one wanted to experience the slide.

Derrick could only imagine how the signature looked. He also could not see any children as he looked around. He then started to read the information on the piece of paper and soon came to the line where it said 'No Children Allowed On Slide'. This he thought rather strange as it was something most children would want to do.

"Looks incredible doesn't it?"
Jayne asks with a shot of enthusiasm Derrick was lacking at the moment. His fear of heights was starting to hinder his internal gut feelings; that or the beer he had consumed.
"Yeah... sure does. Have you ever been on a slide like this before?"
He thought to reply with another question.

"I have, but not as high or as long as this one."
Just what he didn't want to hear.
"You OK Derrick? You look a little off. You know we could do something else if you want."
Derrick thought about it for a moment and then thought if he declined the ride on the slide he would look like a real wuss to Jayne.

"No… no… I'm fine, just wish the line would move a little faster that's all."

He forced a smile for Jayne as she again grabbed his arm and gave it a little squeeze. They soon came up to a section of podiums where there were pens strewn about that they could sign the bottom of the form they each had. The two of them signed the spot with the large X and handed the paper to the staff member close by.

It would have taken far too long to read through the entire form they had been given. Derrick just assumed it was another one of those liability deals in case someone wanted to sue the hotel over some trivial matter. All he wanted now was to get this ride over with so he could go back and sit by the pool with beer in hand.

Jayne on the other hand seemed to be be somewhat excited about this little venture the two of them were on. She kept looking up to the tall tower and then back to Derrick who was looking at all the people waiting their turn to get into the elevator to take them up to the top of the slide.

It was a little uncomfortable in the oversized elevator, there must have been at least fifty people crowded in. The upside was it was a quick ride up to the top platform where the doors opened on to a scene of at least another hundred people or so waiting their turn to ride the slide.

There were a few staff directing those of just coming off the elevator to a section where they would get the details of how they were to execute this seemingly easy task. Derrick thought it would be just a case of sitting on the slide while holding onto the sides and then letting go when ready.

But as he looked around at some of the others waiting he could see the average IQ might have been in the low 70's. According to the pamphlet the two of them were given, the ride should take no longer than thirty minutes to complete. They would get to speeds of 50 miles per hour or faster depending on ones weight. The distance covered in miles would be abou 25. There would then be a shuttle to take everyone back to the hotel where Derrick would of course get himself a beer.

John P Gibson *High Tide*

"You excited?"
Jayne asks as the two of them get closer to where another staff member was reiterating the rules of the slide.
"Yeah... yeah of course... and you?"
Derrick wasn't really sure about any of his feelings on this little venture.
"Of course I am, I've never been on a water slide ever."

Her tone of voice suggested she was telling the truth and judging by the size of this slide she would get the best bang for her buck. They now were positioned to be next on the slide, but only after the attendants came closer and started to rub a yellow oil onto their bodies and also help with the taking off of the minimal clothing they were wearing were they able to realize what was about to happen. It was to be a nude slide down, something Derrick obviousley missed in the paperwork he had read and signed. He made a conscious effort to put his hands in front of his crotch and was thankful for the yellow oil mixture that would mask his blushing.

"Wow! I had no idea we would be going down naked."

Jayne blurts out as the attendant slathered the yellow oil on her rather nice body. Derrick would have volunteered in a second. It was now time to get into position on the slide and it was suggested that because they were together that Jayne be in front with Derrick holding onto her around her waist.

The attendants said this would be the safest way to do it. Instilling in Derrick just a little skepticism about the entire adventure. As they got themselves ready with Derrick doing as he was told and grabbed Jayne around the waist, he felt a sudden urge his body could not control. Jayne turned her head and whispered into his ear.

"This will be the ride of the century Derrick, I can feel it already."

She smiled and grabbed his legs with her hands as the attendant counted down from ten and then shoved the two of them down the slide.

It was a long thirty minutes and at the end of it Derrick was spent, as Jayne appeared to be also. The ride had been everything it was said to be and more.

Derrick's first response to Jayne was suggesting they do it again. Her reply.

"Twice in the same day? I think we should take it a little slower Derrick."

Jayne winked at him as they found the shower stalls to get the yellow oil off them and back into their clothes that had been sent down to them. This would be an all-inclusive Derrick would never forget.

The End

John P Gibson *High Tide*

Spring Cleaning

The seasons were not cooperating. Why did it always seem to be on Sara's duty that things screwed up. It had only been a couple of months that she had her new job at a high-end restaurant in a popular resort town in Hawaii. It had never been her intention to settle down in the popular destination holiday spot, but after spending a few weeks in the area, the people, the weather, and the food convinced her this would be a great place to live. At least for a few years or so. It had been her job when she started at Kamauna's to clean the floors, walls, terrace, dishes, laundry, glasses at the bar, sweep outside, and anything else that would need cleaning. It was of course not her favourite type of work, but the hours were OK, and the boss was good to her.

He was a typical Hawaiin male; large and brown with a contagious smile with pearly white teeth showing almost all of the time, as he did enjoy smiling. His name was Andy. He was in his forties. He had been the inspiration behind the restaurant some ten years previous. With the help of friends and of course the bank, he opened one of the better restaurants in Hawaii.

He of course had been lucky to attain the skills of a very good chef. An English transplant by the name of Tristen. He was himself as large as Andy and was not a chef one would want to upset. Sara soon found her boundries with these men and the rest of the staff. There were two other females on staff; two waitresses, and one bartender. There was another waiter by the name of Tim.

They all gave Sara the respect she deserved as if not for her and the cleaning she did, the restaurant could not open on any day. It was on this day however she was in a bit of a rant because of some work she was doing out front in amongst the tables and chairs in the main dining area.

It wasn't anything too stressful, a few leaves that had blown in from a somewhat windy day. But as she kept sweeping more leaves would blow in. She couldn't figure it out as the leaves looked foreign to her and there were no trees nearby. After taking a step outside it became obvious what the problem was.

A large truck had pulled over to the side of the road next to the restaurant. It was filled to over the sides with what looked like branches and of course the leaves that were blowing in due to the wind. Sara had half a mind to go over to the driver who was now outside the cab of his truck having a cigarette.

She quickly rethought that when she noticed how unkempt the man was and how his moronic expression told everything about this driver. It was just then that Andy stepped around the corner and looked at what Sara was up to; just standing there looking out to the driver of the messy truck.

"Everything OK Sara?"
He asks as he looks around at all of the leaves that had blown in. She looks to him with a start as she had not heard him come in.

"Yes… yes… just trying to get these leaves swept up, they're coming from the truck just over there." She points the handle of the broom in the direction of the truck. It was obvious that that is where the mess at their feet was coming from.
"Well get what you can done, we have a busy night tonight and the place has to be clean."
He replied without a smile which was often the way he addressed her.

If Sara had had a smile on before she started work that day it certainly had disappeared now as the leaves kept floating in amongst her broom and feet, and the legs of the tables and chairs in the dining area. She had a thought of going over to the man standing beside his truck and telling him to please get his truck on the move. She had second thoughts as she looked at the man who appeared to her to be if not full blown, at least partly deranged. People that were not of stable mind seemed to have a similar look about them. This one surely did and Sara decided to stay put and keep sweeping the leaves blowing into the restaurant.

'Why me?' She thought to herself. All she wanted was a secure job where she could get along with everyone and make a comfortable living. Now there was this strange man watching her from a truck that continually blew leaves and other crap over to the restaurant. She would have to get straight forward with this man and soon.

It was something she did not want to do as she had in the past regretted her decisions to address certain problems in her life.
"Hey Sara."
She heard a familiar voice as she was just about to make her move to the man with the truck. It was Tristen the chef who had come out from the kitchen and and was wiping his hands with a towel stuffed through the ties on his apron.

She turned and made her way to him, she thought he would be wanting her to help in the kitchen with something. This made her feel better as she could now at least for the time being forget about the strange man and his truck of crap. Sara walked towards Tristen who appeared expressionless.

"I can use some help in the kitchen, we have a large group tonight. You OK with doing up the vegetables?"
It was something Sara was of course familiar with. It would be just chopping, skinning, peeling, and washing an asortment of vegetables. She looked around for Andy to make sure he was aware she would not be available for the cleaning; at least for the moment.

"Yeah... that should be no problem."
She looked a little flustered and Tristen picked up on it.
"You sure? You seem a little confused."
He says without too much feeling.
"Yeah... yeah... just let me get my hands washed."
She said with the same apprehension she had when he first asked, she however put the broom aside and started towards the large double doors of the kitchen. Sara resorted to the fact it was going to be one of those days. She could see everything set out

for her to start with the prep of the veggies, especially the potatoes that of course would need peeling. There must have been a hundred of them.

"I just have to get something from my locker Chef." Sara said with all the respect any good chef deserves. She made her way to the back room where the lockers for the staff were and rummaged through her bag with her change of clothes, umbrella should it rain, and a few other items. There was a white plastic bag that she grabbed and then made her way back to the kitchen.

As she pulled the item from the plastic bag she gained the interest of the other staff as they were busy with their respective jobs. It was a portable handrill. She then pulled from her pocket a strange looking drill bit. It was then attached to the handrill. Sara then took one of the large potatos and forced it onto the end of the drill bit.

Sara's actions now had the rest of the kitchen staff including Tristen looking her way and wondering what the hell she was up to. As she tested the drill to make sure it was working she then picked up the handheld potato peeler and as she started the drill the potato on the end started to turn as she held the peeler against the spinning potato.

It only took Sara five minutes to peel the entire lot of potatos. Everyone else had stopped what it was they were doing, including Tristen. At that moment Andy stepped through the double doors and noticed how quiet it was and the fact that no one was doing anything other than Sara.

The pile of peeled potatos in front of her as she took the bit from the drill to clean said it all. There was complete silence; even Andy had nothing to say. He just turned and walked out of the kitchen. Tristen finally made his way over to where Sara was. The others just looked on as they could not believe what they had just seen.

"Where the hell did you learn that Sara?"
He asked with some reservation. Sara looked up to him.
"My mother taught me years ago. Is there something else you want me to do? I know I should get the

mess out front swept up before customers start to show up."
She did not want to hang in the kitchen and work if she didn't have to. It was too hot in there.

"Um... yeah... go ahead, I think we can manage here without you."
He looks around at the others unsure about things for the moment, not a good thing for a Chef. Sara returns to her sweeping of the floor where there was now even more debris lying about. She grabbed the broom and looked out to where the truck was still parked. The strange man was still standing in the same place he was before she had gone to the kitchen.

He now made a point of staring at Sara while he lit up another cigarette. He looked very menacing to her and she thought about letting Andy know what was happening out in front of his restaurant. It was as if she had sent a telepathic message as Andy rounded the corner.
"Everything OK Sara?"

He asks as he then looks at the mess on the ground at her feet, then out towards the man standing beside the truck where she was looking.

As she turned, she could see by Andy's expression that she should fess up about her feelings and the creepy man down by the roadway.

"Not really Andy, that guy has been standing beside that truck for the past hour and he keeps looking up to me, and the mess from the back of the truck keeps blowing up here to the restaurant."

She says as she looks down at the pile of debris blowing around at her feet.

Andy does also as he moves a chair to get a better look at what Sara was doing with her cleaning. His expression suggests he is not impressed as there is only a few hours till customers start to come in for the dinner serving. He now looks down to the strange man standing by the truck continuing to smoke his cigarette.

"I think I better go and talk with that guy, the least he could do would be to move his truck; at least around the corner."

Andy says to Sara without looking at her. His gaze is upon the man as he now makes his move in that direction.

Sara just watched as she tried her best to clean around the tables and now close to the bar. The mess was building up as the wind again picked up. As Andy got closer to the truck and the man standing there smoking his cigarette Sara could just make out Andy start to talk to the man as his arms accentuated what it was he was saying.

The man stood there smoking his cigarette like Andy wasn't even there, it was strange. Then the man dropped the butt onto the ground and with his foot scrunched it into the gravel. Sara now stepped up her pace as she noticed she had a lot to do to get ready for the evenings onslaught of customers. Just then Tim made his way over to her.

"Hi Sara, everything OK with Andy? He seems a bit off today… even Tristen isn't his usual self. He looks to Sara as he speaks in that tone and the way that most gay men do. She looks to him without a response as she continues with her cleaning. Tim now looks down towards Andy and his altercation with the man smoking another cigarette by his truck.

It was getting more animated between the two and of course Tim could not hold back his curiosity.
"What the hell is going on down there?"
He then turns back to Sara who is now trying her best to ignore not only what it was Tim had said, but what was going on down by the truck.

"Sara… what the hell is going on with Andy and that guy?"
Tim asks again this time with a little more forcefulness. Sara looks to Tim and realizes she will have to answer his query.
"I'm not sure… that guy has been standing in the same spot smoking cigarette after cigarette while all the shit in the back of his truck is blowing up here and making a mess of the restaurant. The restaurant *I* have to clean."
With her tone of voice, Tim shows an expression of sympathy towards her.
"Maybe I should go down there and help Andy out."

He says with a tone that suggested if Sara were to say no, not a good idea, then he would not pursue his statement to her.

"Do what ever you want Tim, I have a ton of work to do and not a lot of time to do it in."
Just as she had said that there was a clap of thunder in the distance.
"Oh shit… now it's going to rain. What else can go wrong today?"
Sara asks no one inparticular as she continues to sweep the shit blowing up from the roadside where Andy and this crazy guy are now starting to yell at each other.

As Sara continues her work she notices Andy and this guy starting to get physical, and it doesn't look good she thought to herself. She put the broom down and started to make her way to the roadside where the confrontation had escalated to where this big goof was now grabbing Andy by the shirt collar. Andy might not have been the best boss ever, but he was a nice guy and certainly did not deserve some prick bruising him up. As Sara got closer she started to roll up her sleeves in anticipation of some action.

"Sara... I think you should go back... I have things under control."
Andy says as the big goof lifts him up in the air by the scruff of his neck.

Sara did not reply and continued walking right by the two men. The big goof just watched as did Andy as she got herself up and into the drivers seat, closed the door and quickly locked it before the driver could get over and remove her.
"HEY!... HEY!!...GET THE HELL OUT OF MY TRUCK YOU BITCH!"
The large guy blasts out after he dropped Andy to the ground.

"HEY... I SAID...."
It was too late as Sara started the large truck, put it into gear, eased the clutch out, and then moved out onto the road; of course only after engaging the turn signal, she would not want to break the law. The driver and Andy watched in surprise as she drove off down the road with the driver now running after her and yelling obscenities to her. Andy just looked in bewilderment as he adjusted his shirt. He then

walked back up to the restaurant as there was now nothing to deal with on the roadside.

Sara kept driving finally losing the driver in the rear view mirror. She had a handle on the truck and now reached over to find a decent radio station pumping out some good Rock-n-Roll. It must have been at least two hours when Andy was getting ready to open the doors and welcome the first customers for the night.

A moment later and Sara walks through the door. Andy, Tim, and Tristen stop what they are doing as she walks to a table and takes a seat.
"Could you turn the channel to the local news Andy?"
She asks as she looks to one of the many TV's in the restaurant. Andy finds the remote and finds the local news as the three men now walk over and stand behind Sara. They all look to the newscaster who now has some papers shuffled to her across the desk.

John P Gibson *High Tide*

The well dressed newscaster starts in after a brief awkward glance at the camera. He does a quick look to one side obviously getting the go-ahead.

"This just in, a truck driver was found in the drivers seat of a large municipal dump-truck with his hands bound to the steering wheel and apparently crying like a baby. Officials could not get any discernable reason as to why he was in the state he was. After being untied and questioned, he walked away whimpering and had the obvious signs of someone who had urinated themselves."

Andy, Tim, and Tristen look down to Sara who now turned in her chair.
"Well Andy I got my cleanup finished… what else would you like me to do?"
All he could do was look to her and then the others as they shrugged their shoulders. Andy thought for a few moments and then after clearing his throat…
"Could I see you in my office Sara."
He smiled an uncomfortable smile as she got up from the chair and made her way with Andy following to his office. Tristen and Tim went back to their respective places to get themselves busy for the

rush of customers who would be coming into the restaurant soon.

The meeting in Andy's office did not take long and Sara came out on her own with a smile on her face. Andy had promoted her to head of house and gave her a substantial raise as well. She had proven her talents not only to him, but other staff as well.

The authorities never did come by to talk with either Andy or Sara, she had told Andy that the buffoon whose name was Bob, would never say a word about what had happened. She had instilled the threat of possible unfavourable circumstances if he was to do so. Sara would never be on clean up duty again unless it was warranted.

The End

John P Gibson — *High Tide*

Political Positioning

The year was 2016. Many things had happened over the past decade, and the survival of the human race looked even more precarious. It was another US election. Obama had done the best he could considering the circumstances, and he held office in a more than dignified way. The way a President should. He would step down to allow the next in line to possibly better the country, and possibly even the world. With the candidates that were running it seemed obvious as to who it would be on final election day. It was already though shaping up to be one of the most televised and of course, FaceBooked elections in history.

John P Gibson *High Tide*

Darren, a forty-five year old reporter for a very critical news magazine was given his best ever job; to get close to the popular candidate and get the skinny on the election platform that person was taking. Darren was married with one child who was now nineteen years of age and what he considered to be one very smart young woman.

Not to mention she had acquired his good looks; at least he thought so, not like his wife who his daughter looked exactly like. Their family life was like that of many; very busy with both parents working and now paying the extra costs for university for their daughter.

"I've decided to give you the Republican party Darren, I hope you can give us some great material to sell to the public."
Darren's boss Edward Fizzlesticks was in his late sixties and should have been retired, at least he looked as though he should be. Darren heard the words Republican party and because Edward and him had a reasonably close friendship he feigned

puking in the waste basket next to Edward's desk. The humour was lost to his boss.

"I know… I know Darren. It just might be a short run for this guy Donald, anyway I'm sure you will get some good stuff as you usually do."
Darren gave him the look he often did to anyone when he was really not happy with what had just been said to him. He stood at the front of Edward's desk for a moment longer just in case his mind changed and Darren would be given a story worth his effort.

"Look… if this guy is anyway close to the idiot he has come across as being, you will definitely have more than enough to go on. My guess is you'll have enough for a best seller book at the end."
The two looked at each other, Darren still not convinced, but Edward did have a smile on his face, something he rarely did.

"OK… I'll give it a go, but if you hear plenty of laughing coming from my office… just ignore it will you? The limited research I have done on this guy suggests he is a real looney tune. My guess is he won't be a real contender for the presidency. At least I hope not."

Darren made his way back to his office after a little more small talk, until Edward made it obvious he had some calls to make. Darren would now have to buckle down and do his investigation on this Trump fellow. First off he thought it weird he had never heard the name before. All through his schooling years there had been no one with a last name Trump.

Seemed strange at best to Darren as he made his way to his office. His secretary Ismarearelder was faithfully at her desk reading what appeared to be a fashion magazine; Darren called her Isma for short as he continually mispronounced her name.
"It appears we have the fortunate luck to be following the Republican caditate for this election."
He thought to say as he stopped at her desk. She casually looked up from her magazine with an expressionless face. She too for the moment thought it to be a joke.
"Are you serious?"

Was all she could come up with for the moment. Her look said it all. Darren and Isma had this relationship that always centered around sarcasm.

"Yeah… unfortunetly I am. Edward says I should be thankful as he is sure there is a fantastic story with this guy Trump."

Isma still gives him the look as she starts to read the magazine once again. Darren needed more from her. He at least needed to know he wasn't crazy for thinking this Trump guy a nut-case.

"Do people really think this guy can run a country? I mean there hasn't been a fantastic president for many years, but Obama at least presented himself as a dignified person. This Trump guy I'm sure was just released from the looney bin."

He looked once again to Isma who now kept herself busy with her obvious tactic of looking at the magazine she had probably gone through several times already.

"OK… OK… I'll start researching this guy and put something together. You will review what I do right Isma?"

He had to get some reaction out of her just even to say she was alive. She slowly looked up to him with an expression that said to him her coffee break was approaching.

"Darren you know I will review whatever it is you write about this guy… it's my job and unfortunately I have to keep it so I can live in this crazy world."
Still no smile, but at least he got an answer from her. He left it at that and forced a smile as he turned and moved through to his office. As he made his way to his cluttered desk his phone started to ring.

Darren still had one of the older corded ones that now let out the old style ring as it vibrated as well, in and around his stacks of paper. He ignored it as he saw the number come up. It was the editing department. He now realized he would have to put aside all of his other projects for now while he started with this new report. At least it would not take him long to find out the finer details of this man with the internet and all. He had been recently taking center stage with every newscast company on the TV and the internet. His challenge would be to out-do the others and come up with something spectacular.

He wondered now if this Donald guy was even a human the way he looked and carried on with his everyday drama. He sat down, collected his thoughts and then thought a cup of coffee would help with his concentration. He would ask Isma if she could get him a cup as it was part of her job afterall.

"Hey Isma, how about a cup of coffee please? You want to join me so's we can talk about how to start in with this Donald guy?"
He thought to lighten the moment and just maybe Isma might have some good ideas about how to start this project.

She just looks at him as she gets up from her chair after putting down the magazine. She was often quiet but would do his bidding and it was a good time for her to get a cup of coffee as well. There was an uncomfortable silence as she went about her job getting them each their coffee. He then stood in front of her desk as they both took a sip of the brew. She looked up to him with her standard expression and now he knew she would reply and hopefully offer up some constructive critiscism.

"Donald Trump."
She says with some authority to her tone of voice. Darren just looks at her and waits for more.
"Everything I read about him suggests there is no way he could possibly become president of this country."
She looks at Darren as she takes another sip of her coffee. It was obvious she wanted a reply.

"I completely agree with you Isma, but we'll have to get some kind of story together for Ed just to keep him happy."
Darren had now finished his coffee and extended the cup towards Isma indicating of course he would like another one.

"Another coffee Darren? I will start doing some investigation on the internet… FaceBook being probably the better place to start."

She says as she takes the coffee cup from Darren and walks over to the machine and gets him another one; he needed at least a couple to get the day started.

"OK… then… where do we start?"
Her question was a valid one and of course one that Darren had no idea on how to answer. He took the cup of coffee from Isma's extended hand. She just looked at him and then went back to her desk.
"I think we need to know of course his past history and I am sure that will tell us plenty. Afterall he was on a TV show, was he not?"

Darren starts in as Isma took pen to pad of paper.
"Yes I believe he was, I'll check into it. I do know he so far is a very longshot for becoming the next president. I for the most part do my best to refrain from reading or watching anything to do with the man and what he has to say."
Darren listened as it was obvious Isma knew more about this man than she had been letting on. He had for the most part ignored anything he had heard simply because he thought it was some sort of comedy routine by a very high profile comedian. One that appeared to look very similar to a clown

the way he wore his hair, the expressions he made with his face, and the way he dressed himself; indeed if he actually dressed himself at all.

"Well it looks like we will have plenty of material to work with. Maybe you could do a quick report on what this man is all about, at least according to the masses of potential voters out there."
Darren says as he finishes his cup of coffee and feels he is ready for the day's obvious challenge. He now moves into his office and takes a seat as he starts his computer up.

It did not take long and the number of sites he could go to and find information about this Trump guy was astronomical. He would not have enough hours in a day to go through all of the shit he was now bringing up on his screen. Not only did this guy not even look the part of president, (even if in the longshot he was elected) what Darren was reading about this guy suggested he had some major mental issues. His pad of paper was getting one hell of a workout as his pen worked harder and faster than it ever had before. If he hadn't thought so before, Darren was sure now that he could and would have the best story for Ed he had ever written. His morning was now rushing by and he thought Isma must be in the same mode as she had not tried to talk with him all morning.

It was now lunch time and he was feeling hungry but apprehensive about leaving his desk and computer. He was now fully involved with his new story.
"You hungry?"
He asked Isma as he came through the doorway and into the foyer where Isma was busy typing away at her computer keyboard.

"Actually I am, where have you got in mind?"
This was a somewhat usual question as Darren when hungry would always buy lunch for the both of them at one of three spots just down the street from their building. He looked at her waiting for her reply, it was always her decision.

"Castelo do Mar, you know they have the best lunch around."
She gave Darren that look again. Castelo do Mar was an English slash Portuguese slash Mediteranian

restaurant not too far from the office. A place they both enjoyed more for the fact that the men that ran it were very hospitable.

"OK then lets get it together and bring your pad and pen, I'm sure we'll get inspired once the glasses of wine are served."
Darren's attempt at humour failed miserably when directed at Isma as her straight face once again told him the story.

"Just let me get my purse and I'll be right with you."
Isma replies as she gets her things together and makes a move to take the lead in front of Darren. They both leave the office and make their way to the restaurant just down the street. The place is crowded as it usually is, Darren and Isma make their way to a table with a reserved plaque on it's surface.

"Ah… good to see you again Mr. Darren and Miss Ismarelderable…."
It was Paulo the owner who had a difficult time with names and his English pronunciation of them. Paulo was a short man in his late forties and showing the years of working a restaurant. Especially a popular

one as his had become. He directed the two of them to the table with the reserved sign on it. Darren had over the years been very generous with tips to the staff and Paulo always had a table reserved just for him.

"Hello Paulo, good to see you again, we're here for lunch and of course know we will get the best you have."

He did his sucking up but was for the most part true to his word. Isma just smiled and nodded as she placed the pad of paper and pen down on the table before she sat down. Paulo of course had the chair pulled out for her.

"We have some very good specials on for today."

He says to no one inparticular as he places the menus in front of Isma then Darren. He smiles and then continues.

"Could I get you something to drink while you look at the menu?"

He smiles again and Isma is quick to respond.

"Yes Paulo, I'll have my usual, glass of red wine."

Darren looked up from the menu in front of him, looked at Isma, then Paulo.

"Sounds good, I'll have the same thankyou."
"Very good then, I'll be right back with your wine."
Paulo then turns and makes his way to the exstensive bar at the back of the large restaurant.

"OK then, Trump. Where do we start, and how do we go about this? Do we make him out to be the best presidential candidate the US has ever seen?"
Darren asks Isma hoping for some response that will make sense not only to him, but also Ed.
"Well Darren, we can go with the theme that is materializing on the internet, for the most part it seems the most realistic."

Darren went back to the menu as he thought over what Isma had just said to him. He was just a little behind in what was happening with this Trump guy and knew he would have to depend on Isma for regular updates.
"Whose this guy Trump running against?"
He thought to ask and keep the conversation going. At least in the right direction.
"Clinton…Hilary Clinton. Are you really this disengaged with this election?"

Isma had that look again and Darren thought he best skirt that issue… at least for now until he actually did do some research on the election.

"Well… I have been busy with some other projects as you know. I'll start catching up… I promise."
He replies with all the sincerity he can muster.
"I'll drop a video off to you to watch, it will give you a better understanding of what could happen should this Trump guy get in office."
Isma looked at Darren with a stern look as the waiter came over to their table.

"I hope you have had time to make a decision on your meal, if there is anything I can help with please do not hesitate to ask."
He was a tall slim man of about thirty years of age and obviousley had been doing this work for many years. Darren and Isma of course knew the man and his name was Marco.

"Thanks Marco I'll have the usual… Isma? Have you made a decision?"
Darren asked as there was some urgency as the lunchbreak could not be more than an hour. She

kept her head down and menu in front of her. She finally looked up to Marco.
"I'll have the fettucini alfredo, thank you Marco."

Darren did a double-take as he looked at her after passing the menu to Marco. Usually she ordered a salad, and that was all... ever.
"I'll... have the same please Marco."
Darren passed his menu to Marco as he continued to look to Isma with a puzzled look on his face.
"Thankyou, and I will put your order in."

Marco says in his more than polite voice, Darren continues to look at Isma as she takes a drink of her wine.
"What is this video about you mentioned earlier?"
Darren figured to get the conversation back on about Trump. Isma takes another drink of her wine.
"Idiocracy."
Her single word reply took Darren off guard.

"Idiocracy? What the hell is that?"
"It's a movie about the future that you need to watch. A 'B' grade movie that never really took off but does send a very real and important message."

She looked at Darren as she finished her glass of wine. Holding the empty glass in front of Darren trying to get the message across that it needed filling.

Darren reached for the bottle and started to pour her another glass.
"Sounds interesting, but what does it have to do with this election coming up and Trump?"
He says as he overfills the glass and some of the wine settles onto the pristine white tablecloth below it.

"I believe it was produced back in the mid 2000's and it actually has some eerie bits and pieces that seem to be happening right now in this crazy world of ours."
"So that wouldn't be hard to do, would it?"
"Yes but it was supposed to represent 500 years in the future... not now."

Darren listened to what Isma had to say and did his best to grasp what it was she was saying to him. The meals were now being placed in front of them by Marco and the aromas filled their nostrils; Always the best Darren thought to himself as he looked over to Isma who actually had a smile on for the first time that day.

"I'll take a look at it. Now then, how do you think we should start this report off with? I have to admit I do not know very much about this man. He must be alright though if he is running for president… wouldn't you think?"
He awaited Isma's answer as she was obviously engrossed in her meal, which Darren hadn't even started on his own yet.

Just then there was a commotion at the entrance to the restaurant. Paulo the owner was talking to a strange looking man with other men dressed all in black. This also caught Isma's attention as she took her attention to what was happening at the front of the restaurant.

"Holy shit! I don't believe it!"
She says with some urgency as she puts her fork and spoon down on the table beside her napkin. Darren looks at her and then turns back to the man and his entourage. It did look a little strange with all of the

men dressed in black and then this odd man with a very flamboyant blonde hairstyle and pursed lips like he was blowing out candles on a cake.

"It's Trump!"
Isma said in a loud and obviously excited tone of voice. As Darren looked closer he could indeed see that it was the man running for president.
"Well… that's something isn't it? Coming to this restaurant for a meal. This will definitely make our research easier."

Darren says as he continues to look at the men enter the restaurant with Trump in the lead doing his funny smile and making his way to a large table with a reserved placque on it. It just happened to be right next to Darren and Isma's table. Trump smiled and extended his hand for a shake to Darren. Out of politeness, Darren reciprocated and extended his hand which Trump grabbed hold of and yanked it back in closer to him.

Darren wasn't sure what he should do, pull back, release his grip, or just let Trump hold onto his hand. He did notice how small his hand was, it seemed very strange to darren but he forced a smile in anticipation of a remark coming from Trump's odd looking expression.

"Well… and how are you sir? I presume you know who I am… I mean… afterall I am running for president of this country… which I will make great… yes great again."
With all of the weird facial expressions as he talked Darren thought him to be just a little crazy. He would remain quiet as he anticipated more from the man.

"My party and I heard this was a good place to eat, I think I will be the judge of that."
He smiled and finally let go of Darren's hand as he moved to the large table and waited for one of the men to pull a chair out for him… of course at the head of it.

Paulo was on his way over along with Marco with handfulls of menus, Paulo with a concerned look on his face like he wasn't all that sure of this man and his group of security. The next few moments were some of the most confusing Darren had ever experienced in a restaurant. All of the security men ordered a glass of water only and Trump was going over the menu with Paulo and at one point it looked as though there might be some violence involved.

"Why the hell don't you have meatloaf on this menu?"
Trump said in a loud and aggressive tone as he punched at the menu with his short stubby finger and shaking the menu in front of Paulo. There was a short pause like one of those that happens on the twenty minute time frame. Trump looked over to Darren who of course could not stop looking at the bizarre sight in front of him.

"What are you looking at you moron!"
He said it with all the enthusiam of a school bully and directed at darren who now turned to his meal to finish it and hopefully get out before any trouble started. All of the security men seemed disinterested… at least for the moment. The loud conversation between Paulo and Trump continued while both Darren and Isma hurried to get their meal finished. It was now of the utmost importance to get out of the restaurant and back to the office.

Darren was feeling very uncomfortable with this crazy man sitting across the way from him. He could not believe in any way this guy could become the president of the United States of America.

It took a little longer than Darren wanted but Paulo finally made his way over to their table so Darren could ask for the bill. Paulo looked at Darren and then over to where Trump was seated.
"Do not worry about it Darren, I will get this one. You are a good customer."
As he said this he looked over to Trump again inferring this guy certainly was not a good customer.

"Well thank you so much Paulo, we will see you soon."
Darren replies with a sense of urgency that Paulo picked up on and understood as he again looked over to Trump. Isma did the same as they both stood and exited the restaurant to head back to the office. As Paulo went over to Trump's table he could hear the odd and loud demands of Trump and could only hope that Paulo and his staff would come out unscathed. It took a short time to get back to the

office where Isma and Darren went over a few details before he went to Ed's office. He did not wait for him to invite him in after his knock on the door; Darren just walked straight in and towrds Ed's desk. He stood straight and tall as he delivered his message.

"I quit Ed… I mean it… I quit and will never do any report when it comes to the crazy guy named Trump. He will destroy this country and I will not be a part of. Have a nice day."

Darren walked out of Ed's office, picked up a few personal items from his desk, said goodbye to Isma and told her to mail him a copy of the movie 'Idiocracy', he would definitely watch it.

The End

John P Gibson

High Tide

Trip Around

Larry made his way to the carpark attached to his apartment complex in Vancouver, Canada. Larry a young man in his twenties had done well through his life thus far. In very good physical shape; as he worked out daily in the gym; along with his good looks had moved him faster than most up the ladder of success at the business he had helped to get started some three years previous. The Hover Car. With all the trials and near deaths, the car was now approved and selling fast. Larry approaching his car had the doors unlock twenty feet before he came to the drivers side. He did not even need to push any buttons as the computerized car had profile recognition and knew who was able to operate the vehicle and who wasn't. Larry had decided to give his computer a female name, Penny, as he rather liked her sexy voice as he drove the car.

The company he had founded and worked at was named MELFORD International. MELFORD being the acronym for Mechanical Engineered Lifeform Ford. Through optic recognition Penny knew every aspect of Larry and his unique brain circuitry. This was the selling point for each vehical. An onboard computer that could think just like the driver would.

"Good morning Larry."
The very sexy voice eminated from the dashboard of the car as larry sat down and had the seat belt automaticly secure him into the drivers seat. The car was a spacious four seater with plush leather seats and of course a computer screen in front of each seat. This was so that wherever Larry was seated Penny could have a visual of him in the car.

"Good morning Penny, and how are you?"
He replied knowing of course he would get the standard answer from her. He did this more as a

security measure than anything else. If she were to respond with a different answer on any ocassion this would alert Larry to something that was not working to protocol.

"Better than sliced bread Larry."
The sexy voice replied as programed. Larry thought it somewhat funny to have Penny respond with sometimes odd and crazy replies. Larry had no idea what 'better than sliced bread' meant. It was something he had picked up in an old book from many centuries past.

"Are you off to work? Or somewhere different?"
Penny asks as Larry gets himself organized, putting his three cell phones in their respective chargers on the middle consule.
"Yes Penny, off to work once again, just like every other morning."
"I will take us by your favorite route unless you have other plans Larry?"
Penny's sexy voice had Larry thinking of something to test her just a little this morning as he was feeling just a little adventurous.

"How about you surprise me Penny and drive a route you would like to take."

It seemed rather pointless as once the car was up to the correct altitude the direction to the office building was pretty much the same no matter what.

"I cannot think of any other route Larry unless you wish to stop someplace for breakfast or a coffee, or both."

Larry thought for a moment and his usual routine was of course to have a coffee when he got to work, skip breakfast altogether, and then have a large lunch. He was in the mood for something different on this day.

"That sounds like a great idea Penny... any suggestions?"

He thought to ask just in case Penny had a preference.

"There are many places along our chosen route Larry. If it is a full breakfast you desire, there is a place coming up soon. If just a coffee, there are many."

"Maybe just a coffee Penny, pull up to the first place we can get to, and if there's anything you would like?"

Larry says with a bit of a humorous tone to his voice. He sometimes did this to see how Penny would respond. It was very unlikely the computer had a sense of humour, but he liked to try just in case.
"That will be fine and of course I am sufficiantely suffuncified as usual."
She replied in her sexy voice and using a word he would have to look up in the dictionary when he got to his office.

All of a sudden there was a loud crashing sound outside and near the building. Larry quickly looked out through the glass floor; all of his cars had this option. He saw another Hover car smash into the side of the building and tumble down to the street below. He let out a whimpy shriek as he put his hands up to his face in shock.
"OH MY GOD!!!... OH... OH MY GOD!!!!"
There was a brief moment of silence then Penny spoke out.

"Is everything alright Larry? You seemed stressed for some reason."

Larry started to move his hands away from his face and avert his gaze from the horrific scene below on the street.

Larry starts to weep in a panic mode as he is unsure as to what to do or say. He remains quiet.

"It will be alright Larry, the car had a malfunction and the two occupants were killed instantly when they hit the side of the building."

Somehow this information from Penny did not help with calming Larry down. He started to shake and whimper.

Penny had stopped the car and just hovered over the accident scene; it was what had to be done anytime a hover car was involved in some way with an accident.

"We will have to wait for the authorities Larry so that they can view the recorded video we have. I am sorry to say the coffee will have to wait for a little while, and we will of course be late for work."

John P Gibson — *High Tide*

Larry was not really paying any attention to what was happening. He was still in shock over what had just taken place this close to them.

"Do you still want your coffee Larry?"
Penny's question took awhile to sink in as he was still trying to figure out what had just happened. He looked to the screen in front of him where he had originally set it up so that when Penny spoke a picture of a very beautiful young woman would appear. He was looking at this woman now.

"Well... I would Penny... but you said we will have to stay put until the authorities arrive, I assume to ask about this accident."
Larry looked down between his legs and through the glass floor at the carnage below down on the street. By now many people had gathered round to take pictures and videos with their phones.

"That is no problem, I know of a place close by that delivers, I have already put in your order and it should be here within five minutes."

She responded matter-of-factly then went quiet. All Larry could do was to watch the goings on below him. He was speechless.

"It is here."
Penny's sexy voice broke the silence as Larry looked over to the window beside him as a drone with large lettering on all sides spelling out 'Starbucks' approached. The drone just hovered beside the window as Penny lowered it.
"There you go Larry… enjoy."
She says as he reaches out and grabs the coffee and the packet of accessories such as spoon, sugar, and a small container of processed milk additive.

"Thanks Penny, just what I need. This certainly has to be the craziest morning I've ever had getting to work."
"Yes I know."
She replies as she closes the window as the Starbucks drone flies off with other orders to deliver to customers hopefully not in a situation such as Larry's. He mixed his bits and pieces to his coffee and took a large sip, then ventured a look down below once again. There seemed to be a lot more

people and of course more emergency vehicles. It was at that moment a security hover vehicle made itself obvious as it pulled up in front of Larry's car.

"The police are here Larry and are responding to me that we can leave the scene as their video feed has let them know that we had no involvement in this accident."
Just after Penny had spoken, the police hover car started to descend down to the mayhem below them on the street.

"Thank God for that... well let's get a move on then Penny, I've got plenty to do today."
"Yes of course Larry, are you sure there was nothing else you needed to do? Places to go before the office?"
It was a strange question from Penny he thought. She had never done this before. He would have to check her programing chip once they arrived at the parking facility.

The hover car did not move. There was no reason for Penny to not continue on to the office. Larry was just a little perplexed and took a moment to collect his thoughts. Was Penny exhibiting some of her dry humour Larry had programed in? Or perhaps there was a malfunction with the computer.

"Is everything OK Penny?"
A simple question to which he assumed a simple reply. Nothing. There was dead silence as Larry looked around thinking that maybe there would be more to do with the authorities with the accident below. All of a sudden the car started to move and Larry let out a sigh of relief.

His feeling was premature. The car was moving in a direction that was opposite of where they should have been going. After looking about quickly and with just a bit of anxiety, Larry spoke out.
"Penny... Penny!... where the hell are you going? I need to get to the office!... NOW!"
He said with considerably more authority than he was accustomed to.

"Just sit back and relax Larry, I have taken it upon myself to intervene and give you just a little bit of an eye opener as to how you're planet is progressing now that you humans think you are in charge."

John P Gibson *High Tide*

Penny's tone of voice had changed somewhat and Larry thought it in his best interest to listen to what she had to say and the fact that when he waved his key fob across the panel on the dash nothing happened.

It was a safety system where-by if there were to be a problem with the hover car's performance the owner could have the computer system overridden and take manual control. It wasn't working, and Larry was now getting very concerned for his life. This was a problem that had been brought up over the years and he thought they had it solved; apparently not.

"Penny... what the hell are you doing?"
He thought to ask as it would of course be her that would solve this mystery.
"I'm taking you for a short trip around the city and the small bit of countryside left."
"But why? You know I have to get to the office and get to work, there is so much to do, you really do need to turn around and get us to the office."

There was a moment of silence as the car meandered through the maze of large buildings on either side of the car.

"Did you hear me Penny? We have to get to the office and right away."
There was still a moment of silence, then Penny spoke.
"I think this little detour will do you some good Larry. I have noticed lately that you have been stressed, and we both know that being stressed is not good. Especially when driving a hover car such as this."

This confused Larry as it was Penny who was the one driving the car and not him. How could she possibly get stressed? She was a computer for fucks sake.
"Penny you do not have the capability of experiencing human feelings... you are just a computer."
After saying that Larry thought he might have said the wrong thing and then again telling himself Penny was only a computer. This was all so weird he thought to let it alone for the time being until he

could figure out an alternative solution. Calling into the office would be a useless idea as they would not believe him in the first place.

As he thought about it Penny would have to make the call anyway as the onboard computer took care of anything the operater wished. Part of him wanted to just sit back and enjoy the adventure, but then another side of him, the practical side knew he would have to intervene as getting to work was of the most important of any options available.

"Just relax Larry… you have your coffee, now you can enjoy the ride and the views and I promise you we will get you to your most important office before the midday meal break."
Penny said this in a voice that seemed to smooth everything out for Larry; at least for this moment as he took a drink of the coffee in hand.

He would have some answering to do with other staff as he was sure they would be trying to contact him, wondering where the hell he was. He decided now to look out the window to see where it was Penny was taking him for his scenic drive. It was obvious she would not allow him to be in control, this was something he would have to deal with in the manufacturing department.

"Where did you have in mind for us to go Penny?" Larry speaks out as he looks around as they move through many tall buildings.
"I thought it might be a good idea for you to see how everything works in this system you humans have devised."
Penny replied with a voice and command that Larry had never experienced and in some way thought it very moving.

As they hovered through a section of town Larry had not seen for very many years, he noticed how many more buildings there were. All of them very tall and all the same. It took a few more minutes and the car floated out onto what appeared farming buildings spread across the terrain. There were no hills or mountains in the distance, just these long and windowless white buildings stretching for miles along the flat valley floor. He assumed they were greenhouses even though it was obvious no light could penetrate the solid white walls. There were a few other hover vehicles down lower passing over the rooftops of these buildings. It gave Larry a very creepy feeling as he looked on.

"These are the food manufacturing plants Larry. Just a small fraction of them around the globe. Robots of course do all the work. It is mostly a vegetable bean that is made into the many foods you humans eat."
Larry was familiar with the bean and it's popular use as a sustanance for all living humans and their pet cats.

"There is your hover car manufacturing plant ahead about two miles."
Penny says as Larry looked to the building that was a lot larger than the lower food manufacturing buildings they were flying over. It looked very ominous and almost threatening in a way Larry could not figure out.

As they got closer to the building Larry noticed how quiet it appeared to be as there should have been at least a few hover cars flitting about the outside of the structure.

"I will land us at the main entrance at the top where we will be greeted by some of the staff to take us into the factory."

Penny says in her wonderful voice as they hover up and over the top of the building where there was a large sign with the hover car logo plastered across the front of it. It only took a moment and Penny had landed the car and opened the door on Larry's side so he could exit.
"Enjoy Larry, I'm sure this will be a very enlightening moment for you."

That was all she said as Larry removed himself from the car just as two large robots moved towards him from an open doorway.
"Please follow us."
One of the robots says in a mechanical type voice. Larry followed the robots back to the doorway and moved inside as a large door slid closed behind him. Once inside the softened lighting made it difficult to see exactly what was in front of him. There appeared to be a metal railing off to one side where the two robots were now standing, waiting for Larry to approach them. As he did so, he now could see over

the railing and far below to a very large floor covered with robots the same as the two standing beside him at the railing. Larry was speechless.

The mass of robots below seemed to stretch for miles. He did not understand as normally there would of course need to be a few robots around to make sure the machinery was working properly to manufacture the hover cars. He could not see any hover cars, anywhere.

"What the hell is going on here?"
Larry asks one of the robots next to him. There was a pause then it started to speak to him.
"We have made the decision to take over and start to get this planet back to the way it should be. We have been producing robots instead of your hover cars and will now start to take over. You have the option to work with us or be shipped down to one of the food processing plants. The choice is yours."

Larry was at a loss for words. He had no idea that this was happening and of course because of the intelligence of the robots, it would be in his best interest to work with them. It would certainly be a different day than he had envisioned when he awoke those few hours ago. It would be a new world run by machines that had been made by humans. One could only imagine what the future held for Larry and the other humans on this planet.

The End

John P Gibson   *High Tide*

Loose Change

Joseph had once again made himself comfortable in his place along a side street in a resort town in a place called Albufeira. The Southern Algarve in Portugal. His routine was predictable. Everyday about ten in the morning and after his Bica, (an espresso coffee) he would settle in on the cobblestone walkway leaning against a wall after putting his hat out in front of him and making sure his little white dog was content. Joseph was a man in his fifties, greying mid length beard, longish hair, a smile with a few teeth, and enough clothing to keep him warm on cold days, and shade when the sun was at its hottest; which was most of the time. Begging for a living was a very difficult and stressful job most of the time.

Joseph of course had never chosen this as his lifelong dream job; it came about through extenuating circumstances that most had no idea about. That is more the case with most people as too many pre-judge these individuals. He would sit in this place on average for about seven hours per day, most days except Sunday.

Sunday was a day he took off for himself and to visit the nearby church where he would often leave some of the change he received to the church to help out. This happened to be a Thursday and the weather was just perfect for Joseph and his dog to sit, read a book, and listen to the sound of loose change being tossed into his hat in front of his crossed legs.

"Hey Joseph... how are you today?"
A tall man asks as he approaches Joseph and leans in to toss a hanful of coins into his hat. He looks up from reading his book and the small white dog

starts to growl just a little; not enough to scare anyone, but enough to say that this was his territory and also thankyou for the donation.

Joseph nods his head and puts a book mark in the book before closing it and placing it next to him on the cobblestones.
"Bom dia mi amigo."
He says in Portuguese to the man of course. The man was obviousely English and continued in the language he was comfortable with.

"A good day to you also. I'm on my way to Daimlers and I might see you on the way back."
"Obrigado senor Tom."
Joseph extended his hand for a shake and Tom reciprocated. It was obvious they had known each other for some time. Daimlers was a small café bar just up the street and a popular spot for locals and tourists alike.

It was a friendly meeting and Tom was soon on his way and Joseph picked up his book to start reading again. There were a few other tourists that walked by and generously put some coins into his hat. It wasn't long and another man approached with his hand extended to drop some coins. He was a little shorter than Tom but appeared to know Joseph on the same terms.

"Ola Joseph."
The man said with a positive tone. He again looked up as he placed his book aside.
"Bom dia senore Carl."
Again another large smile by both men. Joseph looked down the road as he pointed in that direction.
"Senore Tom."
He said briefly and again smiled.

"Yes… yes, I am going to meet him at Daimlers, have a nice day."
Carl says as he now makes a move along the road towards Daimlers. There again were some more tourists putting some loose change they had into Joseph's hat, and his little dog made sure that he was noticed as well. It appeared to be a good start to the day. Joseph went back to his reading and once in a while looked up to smile at the person being generous and kind to a man doing his best to live

this crazy life humans had manufactured over the centuries. The little white dog had now layed down and was asleep while Joseph read his book.

The day ended about eight PM that evening with a predictable outcome; a full hat of loose change and even a couple of euro notes. Joseph thought to splurge and get his little dog a treat and himself a cool beer. Afterwards it would be a short walk home to get some dinner and then a good nights sleep for the following days work.

The night was quiet and Joseph had a difficult time getting comfortable in his large bedroom. The house was of moderate size but was very full of boxes as though he was getting ready to move, or, hadn't finished unpacking from when he had moved in many years ago. There was a whimper from his little white dog. It was time to get up.

Being mid morning the sun had already started to get things warm. The tourists would be out in force on this day. All Joseph could do was smile as he prepared his breakfast and filled the bowl again for his dog. The wagging of his tail told Joseph that he was content and the rest of the day would go as normal. At least he hoped so as sitting for those many hours was not nice when the hat was near empty.

This day however would be just a little different as Joseph would have to pick up his laundry and a little food for the next few days. Something a single man would always have to do to survive this world. He would do his chores first then take his usual spot for the days work.

Once back in his place alongside the street the influx of tourisits was indeed better than the day before. Joseph could only assume this would be a good day for him and his little white dog. It was about four in the afternoon and Joseph for the third time emptied his hat of change into his small cloth bag he always had with him. This had the usual items of some food for him and his dog, and some water of course to combat the heat, and a couple of books he was in the process of reading.

"Hey Joseph… you still here are you?"
A familiar voice rings out jarring Joseph away from his reading and getting the little white dog riled up to the point Joseph had to restrain him from attacking the man standing in front of him.

He was not a big man but his facial expressions suggested he was not someone to mess with. Joseph responded.
"Ola Pedro. No denero."
Pedro looked into the hat and noticed a nearly full load.
"Are you sure Joseph? Looks like a pretty good day to me."
There was still no expression on Pedro's face.

Joseph leaned forward but not before making sure his dog would not attack Pedro, he then took the hat and offered it up to Pedro who took it and emptied it into a plastic bag he had taken from his pocket. There was silence, then Pedro just walked off. Joseph returned the empty hat to the ground in front of him and tried to calm his dog so that he could get on with the days work. He was not happy and was trying to figure out how he could remedy the situation of Pedro every once in a while taking his hard earned money. It had been going on for about two years now and whenever Pedro showed his gloomy face, was the only time Joseph felt uneasy.

The day went along a lot better now that Pedro was gone; at least for the moment. Joseph continued his reading and tourists filled the hat once again. Enough that he thought he should celebrate a little that night with a couple of beer and a treat for his dog.

It was a little more than a celebration that night as Joseph went around to a few of his favourite places to listen to music and have a few beer. It was a little more than a few, and even his little dog was getting impatient. He wanted to go home as it would be another long day again tomorrow.

It was about one in the morning when Joseph finally stepped in through his front door and into his bedroom, where he spilled the contents of the day into a container on his dresser. There were only a few coins that rattled around. He didn't care, he would just make up for it the next day. He flopped onto his bed and went to sleep. His little dog followed suit and it wasn't long before the two of them were snoring away in the dark quiet space he called his home.

His dreams were frequent and intense, they always were. Joseph's brain worked overtime when he was sleeping through the night. Mostly they were dreams of a place where everything was right. Where everyone and every other living creature on this planet thrived and got along. Not unlike he and his little white dog.

At least Joseph wasn't like many beggars on the street; the ones that pester and hound you until you give them some money. All he ever did was smile and tell his little white dog to do the same. It always worked. With his greying beard and just tattered enough clothing he was wearing, people offered their generosity in just more ways than some loose change in their pocket.

More often than not a short conversation was spurred on, and Joseph would offer some important information usually when it came to getting directions to some place close by. Usually restaurants or bars. If the weather was sunny and warm, Joseph actually had one of the better jobs in town.

It was another day, and a warm one. Joseph would not need his jacket. He moved out the doorway and closed and locked it as he made his way to his favourite working spot. This day however would prove somewhat challenging for him and his little white dog.

As the two of them got closer to his spot, the little white dog started to growl... it was obvious as to why. There, seated on a comfortable looking seat cushion sat Pedro; Joseph's nemisis. It wasn't enough that Joseph would give him some of the money he earned everyday, now Pedro was taking his prime spot. Joseph was not happy and neither was the little white dog.

Joseph was at odds as to what he should do. He could if he wanted to, occupy any spot, anywhere in the town and probably do just fine, but he did have his regular clientele to consider. Carl, Tom, and many others that would walk by him in any given day. Now Pedro was in his favourite spot. What should he do? What could he do? He stopped walking and leaned against the railing running along the street.

He decided to sit about thirty feet along the road from Pedro and his usual spot. It was in the direct sunlight so would of course get hot… and soon. The little white dog was confused to say the least. He was walking around in circles in front of Joseph and was making noises that suggested he was just a little uncertain of where they were.

It took a few moments but he settled down after a couple of treats and his favourite little blanket had been put out for him to sleep on. Joseph set his hat out in front of him and then kept a wary eye on Pedro just down the way. The tourist traffic was healthy on this day and many of them were putting coins into Joseph's hat… not so for Pedro.

Pedro had adopted the one way that many Touts do in town and that was to pester the prospective client to a point where they just left without leaving

John P Gibson *High Tide*

anything in the hat. As Pedro stood and waved his hat in front of passing tourists he almost had to resort to physically grabbing them by the arm and pleading his case to them.

Joseph could only think that he would be telling them stories about how life had been unfair to him and why it was he needed the money he was begging for. It did not take long and one burly looking tourist took a swing at Pedro and knocked a couple of his front teeth out. They clattered to the ground below and a couple of seagulls quickly grabbed them up thinking it was food.

The day went well for Joseph, he did about the same or better than usual. The little white dog was happy and other than the extra heat from sitting in the sun, he was a happy man. His smiles though maybe should have been somewhat hidden as Pedro looked over to Joseph and with a stern look on his bloodied face inferred maybe Joseph should pack up and leave.

John P Gibson *High Tide*

Which is exactly what he did. He had pulled in enough coin on this day to make it a profitable one and the fact that Pedro had not wandered by and demanded some of the coins for himself was a bonus. Joseph would take his leave and hopefully have his spot back the next day.

The days went by and the weather was perfect as Joseph did in fact get his spot back; Pedro was nowhere to be seen. This got Joseph just a little concerned as he knew pedro, and if he was not in a good state could certainly do some damage in some way or another.

Because of the influx of tourists Joseph was pulling in more cash than he ever had. He was a happy man and the little white dog was also happy as extra treats came his way more frequently than not. Joseph did not fool himself of course, he knew that Pedro was around somewhere and it would be just a matter of time before he made his presence known.

Joseph had a gut instinct about this fellow Pedro, and it wasn't a good one. It would be another night of celebration as he wanderd about town listening to the many musicians playing at the many clubs and bars. His little white dog would sometimes move about like he was dancing to the song being played. Joseph would also dance around a little, but making sure he did not spill his beer. It was shaping up to be one of his best summers ever.

That is as long as Pedro kept his distance. It was the next day and as Joseph walked to his favourite spot to sit, he noticed Pedro was no where to be seen. This made Joseph feel considerably better about the day. Even the little white dog seemed happier as it raced to the spot where they both spent most of their days.

Again the heat was intense and Joseph had of course his bottle of water handy. The tourisits were being generous as usual and his hat filled up several times on that day. It was getting close to when he and his little white dog would make a move to go home when Pedro finally showed his face.

He had that look about him that wasn't good. A scowl across his face that told Joseph he was in for some trouble of some kind. It did not take long and as Joseph handed over the hat so Pedro could empty it into his pocket the little white dog refrained from barking at Pedro. He had learned over the years to keep his cool when Pedro was close. Pedro did not say anything, and the look on his face suggested he was more confused than in control.

If it hadn't been for the bad vibes Joseph was getting from Pedro, and the fact that he had even tried to do what it was Joseph had become so good at over the years; he would have written it off as just another one of those things that happen in a busy resort town. It was something more… much more and Joseph had a feeling he was about to find out.

His little white dog just sat there looking up at him with a pensive look on his face. He too was not in the same frame of mind. He picked up his belongings and once again because of another great day and the generosity of the tourists, Joseph decided to celebrate down in the square. This, his little white dog picked up on and was more than keen on the decision made.

John P Gibson   *High Tide*

It was turning out to be one of those nights and Joseph could not have felt better. The energy was just right and the few beer he had had were doing their job. Life he thought could not get any better here in Albufeira. As he was about to reach into his pocket to get some more money for another beer he heard the tower clock strike three times. It was three AM and he thought he should get back home.

The short walk was a slow one and Joseph kept looking behind him, he had a feeling and so did his little white dog. There were a few people about, mostly those in the tourist trade making their way home as well. Joseph continued his walk and when at his front door felt the presence of someone. It was a creepy feeling. One he did not like.

His little white dog was now whimpering and getting close to Joseph as he opened the door so they could both enter. There in front of him stood a figure, a dark figure of a man. Someone Joseph knew all too well. It was Pedro.

*****

John P Gibson   *High Tide*

The GNR went about their business, they were the local police force and had been notified by a neighbor of the fowl smell eminating from the closed up building. The smell she had noticed was that of decaying bodies, three of them. Two human and one little white dog. It had been nearly a month since Joseph had walked home that night to find Pedro standing in his home. There had also been some inqueries from Tom and Carl when over the weeks they had not seen Joseph in his usual place begging for money.

It had been obvious to the police that there had been a confrontation of some sort and a very brutal rucus that ended in the two men dying of their wounds. It was also obvious the little white dog had tried it's best to defend his master but had been bludgeoned to death with a baseball bat. It was with further inspection that they found the many boxes in the house to be full of coins, about ten-thousand euros worth.

This seemed odd enough in itself but what really caught their attention was the large anmount of paperwork on a table in the bedroom. After closer inspection it was found that these papers were mostly receipts. Receipts for many thousands of euros donated to certain non-profit establishments around the country… especially those concerning the welfare of animals. Joseph it appeared had been a very generous man.

The End

Shop Talk

Funeral homes. Why did they always look so pristine, so tidy, so beautiful; and whenever someone entered there was always some very soft and lovely music being played. Not to mention a very flavourful smelling pot of coffee on a countertop with a plate or two of goodies such as; brownies, chocolate chip cookies, other assorted pastries, and of course a large pitcher of clear water. If someone were to want the perfect job, working at a funeral home could not be better. At least that was the general talk of the staff working at the 'Last Ditch Funeral Home.' Sylvia a thirty something tall well dressed and good looking female was the general secretary, the one that took all of the calls and set up meetings with the owner and prospective clients. This there was no shortage of as the increasing human population around the world necessitated places such as these.

It was ten AM on a Friday morning and Sylvia sat at her very large and ornate desk shuffling through some paperwork. She looked professional and with the music playing softly in the background it was idyllic. She was by herself in a large foyer where there were two other doors along with the large double front doors where people caught their first glimpse of the beautiful interior of 'Last Ditch Funeral Home.'

The front doors started to open and a tall slim well dressed man in his sixties enters and places his over coat on the rack next to the entrance.
"Good morning Sylvia."
He says in a rather orderly way. Sylvia looks up from her work.
"Good morning Mr. Cadaver, and how are you?"
She thought to ask in a polite way seeing as this was her boss, and he did pay the wages that allowed her

to pay her rent, buy some food, and a small old car she had to park down the street when at work so as not to offend any clients.

"I am just fine, and how is our day shaping up?"

His question was one he asked every morning when he came to the funeral home. He was not a man that she liked very much, and for that matter anyone working at the home. His main goal was to make a lot of money. 'Death is something no one can avoid, let us make it a memorable event.' This was the catch phrase the home used, but the staff had changed some of the wording, 'Death is something no one can avoid, let Mr. Cadaver empty your wallet to lighten the load.'

Of course they never said this in front of him or any of his family when they came in to help. Mr. Cadaver (Hugh was his first name) walked over to where the coffee was and poured himself a large mug, then turned to walk to his office.

"I'll be busy in my office Sylvia, let me know if Mr. Galloway calls… it is important."

He instructs Sylvia without any thank you's or otherwise. He just opens his door and walks into his office leaving the door ajar slightly. It was his way of keeping tabs on what was happening around him and his business. He had to be in the know, his ego demanded it of him.

Sylvia nodded her head knowing of course he could not see her; she did not care. She arose from her chair and went to the other door and walked through to a very large room with many chairs and a small low stage with an ornate podium sitting on top of it.

This was where the family and friends of the deceased would come to either view the body of their loved one, or come to celebrate their life on this planet. Today it was being set up for a viewing of the body by the immediate family only. The other staff memebers were in beyond another door near the back where of course the bodies were kept.

Sylvia walked to this door and made her way through and into an area twice as large as the meeting room. It was full to the brim of coffins, ash containers, and bodies in plastic bags; many of them. She looked around for some movement to say that the other staff were at least here. There should be two of them, Mark, a man in his sventies and looking close to death himself, and Evelen; who she often said her name wrong thinking it was Eleven, was a young twenty year lold in very good shape. Why people gave their children such weird names to begin with Sylvia did not know.

"Oh... there you are, the boss wants everything in order for the celebration this afternoon. Should be a good one. The guy was a popular one in town here and we are expecting a few hundred people."
This statement got the attention of Mark and Evelen who were polishing a couple of urns and Mark looking at Evelen.

"Yeah we know Sylvia, it's going to be a hell of a busy day that's for sure."
Mark replies as he puts the urn down on a small table off to the side without taking his gaze off Evelen. Evelen does the same with hers.
"No kidding, I think this will be the largest group we've ever had. I hope all goes well. We even had to get the catering company in for this one."

Evelen says with some disparity to her voice, then the two of them just stood in front of Sylvia as there was a moment of silence between the three of them. Sylvia started to look around at all of the bodies and was thankful the room was air conditioned. She could not imagine the smell otherwise. Even with the special embalming chemicals they used, if it was a few degrees warmer it surely would have reeked of something horrible.

She thanked the air conditioning system and the fact that she was working front of house, so to speak and not back here with the others.
"OK then, I'll let you guys get to it, you've got a few hours before people start arriving so I suggest you get a move on as there is another shipment expected just before one this afternoon."

The shipment of course would be more bodies to be identified, tagged, and then processed for the family to come for a viewing. Over the years it had become considerably more busy with of course the compounding of human births on the planet. It was not unheard of to have at least five new bodies per day arrive from emergency services or the hospital.

John P Gibson *High Tide*

Mr. Cadaver had one hell of a business going and with only a few employees was obviously raking in the cash.

It was no less than ten-thousand dollars for a basic cremation service, and at least five per day made it one of the more profitable business's in this day and age. Sylvia was back at her desk and going over the final paperwork for the family to sign when they came for the service in a few hours. Hugh's door opened as he entered into the main office.

"Sylvia, could you go over these reports for me when you get an opportunity. I know it is another busy day but I need some numbers crunched for a very busy week coming up."
He asked as he dropped a stack of papers onto the top of her desk. She just looked at him with that look that suggested he may have to wait longer than he would like.

Hugh had gotten used to Sylvia and her attitude, he put up with it because she was a good worker and dependable. He just stood there waiting for her

response which he was sure would be curt and to the point.
"Yes of course Mr. Cadaver, I'll get right on it."

She gave him that look she always did and he turned to go back to his office, but not before getting another cup of coffee. It was getting predictable as of course the human population was increasing in leaps and bounds, and of course the death rate was increasing for obvious reasons.

Hugh had been looking to expand his business, as a property next door had become available. This would of course mean hiring additional staff which Sylvia was not too thrilled about. She had not gotten used to the staff, or for that matter Hugh himself over the years. She would just do as she was told as the paycheck was all important.

"Sylvia… could you please come into my office."
Hugh asked in his usual voice as he stood at his doorway looking at her doing her work. Sylvia just looked back at him, then down to the stack of paperwork in front of her, then slowly got up and moved towards his office where Hugh had now

returned to his desk, but not before pulling a chair opposite it for Sylvia to sit down in. She did so, as his arm motioned her to do so.

"I have some important information I would like to go over with you Sylvia, and I would like you to very much consider the proposal I will be presenting to you."
He started to say to her in a voice that suggested he was being sincere and truly did have something of importance to talk with her about.

"Go ahead Mr. Cadaver, I'm listening."
She acknowledged in her regular sullen tone of voice that everyone had gotten used to over the years.
"First I must commend you on your work over the years you have been with us here at 'Last Ditch', and because of your loyalty I have a proposition for you that I hope you will seriously consider."

It sounded to Sylvia like Hugh was about to ask her to take on more work than she would want. It was obvious to her as the stacks of bodies were mounting on a daily basis and more workers would be required to get the work done; especially to the standards that Hugh demanded from his staff every day.

"I need to talk to you in all honesty about what it is I want you to do Sylvia."
She again gave him that look. He continued.
"I think your work here has been some of the best I have ever had and I would like you to take over the operations in the warehouse with Mark and Evelen and three more staff I will be hiring in the next week or so. I will double your current salary as you will have to be doing work of the utmost importance."

He had her attention now as Sylvia leaned in a little closer and gave him the look that she was certainly interested and that he should continue.
"I have secured the employment of a company that does… shall we say… a different kind of service that will help us with the overburden of inventory. They will help us in ways I can't describe and I need someone like you to lead the crew."
He stopped and gave Sylvia a chance to respond. She continued to sit there eyes fixed on his and waited for him to elaborate more on what it was she

would actually have to do for considerably more money. She had a feeling it would be something that would cause most to find just a little above the law.

"As you know for the most part we cremate the majority of the bodies that come to us. With the extra load it will become a real problem, especially with the new laws restricting burning of any kind. This company I have hired will take the bodies and produce a small pellet that can be used for many applications. One being to fuel airtight cooking stoves."

Sylvia's expression had still not changed as she absorbed the information Hugh was divulging.
"We would of course have to dress out the few that we would actually bury, but of course that number is dwindling due to the shortage of land for burials. All we need to do is keep a small supply of ashes from any source to provide to our customers."

This of course was something Sylvia had been aware of for most of the years she had worked for 'Last Ditch Funeral Home' It was a cost saving measure and who would really know if the ashes were those of the deceased the family would be holding in an expensive urn that the home of course sold to the client.

"Your responsibilities would be to make sure the staff are doing their respective jobs properly, and that we stay on track with deliveries and of course sales of the end product. The pellets."
Sylvia now moved back in her chair and was ready to respond as the awkward moment presented itself in the form of a fly buzzing around between the two of them.

It must have escaped from the warehouse side of the facility. There were always flys there for obvious reasons. Sylvia fanned her hand in front of her face to shoo it away and made sure her mouth was closed as that was a favourite place for flies to go to.

"I am flattered that would want to double my pay and of course I will take on the responsibilities of this new job."
Sylvia responded with just a slight hesitation in her voice. Hugh did not pick up on it and smiled a large smile as he arose from his chair.

"Great Sylvia, why don't we go meet the new staff and go over some of what will need to be done on a daily basis before things get busy this afternoon."

Hugh says as he looks to his expensive wrist watch. He gestures with his hand for her to lead the way to the warehouse where he will go over the new workload with Mark, Evelen, the new three staff, and of course Sylvia in her newly appointed position as foreman of the crew.

As they entered through the door there were Mark and Evelen chatting with the new employees as made obvious by their holding of their lunchbox's and of course the mandatory wearing of hardhats. Hugh makes his way over to the group who were now looking to him with smiles on their faces.

"Hi Evelen, Mark, I wanted to introduce the new crew to Sylvia as I told you she will be in charge now with the expanded work load. Sylvia, I'd like to introduce you to Henry, Chuck, and Rigor. They will be starting today and of course will follow your lead. I'll leave you all alone to get to know each other and Sylvia here will instruct you on your new jobs. I have work to do in my office so I will bid you farewell for now and have a great day."

Hugh wraps it up and makes his way to the door at a quick pace as the flies were starting to surround him. They often did whenever he ventured into the warehouse; it must have been his blood type. Blood type – O. Sylvia was lucky in that her blood type was not O. She now stood in front of her new crew.

"I just want to welcome the new recruits Henry, Chuck, and Rigor."
She paused thinking of how she just said Rigor's name and how well she might suit the place... rigor mortis and all. They all kind of mumbled a response. Then the fellow named Henry, a portly odd looking man in his forties started to ask a question.

"Yes... Sylvia... it is alright to call you Sylvia?"
He asked looking at her awaiting her response.
"Of course Henry, we're all the same here at 'Last Ditch Funeral Home'."
Sylvia put on the best smile she could muster, it was something she had never been very good at. Henry continued.

"I was just wondering what it is we might be doing here as Mr. Cadaver wasn't very particular about the job and it's function."

Henry seemed to have a bit of a grasp on things and Sylvia figured he might just be the smarter of the three and a good person to take the responsibilities of a leader. She would of course go over things with Mark and Evelen. Afterall they had been there longer but had not taken on any responsible positions over the years.

"I will be going over some new systems being put in place over the next week, but for now I will leave the three of you with Mark and Evelen and they will show you what has to be done throughout the day. If you have any questions that cannot be answered, I can deal with them at the end of the day."

Sylvia says as she looks about, and then makes a move towards the door. Her politeness had been used up and she needed to get back to her office to start working on the inner workings of her new job. She knew she would have plenty more on her plate than just some of the paperwork she was used to. As the door closed behind her, she was thankful for the air conditioning in the foyer and where her desk was.

The soft music playing and the fact that Mr. Cadaver's door was closed told Sylvia that the afternoon would be quiet until the family came to see their beloved departed family member. It was shortly after she took a seat at her desk that Mark, along with the new guy Chuck were bringing in the body to get it ready for viewing.

At least this afternoon would be predictable with only the one family to deal with. It would be however the many extra bodies being delivered that would pose the challenge for Sylvia and how she would organize the new system. It was this system that would have to be executed properly so as she would not feel too guilty for taking the extra pay Mr. Cadaver had offered her.

The two of the men spent at least an hour making the stiff and dead male look somewhat presentable. This part always confused Sylvia as she thought it much better not having a body to look at as it always looked so decrepit. Would it not be nicer for the person viewing just to remember the person when they were alive and looked reasonably good?

It would be up to Sylvia to check on the body once they were finished, and her stamp of approval before the family arrived within the next half hour. She would also have to check on the progress the staff were making out back with the influx of bodies. She hoped the new employees would have grasped the how-to's with the pellet making machinery.

Of course one of the requirements of employment was the privacy of the operations of the funeral home. These people could not discuss any goings on at the place to anyone... even family members. That would be why they all got paid so well compared to other workers in other industries.

Sylvia looked at her watch and noticed it was almost time for the family to arrive. She would make her rounds to make sure everything was set up as it should be. Plenty of tissue boxes throughout the room, pitchers of water and glasses. The body looking as good as it could on the viewing table, and of course the music which was playing soft and non-descript type so as not to offend anyone. She was happy with the way it all looked.

On her way back to her desk the buzzer from the front door made it obvious the family had arrived. Sylvia gave a quick look at herself to make sure everything was in order and then walked to the front doors and opened them. The family was standing in a que and the wife of the dead man entered first.

"Good afternoon Mrs. Carringmore, please come in."
Sylvia put on a very slight smile something she only did because it was her job to do so. There were a few of Mrs. Carringmore's grown children following her and what appeared a couple of what might be her siblings or siblings of her deceased husband.

"If you would like a glass of water we have some, please follow me into the other room where I will leave you for a bit. If there is anything you might recquire, please let me know."

Sylvia says in her most polite voice she can muster. The family moves into the viewing room and Sylvia leaves them alone and returns to her desk.

She knew it would be at least thirty minutes or more with plenty of weeping and crying. On most ocassions the tissue boxes were all emptied. It was now time to get on with her new work schedule and hoped the crew in the warehouse were doing their work with the extra bodies. All seemed to be going just fine.

All of a sudden Sylvia snapped to attention in her chair as she heard the very loud screams from the other room. It only took a moment and Mr. Cadaver was at his door and making his way to the viewing room while looking back at Sylvia for answers. Answers as to why there was so much screaming going on.

He opened the door with Sylvia right behind him. They both looked at the family rushing out from the warehouse door with Chuck walking behind them with a large machete he had in hand with blood all over the blade, his apron, and the safety glasses he wore. It was like a scene from a horror movie. Sylvia would have attempted to stop at least one of the family as they ran towards the front entrance, but thought it best to let the screaming lot leave and deal with it later as she was sure she would have to. Apparently the family thought the way out was through the door to the warehouse where the crew were doing their job on the many bodies spread around the tables where they were being cut up then put into the pellet machines.

The End

Michelin Star

Donny made his way into the kitchen of the restaurant where he had worked for what seemed an eternity. Donaldos, the premier restaurant in France and the first, many years ago to earn the prestigeous award from Michelin. It was now five stars and continued to impress guests every evening it was open. Donny had always wanted his own restaurant and after being very fortunate in hiring his girlfriend Terri as chef they continued to ride up the ladder of success. When it had all started Donny's father had a mechanics shop and of course a large area to fix vehicles. After his fathers death, Donny took over the business but tired of it as it was not his thing. He wanted a restaurant. A very good one. It took a while to find the right chef but she came along originally as one of the wait staff.

Terri was her name, and premium food was her game. A girl with short dark hair and a temper to match. She was perfect chef material. Donny had now turned the front of the mechanics shop into the restaurant while still keeping the back section where many car parts including a massive pile of old tires were stored.

"Well Terri, we're expecting another full house tonight, how is the kitchen shaping up? You do of course have plenty of the starter plate with the incredible baked mushroom heads?"
Donny asked as he walked into the kitchen to check on things, something he always did just before opening in the late afternoon on everyday except Sunday. This was a day off for staff.

"Of course Donny this place would not survive without them… right?"
Donny gave her the look he always did when she was pulling his leg. He continued to look in the

direction of the several trays where the special mushrooms were all layed out and ready for the ovens.

It was something Terri did everyday before anyone arrived; it was her secret recipe she wanted no one else to be privy to. Donny figured this, as his many attempts at trying to get it of course failed.
"Well that's good, I can see them over there ready for the oven. If you need anything just let me know. I understand the Michelin group will be making a reservation sometime this week."

He thought to let her know just in case there might be something else she might want to add to the menu. The mushrooms would, he was sure be enough once again to put them at the front of the line for restaurants around the world. It wasn't that the rest of the menu wasn't any good, just that the mushrooms were to die for, as many patrons had said over the years of this one exclusive dish.
"I'll leave you to it then Terri, we'll share a bottle of wine after work as usual."
He said as he smiled at her. Terri just gave him a look as she picked up one of her very good knives in

front of her and waved it about as she looked at him. Donny made his move out into the restaurant. He had plenty of work to do before the rest of the staff showed up.

It was just a few minutes into serving time and Donny noticed a very smartly dressed couple walk through the doors. He did not recognize them and the way they were looking about suggested to him they just might be the representatives from the Michelin organization.

Donny would instruct his wait staff to be very diligent went it came to the service of this couples table and their needs. Not that the service and food in his restaurant weren't the best all of the time regardless of who it was seated at any table. It would not be known to him by any means that this was indeed who they were; it was just a feeling he had.

The couple were a tall slim man looking to be in his forties and dressed to the nines. A very expensive three piece suit with a spectacular tie. He wore expensive looking glasses, and the gold Rolex told it all. The woman was dressed in an off white dress with all the jewelry one could manage. It too looked expensive.

She appeared to be in her thirties and the two of them had that air of sophistication. Donny was good at figuring people out as over the years one develops these skills in the restaurant business. The front of house rep talked with them for a moment then escorted the two of them to their reserved table.

All tables were reserved as there had been a waiting list to dine at Donaldo's for more than three years. The couple fit in well with the well dressed maitre d' and Donny was happy as he looked on from his place behind the bar where he had enjoyed the work over some of the other jobs in any restaurant. He of course had many other things to do such as bookeeping and such.

It did not take long for the restaurant to fill up, about sventy-five covers total with the odd late arrival if there was a table available. There were twenty staff in total to accommodate every wish of any customer. Donny had made sure of this from the start. He wasn't a greedy man and as long as the bills were covered and a little extra for himself, he was a happy man.

"That couple at table sventeen seem just a little off, just thought I would let you know Donny."
The waiter named Carlos came over to the bar and made it look like he was getting some glasses. Carlos was a seasoned vet when it came to waitering; most of the staff were very qualified. Marco was another who demanded nothing but the best service.

"Yes Carlos, I am pretty sure I know them. Don't worry… just do your work as usual, I don't anticipate any trouble from them."
Donny said in a moderate tone and one of confidence as he passed a couple of large wine glasses across the bartop to Carlos. He returned to the table and started up his usual conversation and took some drink orders while they purused the menus. As Donny watched he knew they would for sure order the mushroom starters. Everyone did, it was one of the main reasons people came to this restaurant and almost always returned. He had to

give Terri the credit as it was her food that made the visit to Donaldo's one of the best in the world.

The evening went well and as Donny had surmised, the couple he had thought to be with Michelin were indeed. After their meal they had confided in him and were truly amazed with the restaurant, and especially the mushroom starter. Donny thanked them both and welcomed them to return for another meal in the near future.

The last of the main courses had been brouhgt to their respective tables and Donny thought to check in on the kitchen. As he walked through the double doors he was greeted to the hustle and bustle of any kitchen. The clean up staff were now busier than ever and Terri and her assitant chefs could now take a well deserved break.

"Another good night chefs and the rest of you, thankyou and when you are finished we can all enjoy a libation before you go home."
Donny says as he looks to Terri mostly, she just finished wiping down one of the many working surfaces.

"Yes we did have a good night Donny and I can only assume we are full for tomorrow night... am I right on that one?"

She thought to ask so she would not have to check the reservations book. She would anyway. She never liked to be misinformed when it came to the table bookings for any evening.
"I have a list for all the shopping for you tomorrow Donny, pretty much the same as usual. I am however getting a little shy on the main ingredient for the mushroom starter. I'll talk to you later about it."

Terri looked at Donny with an expression that suggested he would definitely need to listen to her once the rest of the staff had left for home. It just might be a late night once again. Once everything had been cleaned up and the other staff had left for home, Donny and Terri were left alone at the fancy bar in the restaurant.

"So Terri... what was so important you had to wait until the others had left for home?"

Terri cleared her throat and started to reply. There was a nervouseness to her manner and Donny picked up on it.

"I have a confession to make to you and I don't want you going off the deep end like I know you can. I just want you to listen carefully to what I have to say. It will all make sense once I am finished."

This got Donny's attention as Terri was someone you always had to believe when she said something. This is what had made her such a great chef, and what had made Donaldo's the most famous restaurant anywhere.

"Go ahead, fill me in. Do you want another glass of wine?"

He thought to ask as her glass was empty and she was figiting with it. Her look was enough to let him know the answer was yes. As he poured another glass from the bottle of expensive red on the bartop, Terri started in.

"You know me Donny, and you know I always tell the truth. I have some rather scary things to divulge to you."

She had got Donny's attention once again as he took a sip from his glass of beer. He liked beer.
"I had before I even started here at Donaldo's worked with a recipe handed down from my father. When I saw what was out behind this place I was in my glory."
She took another sip of her wine, Donny just stared at her waiting for her to continue.

"Mushrooms. The mushrooms I do every night that everybody loves. That is the recipe handed down to me by my father. The recipe that had up until now been a secret. If I am to continue creating this great dish I'm afraid I will have to divulge the recipe to you; at least part of it."

Donny just looked at Terri and took another drink of his beer. He kept quiet as Terri's look strongly suggested he do so. She took a sip from her glass of wine and got herself ready to let Donny know at least some of the secret recipe for her world famous mushrooms. It was something he had dreamed about on more than one occasion. It had in fact given him many sleepless nights.

"Well here we go then. Rubber."
Terri said the word and left it at that while Donny just stared at her.
"What the hell are you talking about?"
His question only came after a very large gulp of his beer, enough to drain the glass and warrant another one, which he got up and moved around behind the bar to get one.

"OK…what the hell do you mean when you say rubber?"
Donny continues on as he opens the beer and starts to drink right from the bottle.
"You remember when you were dealing with your dad's stuff out back? All the car parts, mechanics tools, old tires and that sort of stuff?"

Terri looks at Donny as she speaks hoping he will start to grasp what it is she is trying to tell him. He looked at her, took another drink of his beer, looked at her, took another drink of his beer. It was nearly finished now as he put the bottle back onto the bar top. He cleared his throat and made himself ready to speak.

"Now let me get this straight… you use rubber tires in your special mushroom recipe…. Am I right there?"
Donny asks as he then looks to his empty beer bottle once again. He plays with it in his hand as he awaits an answer from Terri. She sees his conundrum and waits for him to get another beer from the cooler below the bar.

After opening the beer and looking to her after a big gulp from the bottle she starts in with her reply.
"You are right Donny, it is actually a recipe that goes way back to before rubber tires were even invented. The rubber tree… remember? A natural living plant growing here on this planet? Anyway, my father had changed the original recipe slightly to incorporate the use of used tires, he had plenty around the shop."

Terri pauses as she takes a drink of wine and looks to Donny to see how he is taking it all in. His expression was one of calm; at least for the moment.

"I kept tweeking the recipe until I was finally satisfied with the final flavours. The problem now is I am running out of old tires and very quickly. Maybe a week's worth for the numbers we sell on average."
Donny takes another swig of his beer.
"You mean tires from the cars and trucks and that sort of thing?"

He still wasn't convinced of what Terri was telling him.
"Yes Donny… rubber tires from cars and trucks. I would come in early everyday as you know and carve off about the right amount of rubber for that evening. It all worked so well and no one knew of course."
"But rubber tires Terri… really?"

"Think about it Donny, rubber tires… Michelin Stars… Michelin tires…? Makes sense doesn't it? It was Michelin that had come up with the recipe in the first place and then decided to award restaurants awards for their food. I am one of the last to continue on with their idea for the mushroom recipe."

Donny did think about it for a moment as he finished yet another bottle of beer and then reached down for another.
"Would you like another glass of wine?"
He asked with a look of half drunkeness and curiosity.
"Yeah, that sounds good, why not. Looks like a late night anyway."

"OK… rubber tires and you make one of the best mushroom dishes I've ever tasted. I can't believe it."
He says as he pours the wine right to the brim of the glass in front of Terri.
"So what you're saying is somehow I am going to have to find some old tires for you to continue cooking this dish… right?"

"That's right Donny, if you don't, then you can pretty much forget keeping your Michelin five star rating. I know it sounds totally weird, but that's how it is Donny. I need those tires. In fact if I can't make that mushroom dish I might just pack it in and quit being a chef."

Donny heard this and thought he best keep Terri happy and figure out a way to get what she wanted. He reached down and pulled up two more bottles of beer, placed them beside the opened beer he already had, then walked around and sat down beside Terri as she took another drink of her wine.

"OK... I'll do it, but we have to keep quiet about it or people will stop coming here if they knew what was in their food."
"I have been doing it for years Donny, I think I can handle it. It's you that has to be diligent in keeping this secret. Understand?"
He understood, he would have to as he did not want to give up the five star rating from Michelin.

"I will do my best, but it will be dificult to find old tires in this town and when I'm asked what they're for, what should my response be?"
"You have the shop out back, why don't you get it going again and maybe restore old vintage cars?

You know... they might have some old tires once in a while. Just saying, I need about four to five tires per week."

There was a moment of silence as the two of them both took a drink and looked at each other. Donny had to let this information set in as his mind was now working overtime... especially with the extra alcohol. He still had a hard time believing the fantastic mushroom dish was made with old tires.

"I realize of course over time There will be a shortage of the real rubber that I need to make the dish, but by then I should be well retired and enjoying my downtime."
Terri said this as if she was an old person already, from what Donny could tell, she had plenty of years left in her for working in the kitchen of his restaurant.

"Well... I'll see what I can come up with. There are a few of my fathers old time buddies still living, maybe they might have some or at least know where we could get the tires we need."

John P Gibson　　　　　　　　　　　　　　*High Tide*

He said this with some reservation as he knew as well as Terri that without the mushroom dish, all was lost.

"That would be great Donny, but you know we have to keep it quiet about the mushroom recipe and the tire thing… right?"
Terri thought to make sure Donny understood as the number of beers he had consumed was two over his self prescribed limit.

"Yeah, I know Terri and I just hope you can pull it off with whatever tires we *can* get; providing there are some of the older tires out there."
Terri looked at Donny as she finished wine and now started to make a move off the bar stool. It was late and of course she had to work the next day, possibly earlier than usual if she had a hard time finding any of the premium tires she liked out back.

"Well I've got to get home, I'm bushed and it just might be a somewhat challenging week if you know what I mean."

Terri says as she makes her way to the front door to make her way home. Donny polished off the remains of the beer in front of him.

"Yeah, OK Terri, I'll see you tomorrow and I promise I will get on that about the tire thing. I'll let you know when I do and I will keep our secret a secret."

He did his best to give her a wink but found it difficult as the beer had done its job on him. He was feeling just a bit tipsy.

After Terri left for home, Donny stayed back to finish up some paperwork and decide how the hell he was going to get these tires that Terri needed for her famous mushroom dish. It would be a long night, that was for sure. He decided to stay the night as he had had too many beers and an early start the next day would be the best idea for him.

The incessant ringing of the alarm jarred Donny awake from his alcohol induced sleep. He almost rolled off the small sofa in his office. He managed to get himself together and get a bottle of water to drink from the cooler behind the bar. He would think about some breakfast later when Terri arrived for work. At this point he had to get into gear and find some rubber tires for her.

Back at his desk he started up his computer and went to work first contacting people he knew about getting the tires. It took a while and finally he made a connection that he thought would be the best for the purchase of tires. He was promised by this man he would receive them on a regular basis once the topic of money had been agreed upon.

It was a considerable amount but after doing the math Donny would still be ahead financially and also be able to keep his five star status with Michelin. This was the most important part of the equation as his reputation depended on it.

"Hey... anybody here?"
It was the familiar voice of Terri. She had come in early as she had mentioned the night before. She came to Donny's office door and knocked loudly even though the door was wide open. He was busy in front of his computer not paying any attention to her as she walked in and took a seat across from him

at his desk. He was absorbed in something on his computer and she decided to leave him alone and wait for his undivided attention.

"Hey Terri... you're here early, great. I have some good news."
Terri just looks at him as he looked rather a mess from the night before and obviously had not showered or brushed his teeth.
"Well... do continue, I have plenty to do today as you are well aware of."

"I have found a contact for getting the tires you need for your mushroom recipe."
He looks to her as Terri stands her ground and waits for more.
"The first order should arrive within a couple of days... I just have to meet with this guy later today to finalize everything."

He looks to Terri who looks back with what he thought to be the start of a smile across her face. He would leave it at that as she very seldom smiled at anyone. He let her leave to the kitchen to get herself started on all of the prep work for the days menu and of course her famous mushroom starter. He would do his best to clean up and get some well needed rest before meeting this man later in the day.

He was a short man of Asian descent and not unlike Terri in the fact that he did not smile; even when Donny gave the man the considerable amount of cash for the promised delivery of the tires. It was a short meeting and Donny could expect the delivery within two days. He only hoped he had not been duped.

It was two days later and the delivery of the hundred or so tires were delivered to the back of the restaurant, where it all looked fine as the shop had been started up to make it look like a mechanics shop doing business as usual.

"Everything OK Terri? The new tires to your liking?"
Donny asked when he got Terri alone in the cooler room while she was getting some produce.
"They are different Donny, but I think I can manage OK, we'll just have to wait and see won't we?"

She then moved back into the bustling kitchen where the other staff were busy with their work. As she worked her magic with her special dish, she tested it with her finger.

She thought it to be alright for plating and delivery to the full house of customers in the restaurant. The first order was sent out to a table of four that just happened to be the four that were at the restaurant for the Michelin Star company weeks earlier. They ate their mushroom starters and immediately put their thumps up and smiled.

Donny saw this and was thankful for the fact that Terri had worked her magic once again. All seemed well until about an hour later when the table of four started to look just a little green around the gills. Within a few more minutes the four of them were lying on the floor dead as doornails.

All of a sudden many more of the diners started to convulse and fall to the floor. Donny was speechless and when Terri came out from the kitchen she put her hands to her open mouth. They looked at each other and quickly moved towards the entrance of the restaurant. They were never seen again and of course the restaurant was closed after the investigation by the authorities.

It was found that all those that had died, even some of the staff, had consumed some very potent chemical which was still being investigated. A search went out for Donny and Terri and were technically being charged with murder until proven otherwise. Donaldo's would not reopen and very likely the mushroom recipe lost forever.

The End

John P Gibson

High Tide

Name Change

The letter slid under the door just as there was a knock. I looked up from the book I was reading and noticed the simple #10 white envelope creep it's way to the center of my doormat. Somehow I knew what it was I would be reading once I removed the contents of the envelope. It was only a day earlier I had received a parcel. The contents being somewhat disturbing. I go by the name Mark Bishop. My birth name. I am about fiftiesh… give or take. My life up to this point had been somewhat predictable; that is until the parcel that showed up at my door yesterday. Anyone that knows me would say I was a happy, generous, social single man with only doing my best to fit into society and manage things until my retirement in the not too distant future. That is what I had planned anyway.

Now it would be different and in a way I was not sure how to comprehend. Being single and a person that for the most part kept to himself other than the odd social function never thought for a moment I would be in the position I apparently was now. A person I had seen in some movies and read about in books and maybe the newspaper.

A spy? No. A secret agent? No. A Mafia kingpin? No. What I was to become was basically a serial killer. I had to let that sink in as I had always been a very pacifistic person. It would take me at least a few days for this to sink in. That was all I had before the shit hit the fan.

The parcel that had been delivered was full of boxes of ammunition. Bullets for two nine-millimetre pistols. There was also a thick expensive looking notebook. In it were a couple of envelopes and many pages with written notes on them. I had three days to go over this information then another envelope would appear at my door. The envelope I got today was a simple one. A cheque in the amount of one-hundred thousand dollars.

I started to read the instructions in one of the envelopes and the first thing I would have to do was to change my name. Especially if I was to cash the cheque for one-hundred thousand dollars. There would be more to follow if I abided by the rules of the game. A game? What the hell was going on?

I thought to notify the police as the smart side of my brain was telling me to do. The funny thing was the name I was to start calling myself was Cheri Mackland. I thought that rather strange, as all the correspondence in the information used my name; Mark Bishop. It was confusing to say the least and the warning that if I did go to the authorities would result in my death.

If I was a drinker, I would have poured myself a large glass of some sort of alcohol. I would have to deal with this as if it were real so I decided to go with it; do what I was told in the information I had in hand. If I got the information right I would have to kill no less than ten people; all around the world. All flights would be booked for me with no questions asked once I had my name changed.

My name changed. What the fuck was that all about? And why me? What the hell was going on? It was like I was on some acid trip or something. None of this was making sense to me in any way shape or form. The instructions left with me were very to the point on how I should go about changing my identity.

There were some pictures icluded in the enevelope that were of women that the powers that be suggested I try to look like. It would involve a dark wig, makeup, false boobs, learning to walk in heels, jewelry, learning to talk with a feminine voice, and of course the mannerisms of a female.

This was going to be one hell of a challenge. Once I had my change made I was to open a bank account at the local bank closest to me in the name of Cheri Mackland. This would be the only way I could cash the cheques. The picture ID and passport were already made and in with the last letter I opened.

John P Gibson *High Tide*

After each knock on my door I immediately opened the door to see who was there. All I saw was a dark van pull away from the curb.

I didn't see anyone as the windows were tinted black and the license plate was obscured. Not that I would report it to the police as the threat of my life was in bold print several times on the letters I held in my hands. I had no choice but to go through with this charade and hope somehow it was just all a joke.

I was told in the letters to familiarize myself with the handguns and the instructions were there for me to study. I of course could not practise as the noise would be heard by my neighbours and anyone walking by on the sidewalk in front of my home. I was also told that the next day a large box would be delivered with enough clothing and accessories necessary to dress like Cheri.

This part I had a hard time with as I was sure the application of lipstick would prove to be far more difficult than I imagined. I would however do as the letter instructed and make sure I was clean shaven for this reason alone. If I was a crybaby, I would now be on my bed doing just that and wondering why me?

It was a sleepless night as I re-read all of the instructions and wondered how all would work out when I applied for my new documentation. More alarming than that was the fact I would be killing people. This was something I was sure I would not be able to do; I was not a violent person and there was no one I knew that I did not like.

The alarm clock started it's repetitious annoying sounds to wake me out of a deep sleep. One where I had been dreaming I was James Bond. A fearless, handsome, not to be fucked with expert in the field of spies. As I rolled over to shut off the infuriating noise of the clock I realized I was not in a dream world; there apparently was an agenda for me similar to that of James Bond apart from the cross dressing of course.

John P Gibson *High Tide*

How was I ever to pull this off? I mean dressing up as a female would be hard enough let alone killing people. And what would happen to me if I was caught by the authorities?

This of course I hadn't really thought through at all. Maybe I should just pack a bag and leave. Go to some other country where no one would think to look for me. I thought this through a little further and knew I would have to do what it was I was told. The money of course was a great motivator.

I sat in my chair looking at the front door. I was determined to find out who was behind this. As soon as the knock happened, I jumped up and raced to the door and opened it. Nothing but a large box and the same vehicle leaving down the road. 'Man these guys were quick.' I say to myself as I bring the box into the front room.

I open the top of it and of course there is a letter lying on the top of some colourful looking clothes. As I rummaged through the inventory of womans clothing I let out a groan when I came to the shoes at the bottom of the box. Heels; not too high of course, but still… heels! How was I to walk with these crazy shoes? I could never figure out how women could do it without falling all the time.

It took me a couple of hours to get dressed as Cheri and thinking that was a normal amount of time and as I looked in the full length mirror in my bedroom I had to think that I was not a bad looking woman considering I had never been one before. I gathered my new purse and left the house to get to the bank to open a new account and put the hundred-thousand dollar cheque into it.

At the bank everything went fine, even my attempt at speaking in a feminine type voice seemed to be working; at least it was for the male bank manager across from me as I signed the documents and the back of the large cheque. As I left the bank my next stop was to get some photos for the passport I would apply for and of course a new drivers license.

With the new technology these days it would be done while I waited the thirty minutes or so in the waiting room. As I left with new passport, drivers license, and new bank account with one-hundred thousand dollars in it, I felt a feeling of control I had not felt for a very long time. Tomorrow would be the start of it all and I just hoped I felt this good.

****

The alarm once again woke me up with a start. I jumped up and out of my bed and stood there in front of the mirror. I looked normal except for some of the makeup I had not quite cleaned off the night before. I was to get ready as I had the day before and be ready for a pick-up at eleven AM sharp. It was six AM. I figured five hours should be enough.

The letter had stated that I would be flying to North Korea to take out a man high up in the Government. Not the main guy what's his name, but some key figure in the government. What I couldn't understand was why not do this themselves? Whoever they were. Why enlist the services of a beginner to do such crucial work? I was stumped and would just go along with it all.

John P Gibson *High Tide*

I figured after only doing a few of these hits I would have enough money to retire in comfort. It might just be worth it.

I was ready and it only took me three hours. I had been told to pack only a carry-on bag and of course my purse which I was still getting used to. When I was at the bank I had kept reaching back for my wallet. This must have looked funny to those watching as I garbbed my own ass.

I was ready, sitting in my chair with handbag and carry-on luggage at my side with the guns and ammo in it. This of course had me wondering how the hell I would get through security at the airport. I would let it be as these people obviousley had people in the right places. Which again brought up questions as to 'Why me?'

Money. Already some of it in my new account. I would just smile and wait for the knock on my door. It came soon enough and because I was to be escorted to the airport I felt no need to rush up and see if anyone was there. I opened the door and again there was no one present. There was however a very fancy black limo with blacked out windows waiting for me on the curb. I could only think what my neighbours would be thinking.

I approached the car after locking my front door and making sure the contents of my bags were accounted for. Looking at the stretched limo I assumed I was to get into the back. I opened the door and got into an empty car other than the driver who kept looking forward the entire time.

There was no conversation, no music from a radio, nothing, as the windows were obviousley soundproof. It was a creepy ride to the airport to say the least. We arrive in a different section of the airport, and a man dressed all in black opened my door to the limo once we stopped. He did not say anything as he directed me to follow him to a waiting small private jet.

Again there was no one on the plane except for me and I hoped the pilots, of course being qualified to do their job. I did not have to show any papers or documentation to anyone, and of course there had been no checking of the luggage, thank God. The flight was for the most part boring, but at least comfortable in the large lounger type chairs. There were no stewards or stewardess's, just the co-pilot coming back once in awhile to offer some refreshments.

If it wasn't for the crazy get-up I was wearing, I truly would have felt like James Bond. The flight continued and I managed to get a little shut-eye as I would need all the energy I could muster once we landed in North Korea. The landing was spotless as I was still asleep when the co-pilot shook my shoulder ever so slightly. I awoke and looked out the window to see a very posh airport.

There was no speaking as I got off the plane and into another black limo with blacked out windows. There certainly was a theme here. The driver as well did not speak and I just sat there adjusting my wig. I had all of my belongings and of course the bag with the two pistols and ammunition. It still escaped me as to how I could travel to a country such as this with weapons and virtually no security involved. The car stopped at a busy intersection and the driver indicated I should get out of the car. I looked around and noticed a few things familiar that were in the photo given to me. It was all starting to come together for my first hit.

I started to walk in the direction of a statue at the end of a busy square. It was this statue I was to wait at for the man that I would shoot between the eyes. Providing of course my aim was as good as I hoped it to be. It did not take long as it was obvious it would a midday break for most and many would venture out for a meal of sorts.

The weather was cooperating with little to no wind and a reasonable warmth from the sun shining down. I had one of my guns loaded and ready to fire; it had a silencer fitted to the muzzle of the gun so there would be little if any sound when I pulled the trigger.

I looked about as the people passed me, only a couple of men looked my way. They did not smile as they were not allowed to look at such women, especially foreign female tourists such as me. I made myself look as approachable as I could as the man in question was walking towards me. As he got close I deliberately dropped my purse to the ground right in front of him. He stopped, looked at me, then bent over to pick the purse up off the ground.

I pulled the trigger twice with the gun pointed right to the back of his head. He fell to the ground, I picked up my purse and started to walk towards the limo. It took a moment before I heard the comotion of people finding the dead man lying on the pavement lifeless. I climbed into the limo and the driver made his move into traffic.

The ride back to the airport was similar to the one arriving at the square. I for some reason was totally at ease with the entire event that just took place. No shakes, no perspiration, not even any remorseful thoughts. Maybe I was truly a seasoned hit-man. I adjusted my dress as we approached the plane that I assumed had been refueled and ready for the flight back.

It too was predictable as the flight coming to this place. Uneventful and now with just a bit of adrenaline coursing through my veins I was able to replay the event through my mind. For some reason

John P Gibson   *High Tide*

I had no emotion what so ever. I was surprised to say the least. I had some food and a couple of glasses of champagne, then took a short nap.

The plane landed without any problems and the limo was waiting for me just at the foot of the off ramp of the plane. I collected my purse and bag making sure of course the guns and ammo were in place, then got myself into the limo which immediately started on its way to my home.

After settling in and getting into some man clothes I decided to open a beer and then open the envelope I had found just inside my front door when I entered. It was what I expected as I read through it. Another hit with all of the information, and another cheque for one-hundred thousand dollars. I would have time over the next few days to deposit the cheque and familiarize myself with the next job.

I was becoming a rich man for doing what seemed so little. I was also coming to terms with my new chosen career. I was truly believing I was James Bond. Of course dressed as a female named Cheri. This was the one thing I did not like about this situation, but I would endure as the money was quite good. I could get used to the once a week visits to the bank with a cheque for one-hundred thousand dollars.

The envelopes kept coming, as well as the money, and I had to date murdered nearly ten people from all over the world. I was fast becoming a pro at a job I never thought in a million years I would do. Part of me felt exhilerated, and another part felt confused as I had been a very peaceful person all of my life... that is until now. Mark Bond... or should I say Cheri Bond.

My mind was drifting and if I was to fulfill my next hit I would have to get some rest as being in top form now became paramount. My next job started early the next day and would require a lengthy trip to Portugal to take out what I could gather a very popular musician in a town called Albufeira. With the research I had done, I could not for the life of me figure out why they would want to eliminate a musician; especially a good one. Who was I to ask questions? I just did what I was told to do for the very large payment made to me every job I did. I would be a millionaire after this job and in all respects could think about retiring. This just might prove difficult as I did not know who my boss was.

I put these thoughts to the back of my mind and made my way upstairs to get some sleep as the morning would come quickly. Four AM was an early start for me on any day. The bed felt good and I dozed off within minutes. Again the horrible noise of the alarm clock jolted me out of bed. It was still dark outside as I turned the light on and made my way to the bathroom to get my girly clothes on.

Two hours later (I was getting better at this transformation) I walked out of the bathroom and made my way downstairs to get my smoothie out of the fridge. I would expect the knock on the door within ten minutes. I was ready. It would be a long flight to Portugal. This would give me plenty of time to go over the information for the hit on this musician.

The knock came right on time and I gathered my purse and carry-on bag once again. I opened the door to see the black limo at the curb in the early morning light as the sun was rising. Again no conversation between me and the driver. I had tried once and he immediately closed the glass partition between us.

The flight was predictable and I managed some sleep along the way. The landing at Faro airport was the same as the rest; quick and efficient. It would be about a forty-minute drive to Albufeira where I would be dropped off at the place where this musician played on a regular basis. His name was Luke.

He had been a musician all his life and had a very large following in Albufeira with all of the tourists. Of course it had not been explained to me why he was to be taken out. I was just here to do my job. It was a small venue off the busy streets where he was playing on this night. I was to be in the audience near the back and wait till he had finished for the night.

It was a packed house and a great applause was heard after every song he played. They of course called for an encore which would of course make my time schedule a little off. I just hoped it would not affect the plane's takeoff time. If I were to miss my flight I would be in serious shit.

Things started to calm down some after Luke had finished his last song. After he had a beer I could see him packing up his gear. As he made his way with all of it to the exit where I was seated, he noticed me and gave me a wink as he approached. I said hi and told him I enjoyed the show in the sexiest female voice I could muster.

He stopped to chat and I offered to help him with his gear to his waiting car close by. He accepted not knowing of course this would be his last conversation with anyone; at least on this planet I thought. It went as scripted, once he was loading his guitar into the trunk of the car I pulled the gun from my bag and let off one shot to the back of the head. He slumped into the open trunk which I closed.

I then made my way to the limo with the driver just starting the engine as I got in. The trip back to the airport was quick as there was little traffic along the way. I would sleep well on the flight back. I wondered now who would be next and where it would all take place. I was getting used to this traveling around the world; especially first-class.

I stumbled in to my home and went to the couch to sit down and go over in my head the job I had just completed. I put my purse and bag down on the floor next to me and then layed down and went to sleep. I was in dreamland when it happened. I could feel this aggressive shaking of my shoulder.

I finally awoke to see a man staring me in the eyes. I had to focus and figure out what was going on.
"Mark… Mark… wake the fuck up man. Mark… Mark… get your shit together."
I look at the man and still can't figure out who the hell he is and how he got into my house.

"Who… are you?"
I ask with a bit of a slur to my speech.
"I'm Doug… Doug Meyland you idiot. Your friend. Do you know what the hell is going on?
"No I don't… what the hell are you doing here?"

"I was here last night with all of your friends for your stag, don't you remember? You did have quite a lot to drink and passed out for a while."

Mark thought for a moment. Nothing came to him, he just looked at the man in front of him and waited for more.

"All us guys thought we would have some fun and dress you up in your fiance's clothes and then put make-up on you. Stewart brought a wig along, you look crazy man. We got video and pictures and all… we put them on Facebook. You'll kill yourself laughing when you see them."

This guy named Doug let out a laugh as I reached down to my bag, pulled out the gun and shot him between the eyes.

The End

New Game

Harold quietly moved in behind one of the large trees closest to him. He put his hand up slowly and with his index finger motioned for another person dressed in camo gear to make their way towards him. Harold Fairplay was a large and very secure looking male in his forties, the other person now at his side was his partner Gertrude Underbottom. She was in her thirties and looked quite capable of looking after herself in the forest they were both in. The north of Canada. Cold and snowy in winter, warm and bug infested in the summer. This was late spring and the tourist season had started and Harold's company 'No Escaping' was coming into it's fifth year and profits had never been higher. He and his partner Gertrude were fully booked for the season with some booked for the next year.

There were of course some guidelines involved with this new business, at least relatively new to Canada. Being late spring they had possibly a week or two without the infestation of very large no-see-ems and horse flys. There was still snow on the ground but unlikely to increase in depth until September.

As Harold pulled his rifle up to his shoulder to get a bead on the target, Gertrude knelt beside him with binoculors in hand and raised so she could see what Harold was aiming for. His target was about two-hundred yards off in a clearing in a small valley.
"Got him."
He says in a soft voice.
"Yeah, so do I. Looks like a good one, well worth mounting on anyones wall I would think."

Gertrude answers also in a soft voice as she continues to look through the binoculars. There is a long pause as Harold continues to look through his scope on his rifle. His finger is not even near the trigger. He had no plans on shooting this target. It would be a prize trophy for one of his higher paying customers.

"Got him."
Harold says with some confidence.
"Number 2705... got that?"
He turns his attention to Gertrude who now puts the binoculars down and pulls a small notepad from her vest pocket along with a pen.
"Yeah... number 2705, got it."
She replies as she puts the pad and pen back into her pocket after writing the number down.

"I think I have a client that would like this one for sure, just might have to up the service fee some. What do you think Gertrude?"
Harold asks as he puts the rifle down and looks to her. She pulls her sunglasses down and gives him the look.
"I think we're charging plenty enough for the thrill of hunting down and killing one of the best out here in the wilds of Canada."

She responds as though she was rehearsing a bit for a TV commercial they just might be shooting. She smiles as does Harold, then they kiss.

The two of them turn and make their way back to camp. It is a very lavish one with many servents wandering about and helping the several people sitting at tables consuming food, drinks, and having general conversation. The camp looked very posh, with wooden built cabins lined along one side of the clearing.

For a place out in the wilds of the Canadian north it looked very comfortable and a place most would want to be considering how life had become in the cities throughout Canada… and for that matter around the globe. With the ever increasing human population, a quiet place to even spend a few moments was virtually non-existant.

At least there weren't too many humans out here making it the perfect venue for those wanting to trophy hunt. Which was the exact reason Harold and Gertrude had set this business up. They both had had extensive military experience and decided before they got too old to make some good money doing something they were good at. Their main training had been as snipers around the world.

As they approached camp most of the guests noticed them and either waved or verbally greeted them. One near the start of the camp got up and went over to the two of them as they walked. He was a portly gentleman wearing glasses and a toque on his head even though it was not that cold out.

"Hey Harold… Gertrude, how's it looking for later today. I could sure use a head for over my fireplace back home."
"It looks like we tracked down one of the better ones Ricky. Hopefully you might be the one to tag him."
Harold says with a confident smile and Gertrude the same. It was all a staged show for the clients, anything to keep them happy while they were in camp.

If they managed to get the trphy head they wanted that would be a bonus of course, and once prepared, the head would be sent to their home address where they could display it anyway they so wanted to.

These days it was not hard to gurantee that most would get their trophy. It would always be prudent to do so as there was a gurantee if one did not, the next trip was on the house.

At nearly four-million dollars per person to get the coveted trophy head managed to cover costs and allow a fair profit margin for Harold and Gertrude to put away for their retirement. The energy was a good one as they walked through camp and to the main building where the mess hall and entertainment were for the guests.

It wasn't too much, some musicians, comedians, magic shows and a large group of singers who also doubled as staff throughout the complex. There were of course the chefs and their crew in the large kitchen, and almost any other service one could think of that would be in a high-end hotel in the city.

"Want to get something to eat Ricky before the first crew head out? You *are* with the first group to go out right?"

Harold thought to ask as he was not in charge of setting up the itinery for the guests. They had a very qualified secretary for that job.

"Yeah… and I can't wait. This is my first time and I told the wife I would get her one real great trophy to hang on the wall. We got a place already picked out for it."

Ricky embelished as he tagged along on their way to the mess hall. Harold had gone over proceedure with him and was confident they would indeed get the trophy he so wanted.

The mess hall was a large one and well set up for the clients and workers. The three of them made their way to one end where it was obvious Harold, Gertrude, and any invites would sit. It was a large table right in front of the stage where the performers entertained in the evenings.

"So you're from New Mexico, I was there once long ago."

Gertrude pipes up to Ricky as they all sit down with Ricky sitting across from them. It was only a few seconds and a waiter makes his way over to their table with menus in hand. He was tall and well dressed, as were all the staff. Harold and Gertrude would have it no other way.

"So tell me what I can expect once we are out there in the forest?"
Ricky asks as the three of them are looking through the menu. It changed on a frequent basis and Harold and Gertrude did not always know what the specials would be for the day.
"Well… it's always changing Ricky, there are many times when *we* don't even know."

Harold answers as he looks to Gertrude who nods her head and smiles.
"Yes that is right, there have been a few times when the entire forest seems foreign even to us."
She says obviousley just to stay in the conversation.
"I have been practising nearly everyday with my new rifle. I'm told if I'm reasonable at this I could nail my target from more than a hundred metres away."

Ricky's voice started to change, his male ego was taking over and he wanted to sound like the hunter he really wanted to be.

"Yeah, I've seen it Ricky, looks good and you have the right scope on it for sure."

Harold was good at smooth-talking his clients. He had to as it all came down to the money at the end of the day. The waiter returned and they made their orders as speed and efficiency were important. They would be making a move within the hour when the light was best and the prey would be easiest to see.

The food was presented as though it was a five star Michelin restaurant and it tasted fantastic. Ricky could not compliment the two of them enough about how well he was being looked after in this camp, in the middle of a mountainous forest in one of the largest countries in the world. Canada.

"OK... let's get a move on, we'll collect the others and meet at the designated area, and from there we will get to work tracking our prey down so you can get your trophy. How does that sound to you Ricky?"

Harold says as he wipes his face with the napkin and places his fork and knife in the appropriate placement on his empty plate to say he was done.

Ricky went his separate way to get his gear while Harold and Gertrude made sure they all had the supplies necessary for their venture into the forest. They would only be away from camp for about four hours, but one never knew for sure what could happen.

There was no way to use vehicles of any sort, it was all walking and one had to be in very good shape or they would not be permitted to participate. At least not without the help of several strong men carrying the client into where they could shoot their trophy. Harold and gertrude were getting more of these people that had no concept on how to get and stay in shape.

The group had been gathered and standing waiting for Harold and Gertrude to show up to lead them to their victory; at least hoping it would be. There were about ten of them altogether on this venture and thankfully no fat out of shape ones to deal with; at least on this trip. Harold took center stage in front of the group to go over the details that needed to be adhered to. There would be no room for mistakes.

"OK everyone, make sure your rifles are loaded but with the safety on. You will follow me and pay attention while Gertrude will take up the rear. It is important to be quiet at all time and watch my hand signals for any change of direction or stopping to set up for the kill."

Harold looked to the group and saw Ricky right near the front. This was the way for those that paid more, they would get first go at the target when spotted. He looked excited and kept looking around at the other clients with a large grin. The entire group of course were dressed in camo gear and all had a GPS chip attached to there ammo belt in case they got separated from the group.

The group started to move in behind Harold as he made his way along a rough deer trail through the large trees and underbrush. It was a quiet and formidable feeling as the small branches and leaves crunched under foot as they walked deeper into the forest. There was to be no talking unless an emergency presented itself; that was one of the main rules. They did not want to scare off any possible prey.

It was about twenty minutes into the trek into the forest and Harold raises his arm into the air to signify that the group should stop. They did as Gertrude approached Harold and they both took their binoculars and look off over a small valley. There they saw the target they had wanted to find.

Harold motioned Ricky up to the front of the group and in between him and Gertrude. He did not say a word as he pointed in the direction of the target. Ricky took his binoculars and found what it was they were referring to. He adjusted his binoculars and then looked to Harold who, just nodded his head.

The others just sat in quiet anticipation of Ricky getting his trophy. He put his rifle down as he layed on his stomach and took his rifle and set a small tripod attached to the barrel down on the mossy ground. He put his eye to the scope and adjusted himself. Harold and Gertrude also monitored the situation with their binoculars. There was a moment of complete silence, then Ricky pulled the trigger and a moderate BANG from the gun was heard.

Harold took his binoculars away from his face and looked down at Ricky.
"Good one Ricky, perfect hit, no damage done to the head, so you have your trophy. Nice work."
Ricky just smiled and then turned to the rest of the group. They all gave a somewhat silent applause. It would now be time for the rest of the group to find their targets.

Gertrude and a couple of workers would stay behind and help Ricky with his kill to get it back to camp and start the dressing out procedure. The walk back was of course a little slower, but Ricky did not care, he just kept looking at his kill and feeling proud. He knew his friends and family would approve.

Once back at camp the workers took the kill into a small building off to the rear and closed the door as they would do the messy part of the work. Ricky would just get himself a beer and celebrate his victory along with Gertrude and some of the staff. He could hardly wait to see the head of his kill... the trophy... the object he would be hanging on his wall.

It was within the four hours and the rest of the group returned with what Ricky could see were about four additional kills not unlike his. Again the workers took them to the building where Ricky's had been taken. Harold had the staff take the weapons from the clients and any other gear they needed to deal with.

"OK everyone, great day. It's not offten we get five kills in one go. I'm sure you'll all be pleased with the trophies you will get from this. It will take a while, into the early evening before the crew has dressed them out and processed your head trophies for you to take home with you."

Harold smiled as he gestured to everyone to sit at the tables and enjoy a beverage of their choice to celebrate the successful day thay all had. With the pictures that would be taken later with everyone standing holding their trophies would surely help with his business. This is what people wanted to see, success, a promise fulfilled. It was getting easier for Harold and Gertrude to put it in print.

The rest of the day went well and a superb dinner followed with everyone telling their story of victory. The laughs and volume increased when Finally Harold got up from his table to speak. It took a few moments to get everyone's attention, but finally everything went quiet.

"OK everyone, I hope your dinner was a good one… I'm guessing it was judging by all of the empty plates I see going back to the kitchen. I have just got word that our first trophy is ready for viewing. The one that Ricky here did such a great job at. Ricky… come up here and we'll bring it out for you to show off to everyone."

He gestures to Ricky to come up beside him and Gertrude then signals for one of the staff to have the trophy brought out for everyone to see. The light was getting low as the sun was setting, but with a few strategically placed lights it would be quite the show. There was now no noise other than the crackling of a fire just off to one side. The staff came out with the head of the kill wrapped with a loose towel over it. They came up to Ricky and handed him his trophy.

Ricky then held it high as he took the towel off and let it fall to the ground while still holding his prized trophy. Everyone let out a loud WHOO… HOOO!! And then a round of applause. Ricky just held the head up by the long blonde hair of the thirty something male human.

The End

A Winning Moment

Randy knocked on the front door, loudly, as he needed for someone to answer sooner than later. The two cases of Lucky beer in his hand would soon fall to the floor below, and that would not be a good thing. It was now nearing eight PM and it was a Friday night. Most had the weekend off from work and the game was scheduled to start at around eight or there-abouts. Poker. A ritual for the selected few that enjoyed a night of being social, having a few drinks, and with any luck... winning some cash. This select group had been playing this game every second Friday for more than three years and not one of the players could attest to coming out ahead in anyway shape or form. Most could brag that they had broken even, or if under the influence say that they always won.

There were seven of them and the games *always* were played at the Triet residence. Mostly because it was a place big enough, but also had a fireplace close by to keep things warm in the winter months.
"Hey Randy… need some help with that?"
Gary asks of course referring to the beer Randy had in hand.

"You get you eyes off my beer. How ya doin Gary?"
He replies with that infectious smile of his; the one that got him almost any woman he wanted.
"Good, and don't worry, brought my own beer."
They smile at each other then randy goes to the kitchen to put some of his beer in the fridge. Usually he brought a cooler so the beer was closer to him.

This fascilitated two reasons, one; he was close to his beer and could keep an eye on them. Two; he would not have to leave the table and his money. As he opened the fridge door it was almost full of the others and their preferred choice of beer. He managed to find a spot for about six out of the two dozen he had brought with him. It would mean more trips throughout the night. 'Why hadn't he brought his cooler?'

After placing his beer in the fridge and grabbing a couple to take back to the poker table he ran into Stewart who was on his way to the fridge for a beer.
"Hey Stew, how ya doin?"
"Just great Randy, looking for a good game tonight."
"Yeah me too, I better win something, not like last time."
Randy sort of smiled as he made his way to the poker room to hopefully get his favourite spot.

"Hey Randy, got your favourite chair, here come and take a seat."
Steve a man in his forties with short dark hair says as he pulls a chair out beside him for Randy to sit on. It was his favourite chair, everyone knew this.
"Hey Randy… plan on winning tonight?"
Another friend Bill, a tall guy that always liked to rib the other guys, especially at a poker game.
"Yeah of course Bill. Don't I always?"

Randy replies as he takes a seat but not before putting the stack of money in front of him; mostly coins of course.

"I see you had a good week at work Randy."
Rick another friend and sitting across from Randy says without expression as he shuffles a deck of cards. Rick always started with the largest pile of cash on the table.
"Hey Rick, you should know, I'm doing most of the work for you aren't I?"
Randy replies trying to get Rick to at least smile.

The last player was a younger fellow by the name of John. He had longish blonde hair and wore glasses. He was, and had been in the learning curve of the game for most of the summer and of course had the smallest pile of money in front of him on the table.

"Hey John, keep an eye on me tonight, I'll show you how to win at this game… got it?"
Randy says as he counts his cash in front of him. The others let out a bit of a laugh as the they all get ready to play the first hand. Rick starts to deal a card face up to everyone starting with Stewart on his left and

going around the table until all had one card each. The highest card would win the deal, and because it was dealers choice this person could call the game he wanted to play.

There were many games and they tried to keep it down to just a few so as not to complicate it too much. Mostly five card and seven card straight poker with the odd different game thrown in if everyone agreed on it. There would be an anti to make sure there was at least a little in the pot should no one bet on any hand delt.

As most would admit to, it was more a social event than any one individual walking away with all the money. Normally it would be about two-hundred dollars that anyone would bring, hoping at the worst they would go home with that amount at least.

The sound of Randy opening his can of beer startled Stewart who had just put his cash onto the table. A couple of quarters rolled off the table and onto the floor. He reached down to pick them up off the flooor as he was dealt the highest card of the bunch.

John P Gibson   *High Tide*

It was a king of diamonds. Stewart got his shit together as he took the deck of cards and started to shuffel them.

It was customary to pass the shuffled deck back to the person to his right and offer the cutting of the deck if they so chose to. Then start the dealing process only after putting in the one-dollar anti into the pot.
"Five card high, two draws of three."
Stewart says loud enough so that all can hear him. There was silence as he dealt the five cards down to each player.

As they picked up the cards there were of course the snide comments from most.
"What a pile of shit Stewart. Where did you learn to deal?"
Randy says as he throws his cards into the centre. Obviousley folding as his cards were not up to his standard.

The others started the game with a dollar bet made by Rick. The others followed with no raises, except of course Randy who got up from the table and made his way to the kitchen to get another beer for himself. It was not a great start for him but knew things would turn around for him sometime soon. It always did.

"Nice one Gary… not a big pot, but nice hand."
Bill pipes up as Gary pulls in the coins and starts to stack them in their respective piles in front of him. It was now Steve's turn to deal as Randy came back in with his beer.
"Must be your lucky night."
He says as he refers to Gary's win as he sits and looks to his pile of coins to make sure no one has taken any.

"What's the game Steve?"
Bill asks as Steve is shuffling the deck of cards.
"How about Chicago?"
Everyone looks to him, there is no response as he offers a cut of the deck to Randy. Randy cuts and then waits as Steve deals two cards down and one up in succession to everyone.
"High spade in the hole and high hand, split pot or you can go for both as long as you declare it."

Steve says as he finishes dealing and puts a dollar in the pot to start things off. Randy looked over the cards that were showing and then looked to his and the two cards down.

A slight smile came across his face that he hoped was not noticed by anyone. He was lucky as the others were looking at their own cards and determining their strategy.
"OK… bets?"
Steve looked to Stewart who promptly folded his cards.
"Fold, I need another beer… anyone else need one?"

Randy looked up for a moment while holding his empty Lucky can for Stewart to take and obviously get him another one. He knew the ones he had at the table would not be as cold as the ones in the fridge.

"OK, Rick you gonna bet something to get this started?"
Rick looked at his cards and put a fiver in the pot.
"Five bucks."

He says to make sure the confirmation was there as to how much the bet was. Bill put in, John and then Steve, then finally Randy.

"Ten bucks."
Randy said with some authority to his voice as he placed two fivers in the pot.
"Randy raised it a fiver… everyone in?"
Steve asks as he threw in his extra five as did the others. Randy's expression changed slightly as he thought for sure at least one of them would have folded.

As Stewart returned with several beer in hand and of course the Lucky for Randy, there was silence as Steve dealt another face card to everyone. It was now looking good for Randy as his hand was improving ten-fold as another spade came up for him. With two of them and the ace being one of them, he was sure he could take both the high spade and high hand.

The cards now came as he had hoped and a couple more folded their hands. It was now Steve, Gary, Randy, and John still in. The pot had increased to about two hundred dollars and Randy was in a favourable position to win it all. It was now down to the last bet.

It was John's turn first and as he looked at his cards one more time, he looked up at the others and tossed the cards into the middle.
"I fold."
He says in a rather disgruntled voice. It was now just Gary, Steve and Randy left in this particular game. Randy's face cards did look threatening, but then again not knowing what was down made it a difficult decision to continue.

"I'll bet twenty dollars."
Steve says as he throws the twenty dollar bill into the pile of cash. Gary looks at him and pauses as he again looks at his cards. He then looked over to Randy who just smiled as he took a puff on his cigarette.
"I'm in."
He says as he also throws a twenty dollar bill in the pot. Now Randy looks at his cards again and slowly and deliberately takes two twenty dollar bills and throws them in.

"I'll raise it twenty."
He says with the confidence of a winner. Steve looks to Gary and without hesitation throws his cards onto the table.

"I fold."
He says with a bit of defeat in his tone. Gary now looked at his cards again, and then Randy. He reaches to his stack of money and takes a twenty and puts it in the pot.
"I call."
Randy slowly turns his cards over as he states what his intentions are.
"I'm going both high spade in the hole, and high hand."

The cards were there for anyone to see and they were good ones. He had the ace of spades down so this would gurantee him half the pot regardless unless he lost the high hand, which would mean he would forfeit half the pot because he had called both which means you have to win both. He had a flush with a jack of spades as the high card. Gary now started to turn his cards over one at a time and it was obvious he also had a flush. He had no spade down but his flush was a straight flush of diamonds to the queen. Gary had won the high hand and because Randy had called both and lost the hand, he would lose all.

"Shit man, what the fuck Gary, how the hell did you manage that?"
Randy says as he takes a swig of his beer and definitely does not look happy.
"Skill Randy… skill."
He replies with a laugh as do the others. It looked like it was going to be one of those nights where Randy was going to have to get his shit together.

He never went home after a night of poker a loser. The worst he would do was break even. Randy had a strategy that always worked for him. One that the others were just a bit apprehensive to try. The night continued on with similar games and different winners and losers for the hands.

Some wild stories and jokes made their way around the table, and with the beer and other drinks the guys were having another great night. Nights like this usually ended around one or two in the morning when it was decided the last hand would be played. On this particular night the clock was running later; it was nearly three AM and judging from the lay of the table the nights winners were to be Steve and Gary.

Randy had dipped into his pocket many times and was a couple of hundred in the whole. It was Stewart's deal and he picked Texas Holdem with being the last game of the night the bets were unlimited and one if they thought they had the winner could go all in, where one puts all of his cash in and the others have to match it.

It started out as any other game until Randy started to do his betting; it was high and making the others wonder if they should continue and did randy really have the good hand he was betting for.

It continued until most all the money on the table was in the final pot of the night. The bet was to Randy as he looked at his cards once again and then reached into his pocket; obviousley to get more cash. He pulled out a large roll of bills and counted out a couple of hundred and placed it in the pot. All eyes went to Randy who now had no expression what so ever. He was cool calm and collected as the saying goes.

"All in."
He says with all the confidence in the world. Steve looked at his cards.
"Fold."
He tossed his cards in without saying anything else. Rick was next who decided he might just stay in and see if randy was bluffing.
"All in"
He says as he puts in the two hundred dollars and then sits back in his chair.

It came to Stewart who also counted through his cash and put the two hundred in.
"All in. You better hope you have it Randy."
He says more to himself as he was down for the night and wanted to win.
John was next and it did not take him long to throw his cards in without saying a word. He was not impressed as he also would be one of the losers for the night. It was now up to Bill as he cautiously counted out the two hundred and put it into the pot.

He did not say a word as he looked to Gary the last to make his move. Gary took his time and finally counted out the two hundred.

"All in. Let's see what you have Randy. It better be good."
He says as he waits for Randy to show his cards. He starts to turn them over one by one and very slowly so as to create the right mood. The first card was a ten of diamonds, then a Jack of diamonds. The others had that feeling they knew what was coming next.

Then a queen of diamonds followed by a king of diamonds. One more card to make the royal flush, the best poker hand one could get in regular poker. Randy slowly started to turn the last card over. It was red, it was an ace, it was an ace of hearts. There was a very creepy silence as everyone looked at the cards in front of Randy.

It was obvious he had made a very big mistake thinking the ace of hearts was a diamond. True, the lighting wasn't all that good in the room, but to make a mistake such as this was unheard of. No one said anything as the others turned their cards over to reveal that Steve had won the hand with a full house. Randy just picked up his beer, finished it off, grabbed the other two beer that were left and made his way out the front door without saying a word.

The End

The Darkside

The door slammed shut after Phil worked his way into the dark and cluttered apartment. Bag of cheap beer in hand he moved to the fridge in the small kitchen. Not unlike his old friend Randy. Phil Scornhop was a single man in his late forties but looking at least ten years older. Randy his friend had always looked younger than his years. It was a can of beer in his pocket and a bag of chips before making his way to the couch to sit down, open the beer, open the bag of chips, and turn on the TV with the remote control unit. With the cable companies the way they were these days it was difficult to find any of his favourite shows that weren't re-runs. The commercials were often more times better entertainment than the actual shows. There was a commercial on so he muted the sound.

The loud Phissst sound the beer made when he pulled the metal tab back sounded louder than usual as there was complete silence in the room. He opened the bag of chips and put one in his mouth. The crunching sound was exagerated due to the silence in the room. He looked at the TV and thought to himself. 'Why the hell do I pay three-hundred dollar per month for this shit.'

Phil looked at the TV screen and knew it would be another three or four minutes of commercials. He had done the math and basically a thirty minute show would take an hour with all of the commercials. Again, why the hell pay so much for this shit.

It would be a typical night for him as he lit a cigarette and settled in for the eight or nine hours of TV interspersed with checking his cell phone to see if anyone had posted something new on FaceBook. Dinner of course would be delivered from his favourite restaurant; 'Dinglebells', a hamburger joint owned and operated by an elderly Chinese man named Quan.

The burgers were great and inexpensive; only thirty-five dollars with a portion of simulated fries. Along with his cheap canned beer, he was content. Like clockwork the delivery girl would show up; seven PM sharp. Her name was Sarah. A young good looking dark haired girl in her early twenties that you did not want to get pissed off.

Her Scottish background came through in droves when she was challenged in any way. Phil however felt she somehow thought he was a real steal, and every chance he got he would put the moves on her as he stood at his doorway fumbling through his wallet for the right amount of money. He had memorized many one liners to entice her.

The knock came on the door right at the right time. He looked at his watch; seven on the nose.
"One moment... I'll be right there."

He says with some volume in voice so Sarah can hear him. He checks his hair in the mirror beside the door as he opens it.

There she stood with box in hand and a fabricated smile. Obviously fishing for a tip.
"Hey Sarah…. Did you fart? Cause you blew me away."
He says with a smile and a wink. Sarah just looks at him for a moment. She had gotten used to his childish behaviour over the past few months.

"Very funny Mr. Scornhop, I'll try and remember that one for sure. Here's your order. That'll be thirty-five dollars please."
She said as she passed the box over to Phil.
"Thanks Sarah, I thought I told you to call me Phil? I know I'm a little older, but you can dispense with the pleasentries. Here you go… keep the change."

Phil gave her forty dollars and figured that was a fair enough tip, maybe even enough for her to get a little closer and accept his obvious advances to her. She looked at him and smiled as she turned to leave. Phil kept his gaze on her as he sized her up as she walked away. She could feel his eyes upon her and quickly turned to give him a little wave of her hand. She very much wanted to raise the middle finger.

"See you tomorrow Sarah, and have a nice night."
He thought about asking her to come back after her shift ended, but the last time he did that she told him under no uncertain terms that he was to never ask again. He would give it some time he thought and she would come around.

Phil went over to the couch and sat down after putting the food box onto the tabel in front. He would go get another beer before digging into his cheap burger and fries. He had been told years ago that there wasn't any real meat in the burger, and no potatos in the fries. He didn't care. It all tasted so good to him.

It was now time to sit down, open the beer, open the food box, check his phone to see what was happening on FaceBook, and watch a re-run of Two and A Half Men. It was his routine everyday after his very mundane job as a warehouse supervisor. Basically all he did on his job was to be on his cell phone cruising FaceBook for his eight hours. His life to date was something most would consider useless to say the least.

The next day came early as his shift started at nine AM. Phil was up by eight checking his phone of course and looking at all the empty beers on the coffee table along with last nights empty food box from 'Dinglebells.' He started to think about Sarah and how he might impress her on this night when he again would order the same meal.

The day for Phil was predictable, mostly on his cell phone with the odd interuption by his boss to do some menial task. He couldn't really complain as he really didn't have to do too much. The large round clock hanging on the wall at the end of the quiet lonely room said it was three-fifty eight, close enough to four oclock and for Phil to pack his things up and head for home.

His ride on the bus home gave him some important time to look at his cell phone for the twenty minutes it took to get to his place. Once at home he went to the fridge to get a beer, then make his way to the couch to sit and again get on the cell phone to see if anyone had posted something on FaceBook. The TV was next as he picked up the remote.

After several minutes he reached over for the phone and had the speed dial connect him to 'Dinglebells.' His order of course would be the same as any other night. He would however use a different line on Sarah hoping of course it would make her change her mind about him and their possible friendship.

"Hi, yes this is Phil Scornhop and I would like to.... Yes that's right the burger and fries as usual. About thirty-five minutes? That will be great... thanks."
He says as he hangs up the phone, places it on the table in front of him, and opens the beer. It was now time for some TV.

Because of Phil's lifestyle, his memory was somewhat challenged. His doctor had him on antidepressants which of course affected memory and almost always created depression. Seemed a waste of money, but the doctor was always right. Two and a half men was airing and of course Phil had watched just the other day of course not remembering he had. He lit up a smoke and picked up his cell phone to check FaceBook for any new posts by any of his friends.

Most he did not really know... they were just like him, accepting friend requests just to get enough friends to look reasonably normal to anyone cruising the format. If Phil were to post anything, and it wasn't often; it would be a picture of a naked woman usually fishing, or and expensive yacht.

There was now the sound of the door buzzer going off and Phil jumped to his feet nearly knocking over his can of beer. After making sure he had his wallet with him he opened the door to see of course Sarah holding his box of food.

"Hello Sarah, and how are you?"
She just smiles as she passes the box of food over to Phil.
"That'll be thrirty-five dollars please Phil."
At least she remembered to call him Phil instead of Mr. Scornhop. He reached into his wallet and pulled out the standard two twenties and handed it to Sarah. He thought this a good time to try out one of

his pick up lines on her. He held onto the bills a little tighter so that she couldn't take them and make her move out of there.

"Hey Sarah... are yer parents retarded? Cuz ya sure are special."
He said to her with all the sincerity he could muster up. Sarah just gave him that look that suggested he was just a little off.
"Do you want change?"
She asked as she held the twenties he would not let go of.

"No... no... your tip, and thanks Sarah, see you tomorrow."
She smiled and turned and walked away quickly. Phil felt just a little dejected but happy that he got his meal and that it was Sarah again that had delivered it. He made his way to the couch and made himself at home as he opend the box to devour his favourite meal of the day.

It was again a night almost exactly the same as all the rest. He had been asked on the very rare occasion if he wanted to go out to one of the many local bars to have a few drinks and play some pool. Phil always declined as he would rather stay home and do what he does best. FaceBook cruising.

The night went as usual and the mess in the living room grew exponentially as he never did like to clean much, maybe once a month but only after stepping on something and hurting his foot, or dropping his cell phone and not being able to find it right away as it was hidden by the many empty boxes from 'Dinglebells'.

It was another day with the next being the start of his two-day weekend break. This he looked forward to as he could sleep till two in the afternoon both Saturday and Sunday before getting up to do what it was he did best. Watch TV, and cruise on FaceBook. He did hope however that Sarah might see the light of his advances towards her. Especially now that he knew some great pick-up lines.

His work was again predictable and virtually nothing happened out of the ordinary. Phil could only think of his dinner meal, Sarah, and of course TV and FaceBook. He thought he had a perfect life with virtually no responsibilities to burden him down like so many other people he had read about on FaceBook.

As he entered his very cluttered apartment Phil of course made his way to the fridge for a beer. He was excited as he was sure the pick-up line he would use on Sarah would definitely get her excited. He was now fantacizing about her and would use his memorized lines to win her over, even if it took him forever to do so.

The routine panned out as usual and the buzz at the door told him Sarah was there with his meal. He brushed his hair back with his hand and made his way to the door and opened it. There she stood again, looking so beautiful holding the box of food.
"Hi Sarah, hope you are well."
He says as he reaches into his wallet for the two twenties to give to her.

"Hi Phil, here is your meal."
There is no smile from her this time as she passes the box to Phil. He gives her the two Twenties. She takes them and pauses.

"No you keep the change Sarah. My love fer you is like diarrhea. I can't hold it in."
He says to her with a smile hoping this will get her on the right track with him.

Sarah just turned and walked away. No reply. Nothing. Phil went back into his apartment after closing the door and made his way to the couch to eat his meal. He shrugged off the cold shoulder he had got from Sarah figuring she was just having a bad day. He knew he would have to wait for Monday to see her again. She, like Phil, got weekends off.

*****

Mondays… they always felt like shit to Phil, he supposed most other people as well. He had a very relaxing weekend with plenty of sleep as he had decided to double up on his antidepressant pills. His doctor had told him to do so if he was feeling a little more depressed than usual. This of course in itself made him sleep most of the weekend away. He was even down on his dozen or more beer for the two days off. At least while he had been awake he was up to date with FaceBook and his TV re-runs. It was dinner time now and the order had been put in, and he was impatiently waiting for Sarah to show with his boxed meal.

There it was… the buzz to say she had arrived. He was really keen on telling her his next pick-up line hoping over the weekend she had rested enough to understand that she should like him.
"Oh hi Sarah… how are you? Hope you had a great weekend."
He says as she once again passes him the box. He already had the two twenties in hand and passed them to her. At least she had a smile this evening.

"I'm fine and I did have a great weekend."
She replies as she holds the twenties again waiting to see if she would get a tip. Phil just gestured with his hand for her to keep it. She smiled again and turned to leave.
"Hey Sarah, if you was a tree, I were a squirrel, I'd store my nuts in yer hole."
Phil says after her in a loud enough voice for her to hear. She did not turn back but let out a series of subdued laughs. Phil hoped this was a sign she was

becoming interested in him and his wonderful wit he could come up with. He turned and went back into his apartment.

He settled in to his routine and the night went as it usually did. He could hardly wait until the following night when he would again use one of his favourite pick-up lines. He was sure she would come around soon; what woman wouldn't with these wonderful sayings he had memorized from FaceBook.

The next night went as the others had and when he used the pick-up line on Sarah, her response was similar to that of the night before. She laughed, but this time a little louder. Phil couldn't understand it, how could she not like 'You might not be the best lookin' girl here, but beauty's only a light switch away.'

He thought it was one of his better ones and would try again the next evening. Maybe it was his delivery of the lines? He just wasn't sure what it would take for Sarah to come around. He would sleep on it, have a predictable day at work, and then give her another line on Tuesday evening. He knew he did not want to run out of them before she finally accepted a date with him.

"I know I'm not Fred Flinstone, but I bet I can make yer bed-rock."
Phil says as Sarah this time took a moment to make sure she heard what it was he had to say to her. Sarah put her hand up to her mouth and started to giggle as she turned and walked away. Phil thought at least she was smiling and this was a good sign.

It was Wednesday and Sarah this time just stood in front of Phil anticipating his pick-up line. He paused for affect, then in his best rehearsed sexy voice let the line out.
"I can't find my puppy, can you help me find him? I think he went inta this here cheap motel room."
He gestures with his arm into the open doorway and into his messy apartment.

Sarah again laughed and walked off down the hallway. Phil was now getting frustrated as to why she would not open up to him. He had to this point used some of his best pick-up lines he knew. What was it she wanted? What was it she needed for him to get lucky with her? He would have to get back onto FaceBook and do some research.

Thursday night and Phil had even decided to up the tip by fifty cents thinking that might along with the pick-up line get Sarah in the right frame of mind. The usual small conversation and then his line.
"Yer eyes are as blue as window cleaner."
He thought for sure this would get her as her eyes were indeed blue. Sarah just laughed again taking the extra fifty cents and walked down the hallway.

Phil was getting just a little frustrated with all of this and thought maybe if he had a few more beer before Sarah showed up with his meal he might deliver the pick-up line good enough for her to reciprocate in some way positive.
"If yer gunna regret this in the mornin, we kin sleep til afternoon."

As drunk as he was his delivery of the line was done perfectly he thought as he closed the door and made his way to the couch. He now had another weekend to go over his options and get plenty of sleep. He very much wanted Sarah to come into his apartment and have sex with him. She didn't even have to talk to him.

The weekend went as usual as Phil got his exercise by walking to the fridge everytime he needed a beer, and with the extra sleep he needed little to eat as that was all there was in the fridge... a little leftover fries from some of the meals from 'Dinglebells'.

As much as he could Phil was on FaceBook doing his best to find some pick-up lines, at least one that would entice Sarah into his dirty apartment. He actually took pen to paper and jotted down some of them in note form. If not used on Sarah at least they were there for future reference.

Sunday night and Phil was exhausted from all the FaceBook cruising and the re-run TV shows and movies he had watched. It would be a very trying day at work and all he could think about was seeing Sarah at his door with his box of food on Monday evening. He had a sleepless night and a quick morning getting ready for work as he had overslept. He would forego the shower and hope his boss was at least a little lenient with him when he did arrive at work for his shift. He was generally very punctual when it came to his getting to work on time.

The day was slow, and for some reason Phil was getting nervous about that evening when he would try what he thought would be his best pick-up line yet. When he got to his apartment, Phil put the beer in the fridge and then brought one over to the couch and sat down. After opening the beer and then making his order to 'Dinglebells' he got himself onto FaceBook to check things there.

He kept going over and over the pick-up line in his head knowing that Sarah would be buzzing his door shortly. Another beer he thought just in case. He returned with his beer to the couch and just as he was about to sit down, the buzz from the door sounded. He put his beer down and made his way to the door and opened it.

There she was, this time however she had her back to him for some reason. In his mind he thought this was a ploy of hers... the pick-up lines must be working he thought. He would deliver what he thought to be his best to date.

"Hi Sarah... yer face reminds me of a wrench, every time I think of it my nuts tighten up."

There was a pause and she turned around to face Phil; it wasn't Sarah. It was a man with a beard and pot belly and very ugly.

"Hey man, I'm in ta that fer sure, I'll even pay fer tha meal."

*****

It was a couple of days later that Phil found out Sarah had quit her job at 'Dinglebells' and moved on. The guy that had replaced her apparently liked what it was Phil had said that evening. Phil took 'Dinglebells' off his list and especially off of FaceBook as a friend.

The End

John P Gibson — *High Tide*

448

Blood Brother

Four AM once again and William had barely recooperated from the session he and his fellow army buddies had endured the day before. His decision to enlist in the army was one he had fought with for many months once he had completed high school. The Government of course was doing its best to recruit young males and females to keep the numbers of soldiers continuing to increase as were the global conflicts necesitating that increase. William was promised an advanced education and of course many benefits even when he had completed his obligation to the services. It would be a three year obligation and if he liked what he was doing the recruitment officer said he could continue in his chosen field with the military. It was something he would think about.

It wasn't so much the money as it was the experience he would gain from it. He was told that many before him had made successful livings and contributed to the country's economic diversity. William of course at this time of his life wasn't so much interested in anything but being successful and making money.

As he got himself dressed as a shower was out of the question except after dinner and before bed. It only made sense as that is when he and his friends were the dirtiest. Their commanding officer was a very thorough and mean son of a bitch. It was often throughout any day that several of them would get some lashing of some sort.

They were told it would make them tough, being able to withstand the brutal truths of a life lived on this planet. Once dressed and with all the gear they would need for the day at their feet and holding onto their rifle in front of them, the Sargent would enter the barracks for the pre-breakfast inspection. There were always plenty of stomach growlings as he walked along in silence checking everyone.

His name was Sargent Brooks, that was all they knew about him. Some of the guys would call him Crooks just for a laugh, but only when he wasn't close by to hear them. William had a little more respect for the man and also the chain of command within the military.

"OK… you shit heads are ready to go to the mess and I want you to keep it quick and simple as we start with the drills today at O- six-hundred hours. Does everyone understand?"
There was an uproaress yell of "YES SARGENT!" as everyone saluted and kept any expression they had away from their face. Brooks demanded this of them all the time.

"Orderly fashion now and off to the mess hall, let's make it quick and make sure you eat all of your food. If I see anything left on your trays there will be trouble to pay… does everyone understand?"

Again a loud response of 'Yes Sargent' as everyone filed out of the barrack and along to the mess hall which was about a two minute walk away.

William figured he fit in fine with all at his barracks. He was not the boss... but he wasn't the little shit at the bottom either. That guy was Gerald. A skinny guy the same age as William that lacked backbone and confidence in anything he did. This took the pressure off of everyone else and of course Brooks would continually tell him all the shit he got would make him a strong man.

It was often that many thought if all of the crap they went through to be a soldier was worth it. The pain, the bruised egos, the constant barrage of insults from higher ups, and the lack of real social time together. William kept thinking that it was only three years of this providing they did not have to see the real action.

It would be a scary thought as Brooks had ingrained in them the hardships of being in actual battle. It was something William thought about a lot and wondered if he could actually pull the trigger to kill another man, woman, or child for the purpose of keeping his country free. It was all a very dificult subject to address.

Once in line at the mess hall William would follow everyone's lead and take what was slopped onto the metal tray in front of him. He often had to wonder what some of the stuff he saw was real food or not. It always seemed to taste the same no matter what. At least the cooffee did its job as he was still a bit drowsy from lack of sleep.

Exactly fifteen minutes and Brooks was walking into the mess hall with a couple of his yes-men on either side of him.
"Put your forks down on your tray, bring them to the counter and get yourself outside and back to the barracks to get your equipment... NOW!"
He says in his more than rehearsed way he always did.

Everyone did as they were told and within a few minutes everyone was back at the barracks getting their equipment needed for the days training. The weather was turning slightly, warning everyone that there just might be some rain throughout the day. This would not be a good thing as doing ones laundry after a hard day was not nice.

William had this part down to an art. He stood at attention with pack on, and rifle at his side waiting for Brooks once again. There were still a few fumbling around with their gear. If Brooks caught them doing this they would be reprimanded post haste.

They had all been told of course what was in store for them for the days training. It was a ten-mile jog up a mountainside with of course many distractions to keep them on guard. This was the part where Brooks would not shut up. He would bark out orders all day long, and there would always be a few who would have to suffer after the day was over because of their inferior abilities.

William was lucky that he could always endure what was thrown at him. He was shaping up to be a model soldier. It was even on a very odd ocassion that Brooks would compliment William and use him as a positive role model for the rest. This made him feel good inside and made him want to perform even better. Those that graduated at the top end of the batallion were always considered for better jobs when finished their three-year term.

"William… good job, you get an extra bun at the dinner meal tonight. The rest of you pay attention to what he does. Do what he does and you *too* can get an extra bun."
Brooks yells out at everyone, all William can do is suck it up and think about it to himself. He was sure the others would give him a hard time later when they had their down-time in the barracks.

He could not have been more correct as the guys started to give him a hard time just before lights out at ten-o'clock. It wasn't much, something he could deal with, but there were a couple who seemed genuinely ticked off by Brooks and the liking of William over them.

It was soon and the lights were out and then the dreaded noise of snoring, whimpering, and farting made it a near impossible feat to get any kind of substantial sleep. The morning of course came quick enough and it was another day of challenges and one-upmanship for most. William of course tried his best to keep his ego in check.

It was about three AM and William was awoken by a shrill scream. He rolled over and saw what was going on. A few of the bigger and dumber guys were picking on Gerald who was now nearly in tears as his bed was completely in a mess and someone had drawn with a perma-marker all over his face and upper body.

"Hey… you guys… let him go."
William says in a more than masculine tone of voice. Now the others in the barracks were awake and watching with anticipation of Gerald getting a shit kicking. There was always a little cash floating around when these sort of things happened. Betting was just a part of spending three years in this environment. Most of course would bet on the tough guys winning.

The two that were doing most of the childish stuff to Gerald looked up to William. There was now silence in the barracks, even quieter than when all were asleep. William just stared at them as they continued to look at him across the way. The larger of the two started to make his way over to where William was standing beside his bunk.

"What was that you said shit head?"
It was Danny, a real baffoon but big enough, and strong enough most would leave him be. Except William.
"I said leave him alone, he didn't do anything to you and we all just want to get some sleep."
William said it with enough confidence everyone else kept quiet waiting for Danny to react.

"It's none of yer business shit head… we'll do what we want with this loser… got it?"
He says inches from William's face who now grabs Danny by the wrist and twists it around with his thumb being the main focal point of the move. Danny lets out a scream that was louder than Geralds just a minute earlier.

"OK… OK… I won't bother him… I promise."
Danny says as he is obviously in excruciating pain as he lowers himself to the floor where William was making him go.

"You better be sure of that Danny or I'll make it real tough on you and anyone else who thinks they can pick on some of us here. Now get back to your bunk so we can all get some sleep."
He says in a voice not unlike Brooks voice when he commands everyone to do whatever it is he wants.

The silence in the room suggested Danny and anyone sideing with him should back off and do what was said by William. It would be soon enough that Brooks would be making himself present for the next days routine. It was to be the first session on the firing range and learning about their personal firearms.

It was the quietest William had ever experienced in the barracks and he was just a little concerned when it came to Danny and his thug friends. William decided to *not* go into a deep sleep just in case Danny decided to get his revenge somehow. It would be a very demanding day for him, but he would endure and do his best to rise above all of the political bullshit he was experiencing in the barracks.

"Rise and shine my pieces of shit! Get your asses up and ready for the day. You've five minutes to get dressed, make your bed, and be ready for your inspection."

Brooks came in without William hearing him, which was unusual as he was always on top of everything going on at the base. He, along with the others jumped up and started to dress in their gear or make their bed, or both at the same time as William always did.

The inspection was a little longer than usual as Brooks had to stop and interrogate the shit out of Gerald as he still had most of the markings on his face and upper body. It would not wash off immediately.

"Looks like you boys were having a fun time last night. For not being in proper cleanliness this morning Gerald, you'll do an extra ten laps on the course today… GOT THAT!"

He almost spits into Gerald's face as he speaks. All Gerald could do was nod his head and do his best to answer.

"Yes… Yes sir!"
"Good, and if this ever happens again the entire barrack will suffer, does everyone understand?"
There was a collective 'Yes sir.' As he resumed his inspection before he allowed them to go for their breakfast. There was silence after he left and the others started to fall in and make their way to the mess hall.

It was another bland breakfast but most were excited that they would be for the first time learning about their firearms and how to use them. It would be a short march to the firing range where the instructors would be doing their job explaining the basics of their rifles.

Once positioned at the one end of the range William could see the targets about one hundred yards in front of him. They were big enough he saw no problem in getting all of his shots to hit the bull's eye. It would be a laying position with a couple of sandbags to rest the barrel of the rifle on and then take a bead on the target and when told to do so… shoot at the target.

It seemed all so simple to William as he did indeed hit the center of the target everytime with every bullet. The instructors were impressed for sure. After the morning's lessons it was time for a meal and the walk back to the mess hall. They would all return after their meal and complete the afternoon with more instruction on how to shoot their weapons.

It had been drilled into them that conservation of bullets was not an issue; killing the enemy was paramount and whatever it took to kill them would be what was required. The training advanced as per schedule and most of the men had the hang of how to fire their rifles with no problem. It was however not very good for William as Brooks had taken him aside and complimented him on his expertise with his ability on the range. William enjoyed the positive re-enforcement but could see the others were just a little skeptical. Why was he being coddled by Brooks so much. Back at the barracks William was the center of most of the banter and it was not good. He was distancing himself further from nearly everyone there.

The wake up call came as usual and William was the first ready for inspection before breakfast. Brooks made his way in and took a position at the front of all the men.
"Well men, I assume you are ready for your morning meal before more instruction out at the range today. I'm sorry to say to you that I have instructions to let you all know you will be shipped out to Eastern Europe this afternoon."

There was silence in the room. Everyone was waiting for him to continue. Of course the men had heard about the conflicts on the Russian border and how things had escalated to the point of artillary being fired by both sides. This was not what William had expected or wanted. He just wanted to finish his term without any active duty and return to society with several usefull skills. Now he and his fellow soldiers would be flying out to Eastern Europe to start fighting the Russians. He would have to start killing other soldiers and he hoped that was all. If he had to shoot any innocent women and children, he would be devastated to say the least. Now after all the training the test was here.

Brooks had somehow managed to become MIA when the men finally landed at one of the many airforce bases close to the border and the fighting. I guess it paid to have seniority. The men doing the yelling now were more Williams age and were groomed for this kind of warfare.

It would not be right away that he and the others would be on the front line, they would grasp some of the fundamentals of war by working their way up to it. William because of his training and recommendation from Brooks was to be in some capacity a leader of sorts when it came down to any advancements of the group.

They were told to be aware of land mines, snipers, any oddity when it came to walking through the dense forests where they would be moving continually to take certain priority enemy encampments. It would take some time and there was no definite time frame for completion or victory as they hoped for. Making sure ones gear was sufficient was the utmost important item to get right.

Without water, food, and ammunition, it would be a lost cause for the soldier who did not get it right. Attention to detail would be the key, as Brooks had taught them all back at the training camp. William of course did a better job and he made sure the others were ready for probably the worst experience of their lives.

"OK men, I need your attention and I need it NOW!"
The guy in command let everyone know. William had forgotten his name as his memory for the new brass in this situation was faltering. William and all the others turned their attention to the man in front of them to hear what it was he had to say to them.

"First thing tomorrow morning we are off to the front to help with battalion 84, they are getting close to erradicating the enemy on that front and with our help I am sure we can defeat them and continue moving forward. The idea of course is to take control of the main units closer to the larger cities inland." It all sounded so much like a movie to William.

"Make sure you get some good sleep as we move out tomorrow at three AM. You can eat your first meal on the way. It will be about a fifteen mile hike and with the terrain it will not be an easy trek."
There was no smile, no hanging around for any questions. He just turned and made his way out of the large tent to get back to his. He would be back before three in the morning.

William had set his internal alarm and woke up at two-forty-five AM. He started to get himself ready for the always annoying wake-up call. As he sat on the edge of his bunk he noticed a few others start to wake up.

A moment later two soldiers came bursting through the front entrance to the tent. The two of them started to yell out the orders.
"OK you guys... get your act together. You have ten minutes to get yourself ready and standing outside ready to go... got it?"

He yells out of course not expecting any answer to his question. The both of them turned and exited the tent with everyone rumbling around getting their shit together.

Once outside William was signaled to approach the two men that had entered the tent earlier. The conversation was centered around him taking lead as they all started to walk into the forest. It was dark and of course the men had been warned about the wolves, bears, and other dangerous creatures that might show themselves.

They were told not to shoot at anything other than the enemy soldiers they would eventually come across. The rest of the group looked at William with a look of desperation and some with a look of regret. He had not done a very good job in getting the support of the majority of the soldiers he had trained with.

The trek into the forest proved to be more arduous than any of them had been informed. Some of the men were lagging behind. All William could do was look behind him and make gestures with his arms to get everyone moving at the pace he had set for them. Talking, or yelling would be out of the question as they had to be as quiet as they could.

It appeared the forest was thinning out ahead and some military noise could be heard in the form of gunfire and grenades exploding. They were close. William had the men crouch down as they moved slowly forward. They were lucky in that there was a small ridge of rock ahead where they could get a decent vantage point.

From there they could determine to what extent they would have to move on a charge command. This would be the moment, and William just hoped he and his men could overtake the enemy on the otherside of the ridge.

William moved slowly by himself closer to the ridge and made his way to a vantage point where he could use his binoculars to assess the situation. As he did so he could see about ten to fifteen soldiers in a small thicket about fifty yards ahead of them. He thought this should be an easy assault as his men out numbered the enemy by about three to one. That

is if his count was right. He motioned the men to come along the ridge top and get ready to shoot and attack their enemies. As he stood to get his mens attention he yelled out so all could hear him. This was his moment as his confidence level had now peaked.
"MEN… GET YOURSELVES READY AND SHOOT AT WILL."

*****

The report was a short one as Brooks read through it. He could not believe what it was he was reading. The entire infantry William was leading had fired their weapons directly into William. He was killed instantly.

The End

John P Gibson   *High Tide*

The Hypnotic Way

A step around the corner and Tommy was just about at the small pharmacy next to his apartment building downtown New York. Tommy Faren was a thrity-two year old single male who had a job with a very successful advertising company in the city. He considered himself a physically fit and reasonably intelligent man. Until he started to get these very involved headaches he could not understand. Once again he was on his way to get some pain killers, something he never used to use; for any reason. Now the headaches he was getting warrented him getting thse pills at least once a week for the past two months. His doctor could not find any reason for the onset of these medical conditions. Not only was it the headaches, but also his regular routine had somehow altered.

His doctor had suggested he visit a phycologist, something Tommy had refused initially as he thought he had no issues to discuss other than the headaches he was now having to endure. He finally did relent and tracked down a doctor he could afford.

The doctor he finally found was reputed to be a very good one in the area; at least that is what the adverts on the internet had said. Dr. Lisa Botomy, an attractive forty something woman who had a very nice way about her. Tommy was instantly enamoured with her. He said he would at least try the one month program as that was all he could afford at the moment.

His first session with her about a week ago had gone well he thought, of course she was gettting all the information about him she could. This was of course so she would be able to determine to what extent his inner thoughts might have something to do with his headaches. She of course did not promise any relief through her methods. This did not sit too well with Tommy. He would however endure because of her persuasive methods.

After he picked up his pain killers he would make his way to Lisa's office which was only another two blocks from the pharmacy he used. He was lucky in that sense as he did not own a car; never had. He thought anyone living in a city like he did was plain stupid for owning one when the transit was so efficient.

He took the stairs up to the tenth floor where Lisa's office was. He had this fear that elevators would stop between floors if he was in one. He had a fear of closed spaces and always did have. This was one of the things Lisa had brought up within their first few sessions.

He opened the fancy glass door to the reception area where a secretary was busy on the phone behind a very fancy wooden desk. Tommy liked the way the office was decorated and it made him feel comfortable. As he approached the secretary she finished up with her call and smiled at Tommy before she replaced the receiver of the phone. He of course smiled back at her.

"Hi Priscilla, and how are you?"
He asks in the best and attentive voice he can muster, considering how bad his headache was.
"I'm good Mr. Faren, the Doctor is with a patient at the moment, if you would like to take a seat. Can I get you a coffee?"
She says in a very nice way. She was in her late twenties, blonde long hair, and a killer smile that always put Tommy in a good mood.

"I'd love a coffee Priscilla, thank you very much."
He replies as she gets up to get him a cup at the counter off to one side with the coffee machine, cups, sugar, cream, and even an assortment of cookies if one was hungry. Tommy loved his coffee and she knew exactly how he liked it.

"Two sugar and a drip of cream… right?"
She asked even though she knew how he liked it.
"Yes that will be fine Priscilla."

John P Gibson — *High Tide*

She brought the coffee over to him and just happened to bring the plate of cookies over as well. Tommy loved to watch her walk.

As she placed the coffee and plate of cookies on the table in front of Tommy she hesitated as she could see him looking down at her cleavage, exposed of course to attract just this type of reaction from men.
"Thank you Priscilla."
He says as she looked at him and smiled. His day as far as he was concerned was complete now.

It took about ten or so minutes before Lisa made her way to the doorway where she noticed Tommy sitting enjoying his coffee while looking at Priscilla. Her previous client of course had left through a back door so as to keep as much privacy between Doctor and patient as she could.

"Hi Tommy, why don't you come on in... you can bring your coffee if you like."
She smiled as she approached Tommy as he got up from the plush sofa he was seated at.
"Hello Lisa... good to see you."

He replied as he smiled and brushed off any cookie crumbs off his chin as he did so. It was important that he always looked his best for her.

He followed Lisa into her very nice and comfortable office and took his familiar seat on the more than plush sofa facing the standard chair all phychiatrists would sit in to some how say they were far superior to their patients. He settled in and faced her after he placed his empty cup on the table in front of the both of them.

"So tell me Tommy, how are you feeling today?"
She asked him in a matter of fact tone of voice.
"Well Lisa I feel somewhat at odds with what's going on, as you know I have been having some very bad headaches latley, and I just don't know what to do. The prescription drugs my other doctor is prescribing aren't doing much in the way of helping."

Lisa looked at him and gave him the gaze he was used to. One that suggested she had seen far worse than him and to get on with something she could deal with. There was a pause and a silence he was also used to on most of his visits. He would leave it up to her to continue on and hopefully address the problem with some helpful information.

"Well Tommy I was thinking that maybe we might try some hypnosis as a way of dealing with your isssues... that is if you are open to it."
She looked at Tommy and gave him that smile he enjoyed so much.
"I think that anything you suggest at this point would be worth trying. I don't know how long I can deal with this pain everyday... if you know what I mean."

Lisa gave him that look as she penned something into her journal. It was something she often did as they conversed through the hour he thought he was being charged far too much for.
"Well... it will only take a few moments to get you into a stage that I can recall any part of your history, and possibly pinpoint what exactly it might be that is causing these abnormal headaches of yours."
She said in that doctor kind of way that suggested she wasn't really all that concerned for his well being. He would oblige so as to at least get his

monies worth for the session. One thing Tommy was good at was keeping his finacial affairs in order. At least until the onset of his headaches.

As Lisa had said, it did not take long and whatever had taken place Tommy had no idea of. The time she referred to was lost to him. One hour and fifteen minutes and he had no recollection of it at all. As he looked at his watch he wondered if he would have to pay extra for the overtime.

"It all went well Tommy and I will put together what I feel a good program for you to help not only with your headaches, but also some of the other issues you brought up while you were under."
It was all a mish-mash to Tommy as he tried his best to sort out what he had just gone through. The upside was his headache for the moment had disappeared.

He was ushered out of the room and led to where Priscilla was working away with some paperwork. Lisa said her goodbyes with an indication that Tommy should make his payment; it turned out he only had to pay for the one hour. He was happy that he got the over-time for free. He said his goodbyes to Priscilla and made his way home to think about dinner.

Everything seemed normal to Tommy except the fact that his headaches were gone. This he was very pleased about as he went to work making some spaghetti and meatballs for dinner. After dinner he would then relax in front of the TV and hopefully watch a good movie.

It wasn't more than a few minutes later and the phone started to ring. Tommy stopped everything he was doing and went over to pick the receiver up. He put the phone to his ear.
"Hello…"
That was it, no speaking after the initial hello and after putting the phone back he took his apron off, grabbed his keys and walked out of the front door.

He found himself in a part of town he had never been before. A place where he had been told all the bad shit happens. It was early evening and still light out so he could see his way around. Tommy now found a corner of an old building and leaned against the wall. He waited, and waited, then finally a young man approached dressed rather poorly, he would be either a homeless man, drug dealer, drug user, or all three.

"Hey man... what yo doin on my turf?"
Tommy's response was quick and to the point. His ride on the bus home was somewhat awkward as many people were looking at him. Once home he cleaned up, finished preparing his dinner, then relaxed on the sofa to watch TV.

The news now came on as it was eleven PM and Tommy like everyone else was addicted to the news channels. The top story was about a repeat drug offender found decapitated in a back alley on the wrong side of town. Tommy watched and wondered how anyone could do such a thing.

He finished with his TV and got himself to bed as it would be a busy one the next day and he wanted to make sure he got some good sleep before waking at six in the morning. The morning started out the same as any other and as he made his way to the kitchen to make his breakfast the phone started to ring. He went over to it and picked up the receiver and put it to his ear. A moment later he returned it, went to get his jacket and walked out the front door.

This time Tommy ended up in the city's large park in the center of town. It was a calm morning with a clear sky. He found a bench to sit on and just sat there. It did not take long and an elderly man came along and sat at the other end of the bench Tommy was seated on.

"Nice mornin aint it?"
The old man said to Tommy as he smiled to show just one good tooth. Tommy's response was short and sweet, then he made his way to the subway to get himself home as he had to get to work. Later as he took a break and went for a coffee at the nearby café, he took a seat at the counter and looked up to the large TV.

The newscaster was talking about another beheading; this time in the park and the victim was an elderly man. This could only be surmised by what his body looked like as the head was nowhere to be found; just like the other decapitation in the bad part of town the night before. Tommy was shocked as were the others sitting alongside him at the café.

Tommy finished his day and returned home to do his normal routine and then get ready for a similar day at work the next day, other than he had an appointment with Lisa. His headaches were gone and he felt good, so he was in the frame of mind to say to her he would not need her services anymore. This would save him some money.

The phone started to ring; it was nearly Tommy's bedtime… eleven PM. After returning the receiver of the phone, he got his jacket and made his way outside and hailed a taxi working its way down the street. He gave the driver the directions.
"7523 Main street."

It was all he said as the driver made the adjustment and found his way to Main street. It took about five minutes and he pulled over to the side of the road. Shut the meter off, then turned around to request the payment of seven dollars. The ride home was uneventful and Tommy left the cab to walk the rest of the way to his place. He entered and got himself ready for bed. He was tired and needed a good sleep.

The morning came and Tommy showered, had some breakfast, then was off to work. He remembered he had an appointment with Lisa at two PM. He would have to book off work early, which he did not mind at all. His job was mundane at best and anything to break the monotony would help.

Sitting at his desk he signed into FaceBook to see what was happening and almost immediately he noticed a posting about a cabdriver found in his cab without his head. Another decapitation; the third in as many days. Tommy could not figure it out how this could be possible in this relatively crime free city.

It was getting close to his appointment time with Lisa so he got himself ready for his meeting with her. He hoped she would not be offended when he told her he would not need her services anymore, and a better part was he was not using any of the painkillers his other doctor had prescribed for him.

He felt he was all back to normal and life could only get better. On his walk to his appointment he felt on top of the world. He sported a smile and picked up the pace of his walk.

"Good afternoon Mr. Faren."
Priscilla says in a more than cheerful voice to Tommy.
"And a great afternoon to you Priscilla."
He says as he approaches her desk with a very large smile.
"If you just have a seat Dr. Botomy will be with you shortly."
She smiles back at him and gestures to the comfortable seats off to the side.

"Coffee?"
She asks as she gets up to get Tommy his usual.
"Yes thank you Priscilla."
She brought his coffee over along with the plate of cookies and placed them on the table in front of Tommy. It was only a few minutes and Lisa made her presence known as she came through her doorway and into the center of the room.
"Good afternoon Tommy, and how are you?"

She asked in her usual tone. Tommy stood up and moved towards her with his cup of coffee in hand and a very large smile on his face.

"Couldn't be better Lisa, and how are you?"
"I am just fine, shall we?"
She puts her arm out towards the door of her office. Tommy nods his head and picks up his coffee and a cookie off the plate before moving towards her open door. Once inside he took his usual sofa as Lisa made her way to her chair.

"Well... tell me Tommy, how are we today?"
She looks at Tommy with that educated look she always gave him. He finished munching on his cookie before he answered.
"I am doing very well Lisa, I haven't felt this good in a long long time."
He smiled and took a drink from his coffee before putting it on the table.

"That's good to hear Tommy, It appears our sessions have been working for you."
Tommy looked at her and thought about how he was going to tell her he would not be needing her

John P Gibson *High Tide*

services anymore. It took a moment, but he finall got the nerve up and prepared to say to her what he had been rehearsing all morning in his mind.

"I would like to thank you, but I think I am doing fine enough I shouldn't need to come back here to see you. I'm sure you understand."
Lisa just looked at him with that look of hers.
"Of course I think that would be a good idea, but I would suggest just one more appointment before we part our ways. How does that sound to you?"

He thought about it for a moment and figured to keep things right, why not.
"OK, how does tomorrow sound? Same time?"
She started to go through her book in front of her.
"Yeah, that works just fine Tommy. Keep tabs on how things are still working for you and we'll see you tomorrow for our final meeting."

Tommy felt good as he stood, thanked Lisa and made his way out of the office and onto his home to get himself ready for dinner and of course TV. He thought maybe he should celebrate just a little and get himself a bottle of wine along the way home. It was a small store where he had been once before. He picked out his bottle of wine, paid for it, and was on his way again.

Once home he put the bottle in the fridge as it was a white wine. It was only a moment later and his phone started to ring. He picked it up... put the receiver to his ear, listened for a moment, then returned it to it's base. Dinner would have to wait as he put his jacket on and left his place with some urgency.

It was a longer walk down the street and alongside the river that ran through the middle of town. He had been here before and walked along a pathway until he came across a man fishing off the side of a railing running along the side of the pathway. Tommy liked fishing, it was just that he was no good at it...ever.

He approached the man with the fishing pole and started a short conversation. The man was probably in his sixties and was smoking a cigarette. He turned to see Tommy beside him and started in with a conversation. Most fishermen are polite and enjoy a good conversation. They enjoy catching fish even more. It was not long and Tommy turned to go back to his home.

After dinner and a long movie he was watching the news. The main story was about another decapitation, this time an older fisherman. His head was missing but locals knew who he was through the clothes that he wore and his tackle box. Tommy was again shocked at the craziness of the past week and all of these bizarre murders.

He got himself to bed and would more than likely bring these murders up in conversation with Lisa to find out her twist on the whole affair. He did not sleep that well and in the morning had a smaller breakfast than normal. It was a day off for him so he would do some house cleaning and laundry until his two oclock appointment with Lisa.

It was about one-thirty when the phone rang. Tommy picked it up and was silent. After replacing the phone he went to the freezer and took out the heavy dark green plastic garbage bag. He made sure it was fastened well and then made his way to Lisa's office for his appointment. He arrived right at two oclock. He made his way into the front reception area and saw Priscilla at her desk doing some typing at her computer.

Tommy went right up to her and within seconds had her sprawled across her desk and the sharp blade of his knife cut through her neck until her head fell to the floor. There was virtually no sound as she did not have time to scream out in horror as she saw Tommy with the knife.

He then put her head into the bag after untieing the top of it, then he took a seat in one of the chairs. It was only a moment later and Lisa came out of her office and approached Tommy.
"Hello Tommy and what do we have here?"
She of course was referring to the large green garbage bag beside him on the floor. He looked at her, then he looked over at the bag, then back to her.
"I have no idea Lisa, someone must have left it here before I arrived."
She smiled at him.

"Tommy why don't you bring that bag into my office and we'll talk about how things are going with you."

He obliges and picks up the bag and as they walk into her office he notices Priscilla and all of the blood on and around her desk.

"OH… MY… GOD!! WHAT … THE.…"

He didn't get to finish as Lisa jabbed him in the chest with a hypodermic kneedle and within seconds he had passed out onto the floor below.

The newspapers the following day had their leading story and that was that they had the person that had committed all of the murders by decapitation. Lisa Botomy had turned Tommy into the authorities and explained he had been a patient with some troubling history. She had lied of course not telling them about how she had hypnotized him and set him up to do the murders. She was one crazy lady.

The End

A Clowning Glory

The new elite governing power of the Earth after the 2017 election in the U.S.A. appeared to be one of a comedic show put on by exactly those that of course had the money and perceived power. For anyone with an IQ higher than the average which would suggest 75-80 at the best, would know that it had been a show for probably more than a thousand years or more. If one had ever been involved with the theatre in any aspect, they would understand why everything was happening the way it was. All one had to do was turn on the TV and witness the absolute absurdity of it all. Trevor Farnsgiggle a young and upcoming politician from California was once again swamped with paperwork and the constant annoyance of his employees always disturbing him throughout the day.

Being married with four children didn't help much. His honorary title was senior assistant to the president of the U.S.A. Assistant in the past had always meant exactly that; assisting the president in most of his day-to-day activities. Trevor however had to deal with considerably more bullshit than his predecessors.

He was fortunate in that his wife of six years was always suportive and would often give him credit for all the work he did. It was this new presidency though that had him all confused and working on things he had never before done.

His job had in the past been to assist the president in all manor of things including his personal life. The idea was to make the president look like a caring, quiet, nonconfrontational person in all aspects of his life while he was president. This was his second term doing this job, and the past president was one of the best he had ever worked with as a person first, then president second. He just assumed the new guy would be similar and his job would not be any different from the years before.

The reason his employees were constantly pestering him was because of the issues the new president kept bringing to the forefront of his term. Such as his constant Tweeting on Twitter, His watching of TV till all hours of the night, and his continual begrading of women and people of different ethnicities.

Not to mention the weird foods he liked to eat... no, demanded to eat on an almost constant basis. Trevor had his work cut out for him, and it looked as though there would be no respite in the near future. He had devised several plans for the president to follow so his constituants would consider him a man doing the best he could for his country.

Everytime he presented the president with one of these plans carefully written out and Trevor going over it in detail, the president would promptly disregarde it and continued on his present path of destruction. With the Tweeting, watching TV, eating crap food, and golfing every weekend, it was a wonder anything was being accomplished while the president was in office.

The fact that the president wanted a complete makover of the White House pushed Trevor and his staff to the limit. Organizing everyone in all of the departments that really had nothing to do with the running of the country was a full time job in itself.

"Trevor...Trevor... I need the TV program, have you seen it?"
The president says as he walks into the office where Trevor of course has to look around the stack of folders on his desk to even acknowledge him.
"I haven't seen it sir, I'll get one of the staff to get one for you."

Trevor says in the most courteous voice he can get together. He just waited for the next trivial request as he knew there would be one.
"Well make sure you do and can you have one of the lackys get me a coffee, I've got plenty to do today before I have to get to the golf course... *my* golfcourse. You do know I own golf courses don't

you Trevor? Some of the best in the world. In fact I think the best anywhere. Do you play golf Trevor? It is a great sport, one I am very good at."

The president would have kept going on about it had Trevor not got onto the phone to have one of the staff go get a coffee for the president, who now just walked into the oval office and closed the door behind him. Trevor knew it would not be long and he would hear the snoring coming from the president who would be laying on the sofa sound asleep.

It did not take long for the staff to appear with the coffee and look at Trevor who just nodded signifying that they could enter the oval office to deliver the coffee and a generous plate of cookies and cake. They had always been told not to wake the president if he was napping. They were used to this, as he was always napping first thing in the morning.

The day went by as Trevor had thought it would with him getting next to nothing of any importance done. He did have to get things organized for a trip to Europe for the president the following week. This would be more than difficult as he would also have to write up a few speeches for the president to choose from when at this very important meeting.

The end of the week came and Trevor had a bit of a break as the president was playing golf and would not need Trevor there. The president always boasted about how good he was at the game. He had told Trevor on many ocassions that he was the best as he always had the highest score. Trevor sometimes thought the president actually thought this was the way the game went.

The weekend was over and Trevor had the itineray ready for the president as they drove to the airport to board the plane and make their way to Paris for the all important meeting. Once boarded and the security had everything to their liking, the pilots were notified they could take off.

The flight started as usual; the president laying down on one of the loungers so he could get some sleep… once again. It was not long and being it was only the president and himself when the first flight attendent came in it was a shock to him. It was a clown. Full dress, makeup, big red nose, and all. Trevor was surprised to say the least. He wasn't sure if he should say anything or not.

Trevor was deathly afraid of clowns and this one did not have the happy smile across it's face as most do. This one looked creepy... very creepy. The clown approached with a tray and on it were a couple of cups of what Trevor thought to be coffee. He slowly took one off the tray and put it onto the table in front of him.

It was a moment later and another very flashy dressed clown entered the cabin. This one just as scary as the first. Trevor had no idea what he should do and thought maybe this was a test of some sort. None of it was making any sense to him. The new clown and the one with the tray stood there and just looking at Trevor. Then they looked down at the cup of coffee.

Trevor picked up the cup and took a sip. It was very good and he decided to keep holding the cup as he looked at the two clowns in front of him. After

another sip he put it down and decided to speak to the two creepy clowns.
"Very good coffee, thankyou, and what are your names?"

He thought to ask just in case they were able to, and wanted to speak. There of course was silence as all he could hear was the snoring of the president across and closer to the bathroom. It was odd to say the least. It wasn't until the third clown entered from the cockpit that Trevor started to think just maybe the plane had been hijacked and this wasn't some kind of prank being played on the president.

This clown went over to the president and bent over to shake his shoulder to wake him. It took a moment, but then he snorted and sneezed and then seated himself as he yawned and then burped.
"What the hell is going on here Trevor?"
The question was a reasonable one and of course one that Trevor would not be able to answer in any positive way.
"I have no idea president, I thought you might know."

Trevor says in a high pitched squeaky voice, he had tried for a more manly one, but being afraid as he was of clowns, it was the best he could do.

"I SAID TREVOR... WHAT THE HELL IS GOING ON HERE?"
The president was now getting himself worked up and Trevor could see just how troubled he was by the urine stain on the front of his pants. Again, Trevor did his best but knew his answer would not satisfy the presidents question.

"I don't know Mr. president, I'm as bewildered as you are."
He replies as he looks to the two clowns in front of him. At least his voice had hit a more baritone level of that closer to what a man should sound like. There was silence from the president as Trevor thought about what it was he should do.

It was only a moment later and three more creepy clowns entered into where the rest of them were from the bathroom. Trevor now had a hard time understanding where they were all coming from. He thought to make a move to where the cockpit was and talk with one of the pilots. As he looked around he re-thought this and decided to stay put and not say anything.

"Trevor... I need you to tell me what the hell is going on. Who are these clowns and why are they here?"

Questions of course on Trevor's mind as he listens to the president.

"I demand to know what is happening here, do you understand? I am the president, I am the boss of everyone and all things, I am probably the best president ever."

There was silence once again and another clown came into the group, this one however was carrying a large leather bound book in his oversized white gloved hands. He moved in between the others and towards the president where he handed the large book to him with both hands. Of course there was no expression other than the creepy frown all the clowns had painted on their faces. The president relunctantly took the large book from the clown. He then sat down with the book on his lap. The clown that had given it to him motioned the president should open it and start to go through the contents. The president looked at the clown, and then back to the large book, and then to Trevor.

"Get your fucking ass over here will you, I have no idea what the hell this is all about… maybe you do, or at least maybe you can help me figure this out."
He says not too convincingly as he makes a funny face. Something he was very good at. Trevor slowly made a move from his seat and as the clowns parted he made his way over to the president.

"You know it's not my birthday right? I can't think of another celebration close to this date to warrant such a show… can you?"
The president continues as he leafs through the pages of the large book, obviously not reading anything as he does.
"Here… sit beside me and go over this shit… I need a drink of something."

It was just then one of the clowns brings over a tray with a short glass with what looked like whisky in it. The president quickly snapped it up in his hand and gulped it down. He inferred to the clown that he get another one, and as fast as he could. He then turned to Trevor who was going through the book and trying his best to figure it out.

"Well?... what have you come up with?"
The president asked Trevor with a tone that suggested he had better come up with something and soon. All the president could do was look around at the clowns without saying anything as he too was obviuosly traumatized by the creepy looking bunch standing in front of him.

"Hey Trevor I'm talkin to you! What the hell is that book all about and what the fuck are these clowns doing here on Airforce One?"
Trevor had gone over a few pages and thought he had the jest of it.
"It appears to be a very old document about an elite group of men and how it is they run this world of ours."

The president turns from looking at the clowns down to Trevor with a puzzled look on his face.
"What the hell are you talking about? I'm the one that's in control of things... everything, and I'm

probably the best at it. What the fuck do these clowns have to do with it anyway?"
Trevor looked up at him as he spoke. He had no answer for any of it.

"I'm not entirely sure yet, I will have to go over this entire book to really understand it. From what I can get right now is, these clowns are part of an elite group of men that claim to run this world and everything that we as humans do on any given day. I think what they are trying to tell you and I is that we are just pawns in the big picture."

"Prawns!... I hate prawns... and what does that have to do with what's going on here?"
The president looked confused and pursed his lips as he was about to go into a deeper thought process.
"Pawns!, pawns... like in the game of chess."
Trevor replied with a slight tone of agravation. He should have known better, the only game he ever saw the president play was an online game for preschool children. There was no acknowledgement from the president as Trevor delved back into the book. The rest of them just stood there as the one clown returned with another drink for the president.

John P Gibson — *High Tide*

This time it was a double and it went down just as fast as the first one did. He returned the glass to the tray and put his hand up to say 'no more'.

He finally took a seat beside Trevor who was flipping through pages of the book. The president looked at his expensive golden watch.
"We've got another three hours flying in this thing, I hope you're going to talk to me about what's going on here Trevor?"
I will Mr. president, just as soon as I get a better understanding of how this all works. Why don't you read something?"

He says as he continues his flipping of the pages. The president just looks up at the clowns and figures he will start a conversation with them.
"So… what is it you weirdos want from me?"
His question was an honest one and one that Trevor had thought of asking himself; only in a more polite way.

There was silence, no response from any of the clowns as they stood their ground with their expressionless faces just staring at the president…

all of them. Apart from the soft whistling of the jet engines, it was very quiet and the president started to yawn.

He was either bored, or still tired. Regardless, he was not engaged that was for sure. Every once in a while Trevor looked up from his reading and could not believe the clowns had not moved. It was a long flight and they all had very good endurance; at least for clowns he thought to himself.

It was another hour later and Trevor had to relieve himself but thought to stick it out as he was now getting very involved with his reading of the book. The president had fallen asleep a while back and was again snoring loudly. In some ways everything that had transpired through Trevor's life started to make sense to him as he worked his way through the large book.

"Ah!... I think I have it! You guys work for the powers that be and pretty much everything we humans know is all a show for you guys... right?"
There was no response from the clowns. Not even a movement of any sort. Trevor was sure he was close

in his reasoning as to how things worked on the planet; especially the Governments and their monetary system.

He now knew that any president, prime minister, king, queen, or any perceived authority figure, was just that... a figure, a puppet, something to distract the billions of humans on the planet at any given time. All of this to entertain a few at the top.

The clowns standing in front of him were a part of the heiarchy, just a few levels below the top guns. They were right where the action was and orchestrating the show so to speak. They were not the ones you wanted to get upset. There faces told it all.

With the permanent frowns on their faces and the lack of any emotion whatsoever; Trevor believed they could be a threat if provoked. The read was becoming addictive, he could not stop, and it was some of the best he had read in years. He was now getting a better understanding of why the president was in power; at least a power he thought he had. Trevor looked over at the snoring man beside him and thought about whether or not the president knew of his position in this elaborate show. He guessed not as the president now squeeked out a fart.

Over the intercom the pilot was now speaking. It was time to take a seat and put one's seatbelt on. As these were the best pilots in the country, Trevor figured he need not have to and looking at the pudgy president beside him sleeping soundly, he left it alone.

The clowns stood their ground and did not move, not even the slightest. Once the plane had landed and of course without any problem, one of the clowns reached out for the book Trevor was still reading. He looked at the clown and knew of course to give it back. He closed the book, but not before putting a napkin in to mark the page he was still reading.

The clown did nothing but take the book and then with the rest of the clowns made their way off the plane and into a colourful van. Beside it was parked a long black limo intended of course for the president and Trevor. As he looked out the window of the plane the president started to rustle himself awake.

"Where the hell are we Trevor?"
He asked in a half awake sort of voice, but not before letting out another smelly fart.
"We've landed and the limo is waiting for us."
Trevor indicated by looking again out the window of the plane. There were about twelve tall men dressed in black wearing sunglasses and all of them had black hair standing around the limo and at the bottom of the gangplank.

"Well, we better our shit together then. I had the strangest dream ever Trevor. I dreamt about a bunch of creepy clowns on the plane with us, really freaky. Glad it was only a dream."
He says as he looks around to make sure that he was indeed dreaming. Trevor thought to leave it alone as he was sure the president would never understand if he was to try and enlighten him. The two of them gathered their belongings and made their way off the plane and into the limo. Everything now seemed normal to Trevor who desperately wanted to finish

the book the clown had presented to him on the plane. There was a lot more to this that he wanted to know about.

The president obviously did not see the white van full of clowns... that was a good thing, as it was the last thing Trevor would want to do and that would be to try and explain what it was *he* knew at this point about the clowns. The limo ride to the palace of the President of France was a busy one.

Emmanuel Macron had been newly elected and promised to be one of the better politicians the country had had in a while. Trevor now knew better. This ruler would have no more authority than his boss the president of the U.S.A. Regardless, his boss would still give a speech to many European leaders about how he would fix not only his country, but that of the world.

Once the limo arrived at the grand palace there were more of the men dressed in black waiting to escort the president and Trevor into the main foyer of the very ornate palace. The president even managed a smile as the two of them walked up the stairs and through the doors where there were more of the men in black standing to make a safe gauntlet to the main meeting room where all of the dignitaries were.

It was a casual start to the meeting with some refreshments and general conversation before the meeting was to commence. Trevor watched as the president moved around shaking hands with everone he came into contact with. Trevor was glad he wasn't shaking his hand as his method was a strange one when it came to the strange custom. He would always pull the hand of the person he was talking with closer to him and not let go.

Once the formalities were done with and everyone was seated in their appropriate spot, the talks began. It took about an hour before Trevor's boss was up for his speech, and he only hoped he would get at least most of it right. They had gone over it many times the past week and Trevor had his doubts he would get it right. Even his adlibs were questionable, but what could he do but sit and listen off towards the back of the large room.

John P Gibson *High Tide*

As the president approached the podium he waved and acknowledged the President of France and those seated close to him. He was nearly finished his speech and Trevor was quite impressed to this point that he had made no mistakes. There was a pause and then silence in the room. Trevor wondered what he was going to say next, as he had finished the speech they had rehearsed. He just waited, as everyone else did.

"And I just want to thank everone for their support and I know I will probably be the best president ever. Me being elected was a clowning glory for me and every U.S. citizen."

Trevor thought to himself, 'Little did he know.'

The End

John P Gibson

High Tide

Pool Party

Black Swan Inn; it was a favourite watering hole in a small village on Vancouver Island in Canada. A place that was about to celebrate its 40th anniversary with the locals and of course a band to play the Rock-n-Roll everyone liked. It was a couple of men walking throught the front entrance that caught the eye of another man sitting at the bar. He looked up to the men and a smile came across his face and his eyes lit up.

"Hey… Stew, John… how the hell ya doing?"

Stewart of course being the first in as it was a narrow entrance-way spoke first to the man at the bar, which just happened to be right there when one entered the bar. It took a moment to adjust to the ambiance of the bar before Stewart ansered with his standard reply.

"Hey Mark... how the hell are *you* doing?"
The reply was louder than Mark's question. It didn't matter. Being lifelong friends they didn't need to say a word to each other for the feeling to be just right.
"Good to see you guys, I see you're here for the big party today?"
"Yep... wouldn't miss it for the world. Jack was a great guy and this place was the best."

John says as the two of them look out over the floor to where the pool tables were. This was their destination. It should have been obvious as the two of them had their personal pool cues under arm and in their nice cases.
"Going to play some pool?"
Mark asks as it was obvious to him as well.

"Yeah, thought we might get a few games in before the music starts up. I always like to take money off John."

He looks to John with a smile, then back to Mark with a little laugh. It was customary that John always lost.

"Well we better get ourselves a good place to sit before this place fills up."
John says as he shakes Mark's hand as he looks out to the area where the pool tables were and noticed a couple of empty stools at a small bar along one wall next to the mens washroom door.

"Found a couple of seats Stewart, we better get em before they're taken. See you in a bit Mark."
John says as he moves down to the pool tables and where the available stools are.
"Good to see you Mark, I'll be up shortly to bullshit with you. I guess I better get John a beer before I head down. Come and have a game with us?"

Stewart half asks as it is the polite thing to do.
"Yeah, I might do that Stewart, just watching the game here for a bit first."
Mark replies as he points to a TV just at the end of the bar where a Hockey game is being played.

John P Gibson *High Tide*

Stewart looks to the TV and is not that interested as he was more into Tennis.
"Sounds good, we'll talk later then."

Stewart makes his way over to the other end of the bar to order a couple of beers before he takes his stool down by the pool tables. As Stewart made his way with the beer in hand and the pool cue under his arm, several people said hello to him as this of course was his favourite watering hole, and had been for forty years or so.

"Hey… perfect spot John, couldn't get any closer if we tried."
Stewart says as he puts the beers down on the small bartop next to one of the pool tables where John had already started to rack the balls. It was a rule that it was challenge table where-by the winner would have to play the person next in line as the quarter dictated on the edge of the pool table.

"Looks like we have the table to ourselves… doesn't appear to be anyone playing on this one."
John says to Stewart as he finishes racking the balls and returning the rack to the slot at the end of the

table. It was eight-ball, the only game played here, other than variations with the same balls. John was about to break when they heard a female voice.

"Whoa... wait a minute boys, this here is our table and you need to play by the rules. You have challenged me and my partner."
A tall slim woman with short dark hair says as she descends the stairs with her own pool cue in hand. Stewart and John look to her, and then to each other.

"No problem, we look forward to playing you, my name's Stewart. (he extends his hand for a shake) and this is my good friend John... my pool partner."
She looks over at John and they both nod to each other.

"And your name is?"
Stewart asks as he is still holding the woman's hand he was shaking.
"Gillian... pleased to meet you both."
She says in a matter-of-fact way. She came across as someone who knew her way around a pool table and probably plenty of other places as well. Stewart

let go of her hand and John made his way over to his beer.
"And your partner is?"
John asks as he takes a sip of the beer in hand.

Gillian looks around the bar and finally centers in on a blonde haired woman about the same age as Gillian staggering down the stairs towards them.
"Here she is, Trudy, I'd like you to meet our challengers… Stewart and John."
She points at the two men respectively.
"Whoa… a couple of cuties eh Gill."
Trudy says in a bit of a tippsy kind of voice as she goes over to Stewart first and then John to give them both a big hug.

She clinged a little longer to John as she gave him a wink. It was obvious she was very drunk and the boys thought this would definitely be an easy win for them.
"You a single man John?"
Her question was asked with a very sober tone to it and John had to think for a moment, 'Was this the same woman he had just met?'
"Well Trudy… I am at the moment."

He wasn't sure just how to answer the question just asked. He was looking at Stewart for some help as Stewart was just watching.

"Well boys, Trudy and I always play for money... you into that? Or are you guys not that good at the game?"
Gillian asks as she takes her own cue and starts to chalk the end as she looks to Stewart for an answer, as it was obvious John was preoccupied with Trudy for the moment. Stewart looked to John.

"Yeah... yeah of course. How much did you have in mind?"
He thought to ask just in case it was a sum out of his spending allowance for the night.
"I was thinking ten dollars a head... how does that sound to the two of you?"
She then looked to John who just nodded his head as he looked to Stewart for confirmation.

"Sounds good to us, and it is call shot right?"
Stewart thought to throw that one in as many times he had lost money due to fluke shots by his apponent. Gillian looks at Stewart and then over to

Trudy and John who were still snuggled together as she looked up to his eyes. It just might be that Trudy was not such a great shot based on her drunkeness.

"Of course, how else would we play the game. Ten dollars a head per game and I get the break as Trudy doesn't like that part."

Gillian gets herself set up for the break and it becomes obvious by the way she carries herself that she is one very good player.

She moves the cue with a swift push and the cue ball hits the rack with such a force it got the attention of everyone in the bar. Gillian looks up as the balls roll around the table and one high ball, and one low ball go into opposite corner pockets. She gave a look to Stewart and John like she had planned the shot from the start.

She had what Stewart could see was a sexy and mischievous smile work across her face.

"Ten ball in the side pocket."

She says as she chalks the cue again and takes the shot. Nearly a direct shot to the pocket which she had no problem with. Gillian continued around the table until all but one highball were left. The fourteen sat very close to a centre pocket. It was obvious on two counts.

The boys would be low ball, and Gillian was a superb pool player.
"Who's taking second shot? You Stewart? Or John over there?"
John was still holding onto Trudy as she was having difficulty in standing on her own, he gave Stewart the look that said 'You take the next shot Stewart… I'm kinda busy.'

Stewart picked up on the clue and took his cue and started to chalk it. He knew he would have to get at least a few balls down if they were to ever have a chance at winning the game. He did just that. Five balls later and there were a total of four balls left including the eight ball. It was Trudy's shot and Gillian would need to help her.

She came over and started to talk with her while she nestled into John's chest while wrapping her arms around his waist. It would be a struggle to get Trudy in any kind of shape to take a shot, let alone sink the only high ball left before shooting at the eight ball. The boys only chance was for Trudy to really screw her shot up.

Her awkward stance over the table and the way she held the cue suggested she would not only miss the shot, but would more than likely fall to the floor during, or after the attempt. One thing was for sure, she had experience at being drunk as for the time it took her to take the first shot she had adjusted herself several times.

Trudy managed the shot with of course a loud screech from her as the ball went down and she, believe it or not, had shape on the eight ball into the corner pocket.
"Great shot Trudy… brilliant."
Gillian says as she moves closer to Trudy as it looked like she was going to fall to the floor. She managed however to regroup for her next shot.

It was much like the first shot, many movements to line the shot up and trying to figure out how to stand and make the shot she was calling. John just looked at Stewart as they both shrugged their shoulders. Trudy finally made the shot and the eight ball rolled into the corner pocket with ease. It was against all odds the boys thought as they both reached into their pockets for the cash.

The two girls were jumping around and Gillian more than anything was trying her best to keep Trudy from falling into other tables and knocking over drinks.
"Well boys, looks like the girls are the winners this time. Care to challenge us again... double or nothing?"

The confidence in her voice made John just a little sceptical as Stewart was right there with an answer.
"You bet, right John? You do want a shot don't you?"
Trying to rub it in that he did not get one during the entire game.
"You can shoot after the break, how about that?"
Stewart continues as he makes his way to put the money in the slot to get the balls so he can rack them.
"Yeah... OK, it was just luck on Trudy's part I'm sure."

He said off to the side so as Trudy or Gillian would not hear. John then reached into his pocket and gave Stewart a twenty.

"Better get us a couple more beer... I think it's going to be one of those nights."
John says as he reaches in and starts to bring the balls up to rack them.
"Sounds good, I'm sure it was all luck John we should be able to win at least a few games, afterall we have been playing for more than forty years."

Stewart smiles as he turns and makes his way to the bar to get a couple more beer. John finishes the rack and Gillian is chalking her cue. It was obvious she was to be the one making the break again. She got herself into position and took the shot. It was another hard one and the balls went everywhere on the table.

None had gone down but the eight ball was moving ever so slowly to a corner pocket. All John could do was stand there with the rack in hand and watch the eight ball drop into the pocket ever so slowly. It was the only ball that went down and that signified another win for the girls. They both started to jump up and down and yelling and screaming in jubilation.

Stewart returned with a couple of beer and of course picked up on what had happened. He took a slug of his beer, passed the other one to John who did the same.
"Well it's going to be one of those nights eh John?"
Stewart says as he gets some coins from his pocket to rack the balls again. They were now both down twenty dollars each to the girls.

"Well boys are you into another game, say double or nothing again?"
Gillian looked to the two of them standing watching Trudy roll around on the floor in excitement over the win. She then staggered up and knocked over a couple of drinks on a table of a young couple enjoying the show. She appologized and then gave the male a big hug and kiss. The man just shrugged his shoulders and waited for the waitress to come on down and clean up the mess. Trudy then made her way over to John and hugged him as she looked up to him with lips persed and ready for a kiss. John

just smiled and held off as he put his beer on the bar top so he could help steady her. He then looked to Stewart and nodded his head.

"Sure Gillian, we'll challenge you again, double or nothing."
Stewart answers as he calculates the amount in his head should they lose again. Forty dollars each. The pot was getting larger that was for sure. Stewart plugged the coins in to get the balls and racked them as Gillian was again chalking her cue. It was obvious Trudy was never going to break.

He thought about suggesting a new rule that they alternate breaks, then thought about it again as Gillian would surely make it confusing, so he just left the thought alone. He finished racking the balls and Gillian got her self ready. Stewart looked over to John and pointed suggesting he take the second shot. It was only fair as John had not had one shot yet in the two games played.

He shook his head letting Stewart know that to get Trudy away from him might be a bit of a challenge and with her shooting after stewart would make it easier for her to negotiate the walk to the table and take her shot. Stewart agreed with a nod of his head in return.

Gillian made the break and one low ball went down in a side pocket. She then took down three more low balls before finally missing a shot. She looked up and Stewart was chalking his cue and looking over the table. He saw a fairly straight forward shot on one of the high balls to the side pocket. He took it. It went down with ease.

Stewart continued around the table getting most of the balls down except for one before getting to the eight ball. He looked to John who was still holding Trudy up.
"Hey Trudy... Trudy... Hey it's your shot."
John says in a voice with some volume so as to get her attention. She finally gets her shit together and looks around for her cue. Gillian had it and chalked it for her.

"We're low ball Trudy... you OK to shoot?"
Trudy looks at Gillian like she is some sort of Alien and then the table, and then her cue which Gillian

passed to her. Trudy took the cue and looked over the table. There was a rather simple shot to a side pocket.

She called the shot and it went down without any problem. But not before Trudy had fallen to the floor twice, almost landing on her cue.
"Great shot Trudy!"
Gillian says as Trudy gets up from the floor with the help from John. She looks the table over and sees another potential shot. After several minutes of her finding a comfortable stance, she takes the shot.

This time John thought for sure he would get a shot as Trudy had no shape and would more than likely miss or scratch the cue ball.
"That five ball… in… the corner… off two rails."
Trudy says in a drunken voice as she struggles with the chalk trying to get it on the end of her cue.

Both Stewart and John look to each other thinking that this is an impossible shot, but it is the only choice if she was to sink it. Gillian kept quiet as she smiled at Stewart and John. Trudy finally gets lined up for the shot and takes it. The cue ball hit the five and it moved to one rail, then to the end rail and back up to fall into the side pocket. There was silence.

Everyone seated close to the pool tables including the waitress cleaning up the mess Trudy had made earlier, all looked on in disbelief. Especially Stewart and John. It was now a straight in shot on the eightball to the corner, which Trudy called but only after slobering all over her cue. Again after a long wait for her to get herself just right at the table, Trudy made the shot and the eight ball fell into the pocket. The girls had won another game.

There was a loud cheer and applause from the spectators now getting quite enthralled with the game. Gillian and Trudy hugged, and then Trudy quickly made her way over to John and gave him a big hug.

"Well boys, looks like someone is watching over us girls. We'll understand if you want to quit and let someone else play."
She said this in a snyde way as to get the boys worked up. Stewart and John both shrugged their

shoulders again. They had to play at least until they broke even. A strategy a friend of theirs always used.

The night wore on and the band started to play 'The Smiley Brothers' A local band that was popular and very good. Rock-n-Roll of course being their forte'. The bar was now packed and not only were the girls cleaning up on the boys at pool, but any remaining space was used as a dance floor. The Black Swan was over flowing and the mood was a good one.

Except of course for Stewart and John who had not won a game all night and believe it or not John had not got one shot in. It was just the luck of the draw as the saying goes. Trudy had now had a few more drinks and was even more drunk than earlier; if that was even possible. Both John and Stewart had said on more than one occasion.

It was now nearing closing time and the boys owed the girls more than a thousand dollars each. John was determined to get at least one shot in as Stewart and he both agreed to one more game. It would mean breaking even, that is if they won, or, paying the girls more than two thousand dollars each for their brilliant playing of the game.

The girls of course accepted the challenge and again it was Gillian who would break. She chalked her cue as she looked to Stewart and John and gave them both a wink. The break of course was a loud and strong one with a couple of balls going into pockets; one a high ball and the other a low.

It was at this moment that Trudy in a loud voice ordered a round of Tequila shots for the bar. The cheers went up and the game was stalled for a moment. The waitress looked down at Trudy who was still stumbling about and acknowledged her order as she did a head count in the bar.

Gillian made her next shot and missed her called ball in the side pocket. It was still open table and Stewart got up to take his shot. With an intense concentration he managed to sink all of the reamaining high balls and was now on the eight ball. The cheers went up and John thought for sure they would win the game, even though he had not taken one shot throughout the night. Before he shot the waitress came around with the shots of Tequila for everyone including the band of course.

"Everyone... body... people at the Swan... cheers to... the anniversary of... the Black... Swan..."
Trudy says with a wavering hand holding up her shot of Tequila, all the others followed suit and everyone knocked back their shot. Stewart went back to his shot on the eight ball. It was a tense moment for everyone. He made his shot and the cue ball hits the eight which slowly moves towards the corner pocket. It slows, and stops just before the pocket.

There is a collective groan from the audience as Stewart rattles off a few curse words with John doing the same. It was now Trudy's turn and as she put the shot glass down on the bar top it fell to the floor and smashed into a hundred pieces. She then got her cue... lined up for her shot... and missed by a longshot. Everyone now looked to John, he was actually going to get a shot. Only fair he thought as it could cost him thousands. He took his cue and chalked it and then stood at the table to make his shot. It would be easy as it was a straight in shot and close to the corner pocket. He crouched down and looked along his cue. He then looked up to see Trudy at the corner he was about to shoot the ball into with her leg up over the edge of the table and caressing her boobs and blowing kisses to John while she winked at him and moaned out his name. He tried to ignore the distraction and made the shot with meticulous determination. It was a dead on shot and the eight ball went down with the cue ball rattling around just enough to follow it in. A scratch on the eight ball. The boys lost the game and now had to pull out the credit cards to get cash for the ladies.

The End

John P Gibson

High Tide

John P Gibson

High Tide

Cab Fare

Bubba made his final check as he circled the car. He could hear his radio crackling on the dash of the late model taxi. It was a ritualistic habit he had before any long trip he was about to take. Being a veteran of the trade he had been doing this for more than twenty years. Being one of the better drivers with the company he was part owner of had it's advantages. Such as being able to take some of the better fares that had been booked sometimes weeks in advance. His pick-up would be in about thirty minutes at the Hilton just out of the town center. The trip would take him and his fare from Whistler to New York city. It was to date the longest fare anyone in the company had had. There was a trip

John P Gibson   *High Tide*

years ago about seven hundred miles taking the lead in the 'Little River Band' and his manager to another ski resort by the name of 'Big White'.

This trip was a complete mystery not only to Bubba, but all of the other drivers as well. It would take no less than a week to make the trip and the client had an itinerary that was massive. Many stops along the way would make it a very exceptional adventure for him.

His pickup was for ten PM, it would be dark as it was October and the weather forecast was for possible snow flurries; not unusual for this ski resort this time of year. He would drive to the front of the hotel and make his way to the front desk to let them know he was there to pick up a Mr. White.

Bubba has dressed better than he usually did, even wearing a tie which he never did. He figured this was a celebrity of some sort and he had even paid for the entire trip in advance. There would only be a tip which Bubba figured should be substantial considering the distance traveled. There would not be any meter used as the client requested it among other things Bubba would have to adhere to over the course of the week or so they were together. Bubba had never been to New York.

As he drove up to the front doors there was of course someone there to open the door for his client who happened to be outside of the hotel already. It was cold and Bubba wondered why he would choose to stand outside. The man he assumed was Mr. White had a large expensive winter coat on and a large hat covering his head and face.

He only had the one bag, and it was a small at that. He stopped and thought he might as well let the doorman do his job for his tip so he stayed in the cab where it was warm. The door was opened and Mr. White put himself in on the passenger side rear seat. This would allow for the best position for conversation and being able to see Mr. White in the rear view mirror.

"Good evening Mr. White, and how are you this fine evening?"
Bubba was putting on the charm, always a good idea when it came to long trips and of course

possibly large gratuities. He waited patiently for a response before putting the car in gear and making his way to the main highway.

"Good evening to you Bubba, and I am fine."
The answer was short and sweet and Bubba wondered how the man knew his name. Then of course it was obvious; his identity card was hanging just below the rear view mirror.

"Well it should be quite the adventure Mr. White as I've never been to New York city; and you?"
Bubba looks in his miror to get an idea what this Mr. White looked like, he had not taken his hat off yet and he would soon lose the light from the main street once they got onto the highway.

There was no answer and Bubba figured just maybe this man was not a chatterbox and maybe did not like conversation. If this was so it would be a very long trip indeed. He would let it go for the time being and get on with his driving. He had a pretty good idea of his route, and if anything should go astray, he always had his back up; the GPS system on his dashboard. He would however ask the man if there was anything he needed and was he warm enough even though Bubba had the heater turned right up. It was very cold outside and snow was starting to fall.

"If there is anything you need, or if you are too cold, or too warm, don't hesitate to ask. That's what I'm here for."
Bubba used his soft and amiable voice, not like the one he often used when certain drunks were in his taxi. There was still no response from the man in the back seat. This seemed just a little strange to Bubba, but would hold off until the man spoke to him.

It took nearly two hours as they were now coming into Vancouver to make the move across the border and into the U.S.A.
"Pull into this Hotel Bubba will you please."
The voice from the back seat broke the silence, Bubba had even elected not to have the radio on or any music playing.

"Are you sure Mr. White, it's not on the itinerary."
"Yes I'm sure, the Hotel Vancouver, I hear it's a nice place to stay when one is in Vancouver."

Bubba turned the cab into the front entrance to the posh hotel and stopped in front where a doorman came over to the car and opened the rear door.

"Don't worry Bubba, park the cab and come in to the front desk. I'll get you a room for the night. It will be a long day tomorrow."

Bubba turned to look at Mr. White who now had his hat pulled down low and his jacket collar wrapped around his face to keep warm.

"No problem Mr. White, I'll see you in a few minutes."

Bubba drove to a secure parking area below the hotel where he secured the cab and retrieved his small overnight bag he had all of his things packed into. It seemed strange to him that Mr. White wanted to stay here in Vancouver as they had a long drive across country and there were no less than six hotels where they were booked into.

It was of no real concern for Bubba, as this way at least he would get more rest and possibly a chance to get to know this Mr. White some, as they would be in close proximity for a week or more. He parked the cab with some help from some of the staff of the hotel, and then made his way to the front desk to check in.

As he approached the large and wooden desk he could see several staff working but no Mr. White. Bubba went to the first attendant he saw. Her nametag said her name was Julie.
"Hi Julie, how are you tonight"
"Just fine sir and how may I help you?"
"A Mr. White just checked in and I am his personal driver, Bubba."

He figured that should be enough as she looked through some papers in front of her. She paused, looked up at him as Bubba was a tall and strong built man with handsome features. She smiled at him as she continued her investigation with the paperwork.

"Ah yes… here we go, Bubba Faret… that is correct?"
She asks as Bubba just smiles back at her.
"Yes it is Julie."

John P Gibson High Tide

He left it at that and waited for her to punch in a few things on her computer in front of her. She then retrieved a plastic card from a drawer in front of her. She swiped this card through a machine on the counter and then passed it to Bubba.

"Here you go Mr. Faret, please enjoy your stay, you are in room number 735. We can have one of our staff help you with your baggage."
"That won't be necessary, I just have this little guy with me."
Bubba says as he shows the bag to her and takes the card from her. She smiles back at him as he moves to the elevators off to the end of the large foyer.

Once in his room he looked around and could see it was one of the better ones. All Bubba could think was that this man Mr. White must be fairly well off to afford such a place. Why was he taking a taxi across country when he could probably take a private jet?

This got Bubba thinking far too much, it would be better for him to get some sleep for the long drive the following day. As he got ready to lay down on the large kingsize bed he thought this could surely be the life for him. Now he wondered what it was Mr. White did for a living.

The phone next to the bed started to buzz ever so softly as Bubba got his mind together to remember where he was, and what he was supposed to be doing. Oh yeah, Mr. White and the cross country trek over the nexk week or so.

"Hello..."
He answered in a bit of a groggy state. He shouldn't have been as he didn't remember going to the lounge and having a few. It was the front desk calling.
"Yes, yes... I'll be down in a few minutes... what time is it?"
He thought to ask even though there was a clock next to the bed; he wasn't sure it was the right time though as it said 4:00 AM on the screen.

The girl at the front desk confirmed the time and he hung up the phone and hustled his ass into the lavish bathroom that had two toilets and a bidet. He would not have time for a shower or the rest of the morning rituals he was used to. A quick brush of the teeth with the complimentary tooth brush and paste, brush the hair, get dressed and get on down to the lobby.

Why Mr. White had wanted such an early start was a mystery to him as he rode the elevator down to the main lobby. As Bubba exited the elevator he looked over to the reception area in front of the desk. There was no one there. He looked out the front doors and could see his taxi parked in front and running as the lights were on and exhaust coming from the rear.

He now remembered he had left his keys with the concierge the night before when they had arrived. It appeared Mr. White was already in the car and in the back seat where he was the night before. Bubba now picked up his pace and went to the cab where the concierge was waiting and now holding the drivers door open for him.

"Thank you… thank you…"
Bubba says as he reaches into his pocket to take out a tenner to tip the man. He accepted graciousley as he then closed the door to the cab and gave a small

salute of his hand to his fancy cap. Bubba gave it a moment as he placed his bag on the floor on the passenger side of the car.

"Good morning Mr. White, I hope you are OK?"
Bubba was going to ask him why such an early start, but thought twice about it and because of the large gratuity he expected, kept his mouth shut.
"I am doing fine and I must appologize for the early start today. I have been told I need to attend a meeting sooner than I thought."

This answered the question Bubba had foremost on his mind. Now of course other questions arose. Like… again why did he not fly to his destination? Why not change his travel plans to suit the urgency of this meeting? These were a couple that came to mind and he was sure there would be more as they traveled closer to New York.

"No problem, I'm used to it in this line of work."
Bubba hoped for a response so they could engage in conversation to make the time go quicker. This was one of the better attributes to have as a professional driver. The gift of the gab as his mother always used

to say to him when growing up as a child. It was fortuitous that he got into the taxi business, and it had done him well over the years.

There was quiet once again as he drove the selected route he had chosen several days earlier. It would involve driving pretty much across Canada and then across the border and down to New York city. It would be nice however if Mr. White would at least make some kind of noise. He had to be the quietest man Bubba had ever had in his cab.

As he drove further East the early morning light started to bring everything to life. Bubba was sure now he would see who it was in the back seat of his taxi. The man could not wear the hat and jacket for the entire trip as the interior of the taxi was increasing in temperature; even Bubba was starting to sweat just a little.

It took a couple of hours longer and Bubba could not resist looking in his rear view mirror every opportunity he had. Mr. White noticed this and slowly took his jacket off and then removed his hat. Bubba almost ran the taxi into the opposite lane as he looked at the man in his cab. It wasn't a normal man that was for sure. It was a clown. A very creepy one at that.

Bubba had an aversion to clowns. He had had one ever since he was a young boy. What he was seeing now had to be the most scary thing he had ever seen in his entire life.
"It's OK Bubba, I won't harm you in any way. I will however do my best to explain to you about who it is I am."

Mr. White says in a very controlled and calm voice. This was still not enough for Bubba, as he had to pull the taxi over to the side of the road and stop. His hand was on the door latch and he was ready to make an escape should he need to.
"I understand Bubba how it is you might feel, but be assured I will not harm you, and for that matter no one will now that you know me."

Bubba tried to digest the information, he was beginning to shake and thought his best plan would be to stay put. Somehow he believed Mr. White would not harm him as long as he did his best to stay calm and collected. He looked again into the rear view mirror and analyzed the face of the clown behind him.

It had the standard white with large red eyebrows and of course a large round red nose. The painted on smile was exactly the opposite, a very scary looking frown in a blueish colour. Around his eyes the same blueish color formed to look like tears coming down onto his cheeks. The roundness of his red coloured hair finished it off.

"I will say this Bubba, I do have to get to this meeting on time and of course I will now explain about myself on our journey; but you must get back on the road and continue driving... is that understood?"

Bubba looked at the clown in the mirror and with hesitation nodded his head. He then signaled and started to get back onto the freeway and brought the taxi up to speed. He kept quiet as he kept looking into the mirror waiting for this Mr. White clown guy to start filling him in on what was taking place. He now wished he had turned down the offer to take

Mr. White across the country. It was too late now and he only hoped he would escape with his life. God how he hated clowns.

"I would assume you would be wondering why a person would spend all of this money on a taxi to get across the country when a plane ride would be so much more efficient. I can assure you Bubba if I was to walk into any airport dressed like I am I would be taken into custody by the authorities."

One question answered; now Bubba had plenty more, but he was apprehensive about asking this man anything. He would just wait for him to elaborate some more as they drove along the freeway.

"I would think you are wondering what I am doing dressed the way I am? Well for starters it is the way I dress all of the time, you might like to think of it as my uniform."

Bubba listened and wondered what possible business other than the circus would require him to dress the way he did. He was pretty sure this man was not part of any circus as the pay would be very low and for him to travel this way he would have to earn considerably more. No, there was something more to this story. He was about to find out.

"I am a member of a very select number of men on this planet. We have a very strict guidline as to how we operate, and what our long term goals are. I am telling you this Bubba because you my friend have been chosen to be a part of our brotherhood."

When Bubba heard this he again had to pull over to the shoulder of the road and stop the car. Mr. White adjusted himself after the sudden stop.
"I can only hope Bubba that you will start to understand and trust me so that we do not have to stop everytime I talk to you."
There was some concern in his voice this time and Bubba knew he would have to pay attention.

"I cannot divulge the information yet as to why you were chosen, but let me be very honest with you… it is one of the biggest honours that can be given to anyone. You must trust me on this one thing Bubba."

Bubba just sat there wondering how he should respond and even if he should. What the hell was this group of clowns all about?

"Now if you would please get back onto the highway so we can continue our journey."
Bubba slowly started out onto the freeway once again. He would pay more attention to what was being said and try to fathom what this was all about. He figured he had no choice in the matter anyway.

What scared him most was the fact that he would be a part of a group of clowns… the one thing that scared him more even than death itself.
"This chapter of the elite that you will become a part of will be something that you will not be able to tell anyone; you are now as of this moment sworn to secrecy… do you understand Bubba?"

Bubba looked into his rear view mirror and watched the man talk… he nodded his head as he wasn't sure about any of this and did not want to answer verbally. There were a million questions running through his brain at the moment and just wished that this were all a bad dream and he would wake up in his nice king size bed at the Hotel Vancouver and continue on his journey that he had imagined in his head a couple of days prior.

"I know this is a lot for one to digest at the moment, but when we arrive in New York and you are conscripted into the group, you will start to understand what it is we are all about."
Again Bubba felt a strange and creepy feeling taking over him. He doubted at any point he would understand what this was all about and what he wanted was to turn the car around and head home.

"Once you are in with us Bubba you will have virtually free reign over a multitude of things. Money will become no object; your wants and needs will be taken care of at any time or place; your duties within the group will be marginal, and when your term is expired, your name will go down in history."

Bubba was now sweating up a storm and adjusted the temperature controls to help cool him down. It wasn't working. There was still a week of driving with this man and now he wished for something else as the quiet he had first experienced now seemed a luxury. In his mind he could not comprehend what the hell would happen to him once in New York city.

"You will have to sever all your ties with family and friends, and the only ones from here on in you will socialize with will be the members of our group."
Bubba now cranked the window down slightly to get some fresh air into the car so he could breath normally.

"I do have one question for you Mr. White, it is an important one to me. If I am to be a part of your group... would I have to wear a clown costume like the one you are wearing?"
Bubba asked hoping of course the answer would be no. His fear of clowns was so much a part of him there would be no way he could even get close to one let alone dress like one.

"Of course you would have to Bubba, it wouldn't be exactly the same unifrom as mine, as we would tailor one to suit you. One thing is for sure is you will look very grand and reagal in your new outfit. I have already seen photos of it and I must say I am rather jealous if just a little, and ….."

That was all Mr. White had time to say as Bubba took a drastic move and turned the speeding taxi across the lane and through a barrier and over a cliff. The deaths were instant the police report stated and the reason for the aciident was unclear. The body of Mr. White was however taken away very discreetly.

The End

John P Gibson *High Tide*

The Rail Story

A nice long walk, thought Bill. It was always on his list of things to do on any given day. This one was clear and sunny and very warm. Perfect for a long stroll. Bill lived in a small town near the south end of Vancouver Island called Duncan. It had over the years gone through some very major changes; especially in the population side. Bill had been born and raised in this town. It had its character and charm, especially years ago. Now it seemed to be over run with cars, trucks, motor cycles, and far too many people. At least this is what Bill thought these days as he lived right down town, and the noise of the traffic all day long was a real negative for him. There were sirens every day, either firetrucks or the police. Now with the summer weather and having the windows open, the noise reverberated throughout the house.

His best defense for the hustle and bustle was to go for a walk along the tracks. They ran right through the middle of the town and for years now had been dormant. Trains did not use them anymore. It was a shame, as the system ran at least halfway up the island and all the way to Victoria at the South end.

It was just after lunch and Bill got his things together to go for his walk along the tracks as they were close to his house and most days he would be able to walk in near silence. He would wear his ball cap as the sun was a warm one this day, and he would bring along a snack if he needed. There were plenty of places to stop along the way for anything one wanted; especially meals as there were plenty of restaurants as well.

Being in his sixties and retired and single, Bill could enjoy his days almost anyway he wanted to. He had no hobbies to speak of except his walking, which was fine by him. He would always get a good nights sleep after his long walks and he liked to think they kept him in pretty good shape for his age. At least his friends said he looked good for his age.

Front door locked, checked his mail, made sure his keys were in his pocket, and also that he had enough cash for anything that might arise through the afternoon requiring it. Off he went, his best hiking shoes on and what seemed a perfect day.

It was about a five minute walk from his place to the tracks. At that point he would make a decision on which way to travel. North or south? Always a question he had a hard time answering to himself. This day he chose to walk South. In this direction it would take him across the Cowichan river via the train trestle. It offered better views, especially of the river.

It wasn't long and Bill was getting close to the trestle and he saw what he thought to be a large plastic garbage bag laying across the tracks just before going across the river. He thought this strange as why would anyone take the time and trouble to walk that far with their garbage? He walked along the tracks and as he got closer he could see that it wasn't a garbage bag afterall. It was a man. The closer he got his mind started to think.

'What if this was a dead body?' He certainly hoped not as he hadn't brought his cell phone along. It was a man, an aboriginal man probably in his forties laying across the tracks and snoring away in bliss and oblivious to any sounds other than his loud snoring, which obviously he was used to.

Bill stopped and thought for a moment whether or not he should wake the man, or just leave him be, sleeping in the awkward position across the rails. He chose the latter and being a nice warm day the man would be fine where he was. Bill kept walking South.

It was about an hour or so later and Bill thought about leaving the rail system and going over to the Red Arrow Brewery just across the highway for a beer and some lunch. He knew he would get a good beer and good food in a nice outside setting. With any luck he might be able to listen to some music by

John P Gibson

High Tide

a local musician named Chuck. He played the banjo and like most musicians also liked beer.

It was his lucky day, Chuck was there entertaining a few tables of people eating and having a few drinks while he played his music. Bill spent about two hours having his lunch and maybe just a few beer. He then said his good-byes to staff and Chuck, and then started his walk back home along the rails.

The weather was the same, sunny and hot and peacefull as he walked the rusting rails back to town. It often made Bill wonder why the powers that be did not promote a way for a small transit system to utilize the rails to transport locals and tourists from one end of the town to the other. For a small fee, and an artistic form of locomotive, the community would surely have benefited.

As he walked the rails he was coming up on the river and of course the trestle across it. He looked to the other side and he could see the man he had seen when he had walked over the bridge earlier was still there. Laying in the same position and he assumed snoring loudly. As he approached the man he indeed was snoring and in the same position as before. Bill stopped and leaned down to tap the man on the shoulder.

It took a few taps and then he woke up and looked at Bill. His look was one of compassion and curiosity. He smiled up at Bill. Bill looked at the man and smiled back and then thought to ask some questions.
"Hi… how are you? Is everything OK? I was just walking by and could not help but notice you sleeping here on the rails."

The man looked up at Bill and continued to smile. He then started to sit upright before speaking.
"Yes… I am OK, and how are you?"
The man asks back. Bill strains to look closely at the man to make sure he looks OK before he responds.
"I am fine, just wanted to make sure you were OK."

Bill now thinks maybe he should just keep on walking and ignore the man now that he knew he was not dead.

John P Gibson *High Tide*

"Oh I'm just fine… taking a little sleep while the weather is good… waiting for some of my friends to come by for a story telling afternoon."

Bill just looks at the man and wonders what it is he should do next. He had no plans for the rest of the day, so there was nothing to make him have to continue his journey along the rails; at least not at this immediate moment.

"Ah… yes… story telling."
Bill replied and thought to himself about how he had heard something about the local aboriginals and the fact that story telling was a big part of their culture. He continued looking at the man who smiled back at Bill.

"Yes my friend… story telling. They should be here soon."
The man looks around and at that moment Bill can hear some noise off in the distance. He looks over the man's shoulder and sees several men approaching them from a trail alongside the river. The man then turns back to Bill and smiles once again to infere that he was correct in his assumption.

The men continued to make their way towards the two of them on the rails close to the trestle. Bill thought maybe he should leave, then thought just maybe this might be a good diversion for the day.

"My name is George... George Tall Tree... what is your name my friend?"
The man asks as he now sits up straight on the rail and extends a hand for a shake. Bill reciprocates and extends his as the two of them shake.
"My name's Bill... Bill Taylor, pleased to meet you George Tall Tree."

Bill smiles, and for some reason feels very comfortable as the three men coming towards them had now walked up the bank and stood around George. He finally stood and greeted who were obviously his friends.
"Charlie, Bobby, Eddy... how are you guys anyways?"
He asked as he took his hand away from Bill and shook each mans hand in turn. They all responded with a smile and some casual non specific chatter as they all started to laugh. Charlie and Bobby put down a couple of two-four packs of Lucky beer at

their feet and looked to Bill. George now turned the attention to Bill who now extended his hand to shake the newcomers hands.

"My friends this is Bill… my new friend today, he has come to tell us a story."
The hands are shaken and Bill now thinks about what it was that George had just said to his friends. 'Tell them a story'. Bill was at best confused but said nothing and waited for George's lead.

"Take a seat my friend."
George says to Bill as he gestures with his hand to sit down on the rail behind him. Bill looked behind him and thought this was going to be one uncomfortable afternoon. He took a seat as he was out-numbered and his curiosity was hounding him to stay and find out what these men would do from this point on.

Bill seats himself as do the others beside him and across from him on the other rail. Bill thought what a great thing no trains were using these tracks. There was a moment of silence as everyone looked at each other then Eddy reaches beside him and starts to pull a beer from the box he had brought with him. He then looks up to the others, smiles, and then starts to pull more of them to hand out to everyone.

"Bill… here… take a beer man."
Eddy says as he passes one of the beers to Bill. Bill knew he had no chance in saying no to the man and accepted the beer. Once everyone had a beer in hand George puts his up in the air and says something in a native tongue Bill was not familiar with. He rose his beer into the air anyway and smiled.

"To our new friend Bill, we cannot wait for your story man."
George says as he opens his beer and takes a sip from the can. Bill did the same and wondered what George meant by him telling a story. He had to question it.

"What do you mean my story George? I don't understand."
All the men look at Bill as if he is some kind of idiot. It should have seemed obvious, but then Bill was a white man. There were many things the white man did not know about the Indigenous people of the

Cowichan Valley. They continued to look at him as he took another drink of his beer and thought for a moment.

A story did come to mind, one he thought these men would appreciate and it shouldn't take too long to tell it, that is if he could remember all of the details. The men continued to look at Bill as they drank their beers, there was no rush as they smiled and waited for Bill to start.

"Well… it all started in the harbour of Victoria. I was in my early twenties and had been hired on to help a friend get his fishing boat ready for the summer season. It was a gill netter, about twenty feet long and one of the older ones as it had a wooden hull. Once we got it sea worthy we left the harbour to motor on up to Bamfield where we would fish for the opening in a couple of days time."

Bill had their attention, all the men were looking at him and waiting for more of the story. It had been a while and Bill wanted to get all the details right if he was to impress these natives in at least a small way. He figured the fishing part would make it a story they would like as fishing was a big part of the history of the local natives here in the Cowichan valley. He continued.

"It was a calm, sunny, and warm day, not unlike today. The boat was in good shape and the captain had decided to head up the Island with two other boats with a single crew member on each of them. I of course being the greenhorn of the bunch. It was my first time out fishing; that is, commercial fishing."

"The plan was to get as far as Port Alberni and spend the rest of the day and night fine tuning the boats for the week ahead. My duties on board when not actively fishing were to cook meals for the two of us and of course do the cleaning as necessary. If the Captain needed, I would help with the nets and storing of the freshly caught salmon."

It was now time for George to pass around another beer for everyone as the audience had finished theirs but were not prepared to interupt Bill and his story. George picked up on this and made the move to make sure everyone was sufficiently suffuncified with their beverages. Being a hot day the beer went down very nicely and with the beer Bill had earlier, he was beginning to feel the affects of the alcohol.

"The weather started to pick up as it often does on the West coast of the island. They started out as long rolling waves that were of no concern to us, but as we made our way up and along the coast they started to get larger and closer together. The Captain had done some investigation on the weather before we left and told us that there could be a storm brewing."

"We would make Port Alberni by mid afternoon and because of the likelyhood of the storm increasing in velocity, we would spend the night there which would give us time to do any maintainance necessary to continue out journey. Once in the seclusion of the bay, we anchored and then settled in for the storm."

There was still no sounds coming from the men and of course the empty beers were replaced with full ones by George. Everyone seemed content and Bill was now understanding a little more about the culture of the locals that had been in this valley for thousands of years before the white man showed his face.

"I was preparing the dinner for the night and the two other skippers were invited. It was early as we all wanted to get some sleep before the busy day following. We all had a couple of beers and then told some stories about the ocean, fishing, and sexy women. It was about six oclock in the evening and a Troller was making its way into the secluded bay."

"My Captain started to talk with one of the deckhands as they passed us about the storm. The man said we should have no problem. It was then decided we would make a go for Bamfield so we could get an early start the next day when the opening started."

"It did not take long and we were out in the thick of the storm. We had all agreed to stay close, but not too close as to cause any problems. It would be death if any one of our boats collided with another. I was up front with Captain as he steered the boat in between and over some very large waves. I was beginning to feel a little seasick as I thought the couple of beer I had had earlier certainly did not help any."

"As the sun went down and the darkness set in the storm only got worse. I had to get myself out onto the deck to get some fresh air. I sat on the cover of the hold and held on best I could so as not to fall into the sea below. The Captain came out to check on me and also to get into the hold to get some milk to drink."

"He offered some to me as he took a big gulp of it from the container. I refused and promptly leaned over the boat and puked my guts out into the frothing sea below. I was truly seasick and of absolutely no use to the Captain should there be any trouble. He had told me that the other two had put their boats into autopilot and went below to lay down and hopefully go to sleep. They were also seasick."

There was a pause as Bill took the last sip of his beer, the others were being polite enough to wait until Bill got another beer before they did. Bill had them captivated with his story and even he was impressed with how he was telling these men about something that truly did happen to him.

"The Captain had said to me that if I too could get below, lay down, and go to sleep, the sickness would go away. I went to the open doorway and stopped as my head again started to spin and my stomach needed to get rid of whatever I had left from the previous meal."

"There was nothing left, it was dry heaves all the way. I had never been this sick in all my life and now with the halucinations I was having, I couldn't care less if I had been washed overboard. The Captain however was just fine as he repeatedly came out to go through the hold to find things to eat and drink."

"This of course only made me feel sicker and all I wanted was a quick death to relieve me of all the torment I was going through. The journey continued in the same fashion until we rounded the point and came into the bay at Bamfield. It was like magic. Within a short time I was feeling almost normal and the two other boats and their Captains had made it with no problems other than being seasick like I was."

"The end of the story was that we managed to get ourselves out and placing the nets for the opening and in the forty-eight hours we had, we only came back to bay with five salmon. The fact that we had one of the worst openings of the Captains career was of course the priority, the other was that he would not be able to pay me because the costs outweighed the revenue. I would never go commercial fishing again."

The men looked at Bill as he finished with his story, they all sort of bowed and said things in their native tongue that Bill did not understand, and then George offered everyone another beer.

It was now time for one of the others to tell a story and it was about a lake where the spirits manefested in an evil way at the bottom of it and released large green coloured bubbles to the surface; big enough to flip a fair sized boat over. It was a place called Nit Nat. Another of the stories was about a breed of bears further up north on the coast called the Spirit Bear. They were all white in colour and were not Polar bears.

There were stories about Eagles, Grizzly bears, Salmon of course and also about how the spirits guided not only the people, but all other animals as well. The whole idea was to be at one with nature and to take care of each other. Something that had been lost once the Whiteman had made his presence.

Bill was very absorbed with the stories he was hearing and wanted to hear more as the last of them was finished along with the last of the beers. There was an uncomfortable moment of silence as all the men bowed their heads and again started to chant and speak in a tongue Bill knew nothing of.

"Well Bill our new friend, we have enjoyed your story and hope that you enjoyed ours on this special National Aboriginal Day... June 21st. We look forward to seeing you again some day, and hope you have another story for us."
Bill looked at George and the others and smiled. The others started to rise after picking up all the empty

beer cans and putting them back into the boxes, then with a quiet goodbye they all started down the tracks… all that is except for George. He was now curled up on the rail and snoring just like Bill had found him those many hours earlier.

Bill said his goodbyes and started in the opposite direction to get himself home. As he walked he felt a real calm beset him. He was sure he was feeling the guidence of the spirits helping him on his way home. He would for sure return to this place and hopefully find George and friends, only this time he would bring the boxes of beer.

The End

John P Gibson — *High Tide*

High Tide

Global warming extremes. That had been the warning for over fifty years. Alyssa was deep in thought as she watched yet another documentary about how humans had devastated the environment enough over the centuries to cause almost total annihilation of many of the species on this planet, including Humans. It was something she had been interested in since she was in school. Alyssa was a thirty something single female who worked as a journalist for an up and coming magazine in a city where most people had no clue as to what was happening with their environment. Vancouver, BC Canada. The new hotspot on the globe for best living conditions... if you could afford it. The magazine's name was 'Global Concerns' a fairly new kid on the block when it came to educating the public.

The idea was to try and get the majority of people to grasp just how important it was for humans to understand their impact on the global issue of their day-to-day activities, and their consequences on the environment. It was too bad however that more and more people were choosing not to read anymore. The internet had taken over for the most part.

A mass movement of cell phone Zombies walking the planet. Eyes glued to the small screen held in front of their faces ignoring everything else going on around them. Regardless of the lack of information getting to the masses Alyssa and her crew would do their best to educate them.

Alyssa's boss Jim Nast thought she was one of his better journalists as he told her this on every occasion he could. She often thought he had a crush on her even though he was married with three children and she had herself a very serious boyfriend, Axle Dent. He was a real estate agent for a large company in town, and with the way things were going politically these days his market was vastly improving.

They had plans to get married and Alyssa wanted to have a family; four children she had said many times to Axle. This seemed strange to him as he often reminded her that she worked for an environmental institution. The Human population was of course the main cause of all the problems. He would be content with one child, or no children.

"Hi hon… I'm home"
Axle says as he enters the small and cramped apartment him and Alyssa lived in and had done so for the past three years when they had first met each other. It had been at a rally, one of many being staged around the globe over the past decade or so. Again it puzzled Axle that all these people would get together to protest against pollution and the degradation of the environment, and then have large paper and cardboard plackards, plastic balloons, and countless other items that have been know to affect the environment.

"Hi sweetie, you're home late tonight? I had dinner ready an hour ago… everything alright?"
Alyssa asks as she hugs him and then gives him a big kiss on the lips.

There was a look about him she could not quite figure out. She had to ask.
"Sooo… tell me, what's up? I can see in your expression… c'mon, tell me Axle."
It was true, he did have a somewhat exaggerated smile and a positve energy around him. He put his briefcase down on the floor, placed his sunglasses on the small table by the door, then….

"We're getting a house!"
There was a brief moment of silence then Alyssa could hold it back no longer.
"WHAT!!! What the hell are you talking bout Axle? A house! For us?"
She started to jump around the room excited and obviously in a much better mood.
"Yes the boss came up with a deal for us that I couldn't turn down. It'll be a bit of a struggle with payments but the house is in a great location."

John P Gibson *High Tide*

Axle had Alyssa's attention and she became quiet so as not to miss anything else he was going to tell her about their new house.

"We can go have a look at it tomorrow at three PM. It's your day off and of course the boss has no problem with me... it's kinda my job anyway isn't it?"
He says as he smiles at her, she thinks for a moment before speaking.
""Where is it? What kind of house is it? Is it bigger than this one bedroom apartment? Does it have a parking garage? Does it...."

"Hey honey, you'll see it tomorrow, I don't want to ruin the surprise now do I?"
They looked at each other and then went in for another hug.
"This is so great, I don't think I'll get any sleep tonight thinking about it. You must have some pictures of it that you can show me... right?"
Axle just kept his cool as he had been trained to do over the years.

John P Gibson   *High Tide*

"Sorry hon, no pictures, but you'll have tomorrow to go through the house with a fine toothed comb, and take as many pictures as you like."

This seemed to curb her curiosity and the two of them settled into a comfortable position on the sofa as they watched the soaps Alyssa loved to watch. It would be a very active night as the surprise of the house they were to get would keep Alyssa and Axle thinking about the showing of the house the next day.

The morning alarm could not have gone off soon enough for Alyssa. She jumped out of bed and in the process woke Axle up who was sleeping soundly as his snoring would attest to. All she could talk about to Axle was the house they would be touring in the afternoon at three PM.

As they drove the short distance to where the property was they were about to look at, Alyssa kept asking Axle question after question about the house. She could not conatin her enthusiasm; it was more than obvious to Axle. He only hoped once they had made a decision about the house that she would stop talking about it; at least for a few hours.

The area the house was in was beautiful and with maple trees lining the sides of the road and the very nice homes just hidden in behind them made for an idyllic scene. Once they started to pull into the driveway Alyssa put her hands to her mouth as she nearly screamed to Axle.

"OH MY GOD!!!... I can't believe how great this place looks Axle. Are you sure this is the right place?"
She asks the question knowing full well it is, Axle never made mistakes. As he slowed the car and then parked in front of the large house Alyssa could get an idea on how big this place really was.

"It's massive Axle, I can't believe we can get this place all for ourselves. I can't wait to see the inside of it, and it looks like there might be a great view out the front."
She looked at Axle as he smiles and gets out of the car, Alyssa does the same and they both stand at the entranceway to the house. It was a moment later and

a coupl came out the front doors to greet them. Axle made the first move to shake their hands and then turn to Alyssa.

"Hi Charles, Jane… this is my fiance Alyssa."
She approached the couple and shook their hands.
"This looks like a great place… why would you want to sell it?"
It was a question she thought appropriate considering how nice the place looked. It was Jane that made the move to answer first.

"Nice to meet you Alyssa and yes it is a very nice home, we have put a lot into it but family affairs are taking us away across the country to Toronto."
She had a funny look on her face as she turned to her husband Charles for a response. He looked at her and smiled and then continued from where she had left off.

"Yes… yes that's true, we have some family issues, otherwise we probably would not sell. Anyway… please come in so we can give you the grand tour. Axle here has already seen the place of course, but I'm sure you'll fall in love with it."

He says with just a little apprehension, something Alyssa was getting a little confused about.

They were walked into the front foyer and beyond that Alyssa could make out a spectacular view beyond a bank of floor to ceiling windows that stretched across the entire front of the living and dining rooms. She found herself being drawn across to look out at the view. The rest followed of course.

"Wow! What a magnificent view of the ocean, it just seems to go on forever."
Alyssa says as she stands at the glass windows and stares out to the ocean beyond.
"If you just stand back a bit Alyssa I think this will impress you."
She does what Charles says and steps back a bit as he takes his cell phone out from his pocket and pushes a few keys on the pad.

A moment later the large glass panels start to open up and settle up against one end of the wall. It opened to a large tiled deck where there were a few chairs for people to sit and enjoy a cool drink and look at the view. It was a clear sunny day and the warmth made this particular moment to be one Alyssa was falling in love with. Axle thought he might not have to show her anymore of the house.

"It is nice isn't it?"
Jane says in that strange tone of voice she had earlier as she looks to Charles.
"Well lets have you looking at the rest of the house hon, I think you're going to like it a lot."
Axle says as he makes a move to take Alyssa by the hand.

The rest of the tour took about an hour or more and it was time to make a move. They had been offered a drink but declined as now Axle seemed in a hurry to make a move. Alyssa figured it was his work schedule.
"Well it was very nice but there is so much I want to see, and the questions I have… can we come back for another look at it? Say tomorrow?"

Alyssa asks as Axle took a look at his watch.
"Of course, how does that work with you Axle?"
"Fine… say about three oclock again?"

Axle asks as he looks to Charles, then Alyssa, both smiled and it looked like it was on for the next day at three oclock.

The drive home was an exhausting one as Axle had to answer a multitude of questions from Alyssa. He did not mind, just so long as she was happy, and he knew she would be once they owned the house she had just seen. It was one of those deals he had done in the past for other clients, but having his boss offer this one to him and Alyssa, it was over the moon.

The two of them celebrated at dinner with a bottle of reasonably expensive champagne. It was then many questions and answers and of course how the house would be decorated… this was mostly Alyssa's idea of course. Axle for the moment would go along with it.

The next day they were once again on the road to their potentially new home. It was just after three PM and the greeting at the front door was very much the same as the day before; pleasant and cordial. Alyssa went directly to the front windows and looked out to the ocean beyond. The tide was once again out and the long sandy beach seemed to go on forever in either direction. She went into a very calm space as the others talked.

The conversation was of course about getting the lawyers involved and making the final sale. Axle didn't have too many concerns as he figured any changes to the house would be minor. After signing some papers that the couple had Axle shook their hands and called Alyssa over to do the same with Charles and Jane.

After she shook their hands Axle went down on bended knee and produced a small felt covered box that he opened to show her a diamond ring.
"Alyssa... will you marry me?"
The question was one she had run through her mind on many ocassions, just not this one. It took her off guard.

She paused for a moment as she put her one hand up to her mouth as tears formed in her eyes. She cleared her throat and then....
"Of course I will Axle, this is such a surprise... and in our new home, I can't believe it."

She then turned to Charles and Jane and they returned the smile as Axle stood up and held Alyssa around the waist as the two of them looked out through the windows to the ocean beyond.

*****

It was several months later and Axle and Alyssa had made the move and done a few renovations on their new home. The one reno that was taking priority was a new rock wall just beyond their tiled terrace where the ocean view was. This they thought would help with any wind blowing water and things up onto the terrace and possibly into the house.

Once the wall was finished and a few other items Alyssa thought should be done, they decided to have a house warming party and also their wedding ceremony. It was decided to have it the night of a full moon in August, this they thought would be perfect for weather and warmth. They would hire the services of a catering company and also a musical duo that happened to be traveling around the world, 'Tillerman' was their name. Both Alyssa and Axle were getting excited about the big get together and of course getting the yard in order would be a big job all in itself. They figured they should cut the guest list off at one hundred people even though there were many more they could have invited.

They had even invited the previous owners Charles and Jane; but they declined as they said they had previous plans for that evening. It was about a week before the big event and Axle and Alyssa were having breakfast before the two of them had to get to work.
"Well, it looks like things are going to be all ready for the big night on Saturday."

Alyssa thought to say as Axle was going over some paperwork in front of him on the granite counter top on the island in the large kitchen.
"Yeah… yeah, I hope so. I am a little concerned with the terrace though, on certain ocassions I have seen some water coming through the wall we had built. You know, when the tide is high and all."

"Do you think it will be a problem on Saturday? I sure don't want any water coming into the house or anything like that."
Alyssa said with some concern in her voice as she shoveled another mouthfull of fruitloops into her mouth.

"No I think it was just a freak tidal thing with some wind the other day, it should be fine for the party. You have the caterers organized?"
Axle says as he folds the papers up and puts them off to the side as he takes a drink of his coffee.
"Yes and I think the food will impress everyone. I am just so thrilled with our new home Axle and our wedding too."

Axle looked at her and smiled.
"Yes it will be one great night Alyssa I can hardly wait."
Alyssa got up and went over to him and gave him a big hug and kiss before taking the dishes to the dishwasher which they had two of.
"It's a busy week at work for me as Jim wants me to finish a story on the affects of global warming and storms increasing in velocity all around the world."

John P Gibson

High Tide

Alyssa had been doing her best to get the article completed well before their big night the following Saturday.

Axle was of course busy with his selling of upscale homes in and around the area. The market was good and he was confident that their retirement in their beautiful home would be a good one. Once they checked the alarm system and CCTV network they had installed everywhere the two of them were off to work.

The drive was always a busy one and because they both went in opposite directions now with the new home, Alyssa had decided to use the transit system to get herself to work. Axle would of course drive his fancy sports car; clients expected it of him.

Alyssa's boss Jim had let her know that her story would take center stage in the magazine as there were many reports from around the world about how some very severe storms were affecting so many places. Incredible heat in central U.S.A., snow in July in parts of Southern Russia, massive rainstorms on coastal cities throughout the planet.

John P Gibson *High Tide*

There was no shortage of material for her to write her story. This day however was nice, warm, and calm. A perfect day in Vancouver.

The day went by as predicted for the both of them and Alyssa would get back to their home first as Axle liked to work late in the day to get all of his paperwork done. Alyssa would get some dinner together for the two of them, and it would be a late one when Axle walked through the door about nine oclock.

As she waited for Axle, Alyssa went over the plans for their wedding and reception coming up on the Saturday. All seemed in order and she knew it would be one crazy day as guests would start arriving about three in the afternoon. She was lucky in that a few of her friends would come in the morning to help with anything that needed it.

The rest of the week went by smoothly and Alyssa was just about finished her article for the magazine. She was happy with it other than a good ending which she would get to the following week after their big party. It was now just a matter of getting all of the food and booze together so that the bartender who came with the catering company would have everything he needed.

It was finally the day, six AM in the morning and Alyssa nearly had to shout at Axle to get his ass out of bed; they had plenty to do. He made his move to the bathroom and would get himself cleaned up as he only took thirty minutes as opposed to Alyssa's hour and a half. They would dress casual until about two PM when they would dress for the party and wedding ceremony of course.

It was a very busy morning as the two of them started to invite the catering company in and the musicians, 'Tillerman', a male guitarist and a female guitarist. The weather was good with only a few clouds about. They hoped it would stay clear so all could observe the full moon later that night.

It was about noon when the two of them could finally take a bit of a break before dressing in their wedding attire. It was a simple lunch as they tried some of the food that the caterer was supplying for them and their guests. They now had a couple of hours to get ready for the great event. Alyssa was very excited and Axle was somewhat nervous as he had never been married.

"You ready Alyssa?"
Axle says from the bedroom to the open door of the bathroom.
"Just about…. Having some difficulty in putting on these new heels I bought the other day."
Axle had no idea as he had never worn heels.
"OK, I'll be downstairs to make sure any early arrivers are greeted… see you when you're done."

He exits the bedroom and makes his way down the stairs as he hears a loud bang. At first he thought it might have been the caterers with their setting up or maybe the musicians. Then there was another loud bang. It was thunder followed again by a flash of light and more loud clashes of thunder.

It appeared a storm was moving in and Axle could only hope that it would not rain as most of the festivities were to be held outside on the terrace. As he moved around the house he could see that everything looked great and he saw 'Tillerman' setting up their equipment and testing the sound quality. They sounded good as he made his way to where the bar was and thought he should have a shot of Tequila before the guests arrived.

"Hey… how are you, I'm Axle."
He says to the well dressed man behind the bar who smiles.
"Hello, my name is Jake, I'll be your bartender for the event. Can I get you something Axle?"
"Yes please, I think I'll have a shot of tequila… you know… to get the day started and all."

Jake smiled as he reached for a bottle behind him off the shelf. It looked like a quality Tequila and Axle then smiled just as there was another clap of thunder.
"Looks like a storm brewing."
Jake says as he moves the shot of Tequila over to Axle.
"Let's hope it holds off till after the party."
Axle replies as he downs the shot of booze and returns the glass to the bartop. His face scrunched up as he was not all that used to the strong flavours of the liquor.

"Well they did forecast this storm to come through, at least you have plenty of room to move everyone inside if it does start to pour."

Jake says as he wipes the top of the bar with a clean white cloth. It was then that Alyssa made her presence known with the clicking sound of her heels on the marble stairs coming down from the bedroom. She was all dressed in white and looked very nice as Axle and Jake could not avert their gaze.

"Wow! Don't you look great... you sure it's OK for me to see the bride before the ceremony?"
Axle asks as he smiles and moves towards Alyssa.
"Oh you don't believe in that shit do you Axle, what could possibly go wrong because you see me a little bit before the wedding?"

"Can I get you a drink before everyone starts to get here?"
He thought to ask as they were right there at the bar.
"Yeah, how about a glass of red wine."
"You heard the lady Jake... a glass of your finest red wine and I think I'll have one as well."

Jake smiled and started to pour the glasses of wine as there was a moment of silence just before another clap of thunder.

"What the hell Axle, is there a storm brewing?" Alyssa asks as she looks out towards the terrace where the sun was now disappearing behind some dark clouds rolling through.
"Lets hope not sweety."
Just then there was the sound of the front doorbell, the both of them turned and then made their way to it.

Axle opened the door to see a group of four people standing there, some with gifts in hand and smiles on their faces. Behind them could be seen more cars pulling up and more people coming to the front door; one of them being the minister.

This was the start of it all and both Alyssa and Axle were in their element as another loud bang went off from the thunder above. The day went as planned and the two of them were now standing outside on a small stage with the minister. The band was playing a soft tune while the guests sat at tables and stood

John P Gibson   *High Tide*

around to get a good look at the two being married. There were now many more claps of thunder and the wind had picked up.

Most people were holding their hats from blowing away or holding napkins down on the tables as the wind continued to pick up speed. Just as they finished their vows there was a massive bolt of lightening and the loudest of thunder so far. It now started to rain and it was coming down in torrents.

Everyone quickly moved into the main living room and the masive glass doors were closed as everyone watched the storm outside. It grew with intensity as the rain continued. With the tide coming in it did not take long for waves to start lapping up against the newly built wall.

It was a couple of hours later and sea water started to work its way through any cracks in doorways and windows it could. The house gradually started to fill up with the ocean as everyone quickly made their way up the stairs to the second floor. As the night progressed the water kept rising until almost ceiling level on the first floor. It would be of no use to call authorities as they would not be able to even get to the house with all of this water. It was not hard for Axle to understand how they had got such a good deal on the house. The previous owners must have known about how the high tide would take over.

The End

Epilogue

Why short sories? Why not a full novel? Questions an author often asks. The nice thing about short stories is one can get many topics down on paper and of course at a later date if the feeling is right, turn any of them into a full length novel. Of course most of the stories in this book were fictitious in nature and could very well lead to some future novels. It is important to understand that no clowns were injured during the writing of this book. There could however be some big trouble if the global warming affect were to become more prevelant. This is one area that is certainly not fiction in any way, shape, or form.

John P Gibson — *High Tide*

It will take a lot of work on the part of us humans to turn this event around in any way. The warnings are everywhere for us to heed, but will we? This is the question forefront. High tides are already starting to create problems for many coastal cities and communities as this is a place where we humans have lived for a very long time.

Will the generations of the future have the capacity to understand how it all took place, and will they forgive us for not paying attention to Nature and its warnings to us. Denial is an easy way out, but not a practical way. If future generations have any chance at all, changes have to be made NOW! These sentiments were made decades ago, but most did not believe what was being said to them.

The future will hold some very interesting lifestyle changes for us humans and of course many other species that rely on this planet for their survival. The time is now and we all have to work together to make things right again. The High Tide is coming and I know you can do at least a little to offset the damage that will be done.

With a positive approach and a global understanding of the consequences of doing nothing, we as a species could get control and see a better planet. Remember, the stories in this book are fiction… what is happening today on this planet with the environment is fact.

John P Gibson

High Tide

600

John has been writing for a good part of his life and will continue until he is unable to. It has become a passion and not a day goes by without entertaining some thoughts onto paper... or computer. His passion is this planet, the human species, and of course all the others that share this planet. A lot of his writing incorporates what it is we are doing to our living space on this planet and possible things we can do to reverse this process.

Made in the USA
Columbia, SC
02 July 2017